"Informative! Insightful! Inspiring! The authors relay multiple stories . . . that illustrate the numerous innovative ways in which 'going local and staying put' are increasingly becoming the creative edge today of the gospel's engagement with the world. A must-read for church planters and church leaders who desire to read the 'signs of the times.'"

—**Craig Van Gelder**, Luther Seminary, retired

"With eagerness, I invite you to read *Joining Jesus*. Come, turn its pages and explore the God who lives and breathes in the worlds beyond church buildings. Travel across North America with Moses and Christopher as they tell you story after story of Luke 10 people meeting Jesus in their neighborhoods. Your imagination for God will surely grow. And the way you live the Christian life will be lastingly changed."

—**David Fitch**, Northern Seminary

"*Joining Jesus* stands out for its attention to the ordinary and everyday ways in which Christian leaders have discovered and discerned new ways to be church in their neighborhoods. . . . We do not need more Christian heroes, Chung and Meehan say, but rather disciples capable of receiving the gifts of strangers and attending to the emerging signs of God's future in their midst."

—**Scott J. Hagley**, Pittsburgh Theological Seminary

"This book is a theological collage, weaving stories together like a spiritual quilt. It celebrates the active, feet-on-the-ground faith of incredible people. It is a reminder that Christianity is not just a way of believing—it is a way of living in the world. Let this book inspire you to live out the revolution of Jesus wherever you are!"

—**Shane Claiborne**, author, activist, and cofounder of Red Letter Christians (RLC)

"Chung and Meehan have lovingly curated the stories of faithful folk who are embodying the gospel in places as diverse as inner-city neighborhoods, middle-class suburbs, university campuses, and a Navajo community. Abandoning strategic plans and management techniques, these are stories of improvised incarnation, deep listening, and faithful presence. Do you need encouragement about the future of the church? Read this evocative and delightful book."

—**Brian J. Walsh**, coauthor of *Romans Disarmed: Resisting Empire, Demanding Justice*

"These engagingly told local stories teach us a crucial, universal message. When we reach out in faith . . . to embrace communities that go beyond definitions of who 'we' are, wonderful things happen. Most importantly, we grow together as believers into a more profound awareness of who we are in Jesus Christ."

—**Rich Mouw**, Fuller Theological Seminary

"Everyday church leaders receive mountains of sage advice in books, blogs, and podcasts about mission. Yet, they struggle with the thorny and unique challenges of leadership. . . . *Joining Jesus* instead recounts the real experiences of everyday leaders faithfully following Jesus in real places, with real failures and victories. *Joining Jesus* encourages readers, expands their imaginations, and leaves them wondering, 'What is Jesus doing in my community?'"

—**Zachary King**, Director, Resonate Global Mission

"This is a book of people stories, winsomely told by two 'poets of the ordinary.' The stories are the warp and woof of a living tapestry, the fluid dance of congregations with their communities. They open up fresh imagination for 'going local' in today's missional moment."

—**George R. Hunsberger**, Western Theological Seminary, emeritus

"This book is an invitation to reimagine what it means to be the church *in the neighborhood*. Chung and Meehan walk us down the gritty streets of North Philadelphia, to the homeless in Seattle, to neighborhoods across North America, helping us to see, smell, touch, and taste what the Spirit is doing, giving hope to what God can do in our neighborhood."

—**J. R. Woodward**, National Director, the V3 Movement

"If you are interested in the future of the church, where you look makes all the difference, and this book points to such hopeful possibilities. Brimming with fresh stories, *Joining Jesus* will inspire you to shift your attention from old metrics to God's activity at the local level. Highly recommended."

—**Tim Soerens**, author of *Everywhere You Look: Discovering the Church Right Where You Are*

"Chung and Meehan tell us real stories of ministry and church. From page 1 and from Philadelphia to Seattle, *Joining Jesus* invites us to renewal and presence. Inspiring and encouraging, may it be well read in the Christian Reformed Church and beyond."

—**Mark R. Gornik**, City Seminary of New York

"We owe a debt of gratitude to Chung and Meehan for their important work in writing *Joining Jesus*. . . . You will be challenged, heartened, and blessed as you engage with the content. God wants to use the ordinary in all of us to achieve extraordinary blessings for others—if we but let him."

—**Colin P. Watson Sr.**, Executive Director, the Christian Reformed Church in North America (CRCNA)

"What does 'church' look like? . . . *Joining Jesus* is a wonderful field trip and field guide to help us listen and learn about what God is doing in diverse settings so that we are encouraged and challenged as to what evangelism and discipleship can be as we follow God in mission—together!"

—**Jul Medenblik**, Calvin Theological Seminary

"I'm convinced that today we need two foundational pillars that will enable everyday churches to make the turn toward the new era of mission that we find ourselves in. First, we need more stories. Second, we need *deep* stories, those that go in depth into the life and practice of the congregation. *Joining Jesus* is a collection of deep stories, ones that not only inspire but also inform churches across North America."

—**Chris Backert**, National Director, Fresh Expressions US

"This collection of stories is a hope-filled inspiration, especially during challenging times of a pandemic. It shows the power of the Holy Spirit alive and strong in churches today when they intentionally reach into communities, where they join God already at work there. By the grace of God, ordinary people do the extraordinary."

—**Ida Kaastra-Mutoigo**, Executive Director, World Renew, Canada

# Joining Jesus

# Joining Jesus

*Ordinary People at the Edges*
*of the Church*

Moses Chung

AND

Christopher Meehan

FOREWORD BY
Alan J. Roxburgh

AFTERWORD BY
Cory Willson

 CASCADE *Books* · Eugene, Oregon

JOINING JESUS
Ordinary People at the Edges of the Church

Cascade Books
An Imprint of Wipf and Stock Publishers
199 W. 8th Ave., Suite 3
Eugene, OR 97401

www.wipfandstock.com

PAPERBACK ISBN: 978-1-7252-9909-2
HARDCOVER ISBN: 978-1-7252-9910-8
EBOOK ISBN: 978-1-7252-9911-5

*Cataloguing-in-Publication data:*

Names: Chung, Moses, author. | Meehan, Christopher, author. | Roxburgh, Alan J., foreword. | Willson, Cory, afterword.

Title: Joining Jesus : ordinary people at the edges of the church / by Moses Chung and Christopher Meehan ; foreword by Alan J. Roxburgh ; afterword by Cory Willson.

Description: Eugene, OR: Cascade Books, 2022

Identifiers: ISBN 978-1-7252-9909-2 (paperback) | ISBN 978-1-7252-9910-8 (hardcover) | ISBN 978-1-7252-9911-5 (ebook)

Subjects: LCSH: Christian Reformed Church—Missions—North America. | Ecclesiology. | Church.

Classification: BV2063 .J59 2022 (print) | BV2063 (ebook)

01/17/22

This book is dedicated to

Adrian Van Giessen (1959–2016) "God is crazy about you!"

and

Ben Becksvoort (1948–2015) "Gentle Ben"

and

all co-laborers who dedicated their lives in sacrificial, faithful service for the sake of God's mission through partnership with Christian Reformed Home Missions and now Resonate Global Mission.

After this the Lord appointed seventy-two others and sent them two by two ahead of him to every town and place where he was about to go. —Luke 10:1

# Contents

CONTENTS

# Foreword

I write this from my home on the West Coast of Canada in the early summer of 2021. We're all thinking about the long, lazy days ahead—the chance to slough off the restrictions, lockdowns, and burdens of a long, long COVID-19 season. These have been hard days for us all, particularly those of us in leadership of congregations or the systems that serve them. But even in these early days of COVID's ending new questions are rising to the surface and, with them, fresh anxieties. These questions reflect our concerns around what's going to happen to our churches as we enter this new time. We know a lot of things aren't going to go back to the normal we knew before 2019. We wonder about who'll be coming back once things fully open. There are hints that many younger adults with families have settled into new habits that may not bring them back to the usual programs and ministries we want to reopen. But it's not just younger adults. I was with retired friends a few weeks ago. They've been faithful members of a Christian Reformed Church (CRC) congregation for years. He simply said he now had little desire to go back to the Sunday morning church he'd been away from for more than a year. She, deeply involved in the workings of the congregations, shrugged and expressed how tired she had become with the issues being addressed in their church—they just seemed irrelevant at this point. Neither are likely to be "going back."

These are the kinds of questions and experiences creating the tiredness and anxieties many leaders are experiencing just now. What are we going to do as leaders to guide our congregations into this new time? This book is a very important response to these questions. It will help you sort out the kinds of responses that can make a critical difference to the future of your congregation. It comes at this pivotal time in our life as God's people by offering a hopeful picture, a way forward for us in this space of huge disruption. What makes this book an important guide right now is about what it does and doesn't do. Let's start with what it doesn't do.

In a book I recently wrote, *Joining God in the Great Unraveling: Where We Are & What I've Learned* (2021), I quoted the words of a Catholic sister, Mary Jo Leddy, written more than thirty years ago: "our very human tendency is to try to manufacture our own lives. We try to control through what we manufacture rather than trusting in the mysterious process . . . which is God's gift to us and our work." Fabrications are not suited to the life of faith. They don't wear well.

As I look at what's happening in churches as they seek to address the aftermath of COVID I see, as rock solid as cement, a deep-rooted default to *manufacture*. In one sense, this need to manufacture is "our very human tendency." It describes a primary default running through all our actions as human beings: we're wired to manufacture (*homo faber*). But this wiring can distort our humanity and our responses to the disruptions we're facing as God's people. It turns us into creatures driven by technique and the need to manage our outcomes. This side of manufacturing closes us off to the potentiality of discerning what the Spirit is gestating in the midst of a mystery (disruptions and unravelings) we cannot control. When manufacturing is the energy shaping our actions, then we're being shaped (deformed) by techniques of management aimed at controlling our environments and the people around us. We take the disruptive moments that come to us (such as the present) and turn them into processes for determining the outcomes we desire. With this manufacturing we see the disruptions coming at us not as pivotal moments of the Spirit's invitation but a chance to turn them into outcomes we can control. Disruptive mystery that is God's work amongst us becomes another opportunity for technique and program. This is the overarching response of the churches to their anxieties around what comes next.

If you want to step beyond these defaults, this book points to another way. At one level it's a collection of stories about people, like you, discovering, entering, and being with others in their neighborhoods. I love the moment when Momma T explains her desire to engage with *Galatians*. She understood what it's all about and expressed it simply but profoundly—she's a vessel of the Spirit in her community. This kind of ordinary, on-the-ground understanding of Christian life runs through the book. You won't find a lot of "manufacturing" going on here. Some of these stories emerge from leaders who "moved into the neighborhood" to plant churches. But in doing this they discovered far more than just going about another church plant. They entered the heart and pain of the community where they'd come to "pitch their tent" and they were shaped by the neighbors in ways none of them could have imagined.

Don't be deceived. There is far more going on here than stories. We are often asked about how people in congregations can discover stories about their neighborhood. What you will see are ordinary people bumping into their own stories as they open their eyes and hearts to what is happening around them. These stories are gestated, on the ground, by people's commitment to a couple of practices: a commitment to opening our eyes and ears to what is going on in our neighborhoods and to that bigger story of God's presence in our communities. At work behind these stories is a theological imagination profoundly different from that of manufacturing or, often, church planting. It is a theology that takes us beyond "mission" and "doing for" people to ground us in incarnational life. Here we are encountered by a way that wants to take seriously that God is the primary agent in the midst of our massive disruptions. As these pioneers of the local came to dwell with and be with the people of their communities they were discovering fresh, imaginative ways in which the Spirit was at work ahead of them. Only in this kind of "being with" and "dwelling with" does a way emerge amidst a community of God's people to find mortgages for immigrants, or hang out with kids at a Snack Shack, or hear the call to restart a woman's home. These activities don't come from vision statements or strategic plans. They emerge among people learning to be with their neighbor and listening together to the Spirit.

Many churches continue to wrestle with the long winter of COVID. They're asking questions like: What are we going to do post-COVID? How are we going to lead a very different church in this space of huge social-cultural unraveling? While the answers to these anxious questions may be complex, they are also clear and straightforward: we lay down our manufacturing, enter into our neighborhoods to "be with" people and, in so doing, listen to the Spirit. It is not in manufacturing but in discerning that God is present to us. This book of stories is painting a picture of what our churches, moving beyond COVID, are being called to become.

There's a lot that needs to be unpacked here but here's the bottom line—if God is acting in the midst of all the disruptions we're confronting, then this missionary God is already ahead of us, now, today, right where we live, work and pray, in and among our communities. Discernment begins as we take the risk of being with (not meeting needs or doing for others), of entering into relationship with our neighbors and, in that place (around their table, working beside them) learning to listen to what the Spirit is gestating. This is the journey this book points you toward. Embrace it!

These stories are told from within one tradition—the Christian Reformed Church in North America. But their application goes far beyond one denomination. Any pastor or member of a congregation can see him/herself in these stories. A friend whom I hadn't seen for over a year because of lockdowns told his story. When the COVID lockdowns began he recognized that there were going to be a lot of people, in his congregation and in his condominium, who would be locked away and isolated. He made a mental list of who they were. Each week, he would call a number to check in with them as well as knock at the doors of people in the condo to talk with them and just check in. A simple act of love shaped by Jesus. This is how God's great story in Jesus enters and indwells our world—through the kinds of stories that are told in this book.

Alan J. Roxburgh

# Preface

The book *Flourishing in the Land: A Hundred-Year History of the Christian Reformed Missions in North America* (1996) came out twenty-five years ago. It was co-written by Rev. Scott Hoezee, now director of the Center for Excellence in Preaching at Calvin Theological Seminary, and Chris Meehan, who has also helped to write this book. *Flourishing in the Land* told the story of church mission efforts across the United States and Canada beginning in the late 1800s. Faced with many obstacles and challenges, it was nonetheless a successful enterprise in starting new churches and establishing ministries by the small Reformed Protestant denomination with deep roots in the Netherlands. In 2017, the Christian Reformed Church's synod, the governing body of the church, voted to unite Christian Reformed Home Missions with Christian Reformed World Missions, the international mission agency of the denomination, into one agency named Resonate Global Mission. The book you have here, although written in a more narrative fashion, chronicles the work of Home Missions in the years after *Flourishing in the Land* was published and leading up to and beyond the merger of the two agencies into Resonate. This book examines and celebrates the mission work of Home Missions (now Resonate) and illustrates through many stories how the denomination and its supporters have helped bring the love and message of Jesus Christ to communities across North America in a quickly changing, post-Christian landscape.

# Introduction

The COVID-19 pandemic, which began to spread in spring of 2020 across the world, is likely to change, if not shatter, institutions and organizations that have defined us and on which we have depended. Included in this parade of disruption and change will be a shift—a transformation—in how churches operate. We don't know what these changes will be.

But what we know is that life as we knew it before the virus is gone. Like it or not, the pandemic will cause significant disruption and change. The effect of the pandemic may cause some churches to close and others to struggle to stay afloat. But here is something worth considering: The pandemic could result in a renewal in the church. And that is what this book is about—not about the pandemic per se, since we gathered much of the material before the virus showed up. But we are making the case that in the Christian Reformed Church, a small Protestant denomination based in Grand Rapids, Michigan and Burlington, Ontario, and in other churches as well, there was a movement afoot among ordinary people in church communities—mostly low-key and largely taking place without much fanfare—before the virus showed up.

In this movement, churches were growing into close-knit communities, characterized more by the care members show one another and for the love for the world around them than by the traditional approach of focusing mainly on Sunday morning worship or running religious services and programs. Led by those who we are referring to in this book as "Luke 10" people, these congregations and communities, we believe, express imagination, values, practices, and convictions necessary for the church to hold its own and even thrive in a secular, late modern world confused and slammed off its axis by the pandemic. These are people who follow a new paradigm of mission described in Luke 10 in which Jesus sends out seventy disciples two by two to "every town and place where he was about to go" (Luke 10:1).

Stories in this book are examples of churches that, long before the virus hit, realized their role and even their salvation lay in leaving their church buildings and connecting with what the Holy Spirit was doing in the neighborhoods. It was the compelling move of the Spirit that pushed these churches to change. Guided and sustained by Luke 10 people and their vision for living in a sacred, shared community, some churches have been doing this—going local and setting up ministries in every town and place—for years.

In the towns and places we visited, we saw how, formed by a fresh understanding of their Reformed faith, CRC communities have been connecting with others, building deeper relationships and finding themselves sharing the renewed faith in churches and neighborhoods, in schools and health clinics. Over a three-year period, we visited a church that has brought Christ's love in practical ways to a neighborhood in North Philadelphia; saw firsthand the expansion of local leadership on a Native American reservation in New Mexico; experienced God at work in the midst of busily expanding cities such as Vancouver, British Columbia. We stopped for a stone soup supper in St. Thomas, Ontario; took part in a Bible study on Galatians in a bullet-riddled home in Detroit; joined an Advent service in a home in Edmonton, Alberta; ate dinner with a community of people from a church in Tucson, Arizona; walked the neighborhood where a couple is working to obtain mortgages for Latin American immigrants in inner-city Kansas City, Missouri. What we saw happening was a fresh expression of the Reformed theology addressing and seeking to redeem every "square inch" of creation, taking hold and forming deeper roots in the minds and hearts of people as they join a growing movement focusing on local settings. As Luke 10 people, our eyes are turned from the bright lights and attractive stages of the larger churches to a different place. Instead of looking beyond us at what others are doing, we look to the ground on which we stand, to people we can touch by simply reaching out to them without journeying to far places. And yet we see and want to be part of something larger as well. Whether in prayer or practice, churches we chronicle are seeking to join a movement that is laid out in article 41 of the CRC's *Contemporary Testimony: Our World Belongs to God* (1986): "The Spirit calls all members to embrace God's mission in their neighborhoods and in the world: to feed the hungry, bring water to the stranger, welcome the stranger, clothe the naked, care for the sick and free the prisoner." While it is not easily followed or achieved to address or tackle these issues, it is the calling of God, sifting and shaping us by the Spirit, that many church communities have come to realize is theirs to take on—and to do it in fresh, creative ways.

As author Alan Roxburgh in his book *Missional: Joining God in the Neighborhood* (2011) writes, if we are to respond to this calling, we must open our eyes and imaginations to the stuff that is right before us. And seeing what we see, we need to become poets of the ordinary. On page 173, he says: "The poet is the one who listens to the stories that lie beneath the stories people tell and gives voice to the music beneath their words. The poet is the one who, in such listening, offers ways in which people can connect this music to a larger story, a larger movement." The poet is kind of a secular priest. Not necessarily ordained, poets are certainly those who pay close attention to what people say, especially about their encounters with a mystical, hard-to-place God in their everyday lives and circumstances.

These poets learn and can share the stories that define the character and the purpose of a community. Shaped by the Spirit and the stories, as sacred poets, we venture out to meet those who will walk the road with us. As we go, we look for ways in which we can participate in the work of God in the world. And as poets, we seek to point to the larger story—the grand and vast and ever-evolving story of God at work in a world that in some places—often right next door—has begun to express a greater hunger to know God. The poet crafts words into sentences that allow us to look into the deep well of human experience—the well that holds the holy water that nourishes life. By reading stories about the Luke 10 people, you see how this holy water fills us and buoys us up in the world; it gives us energy, and allows us, in the right time in the right place, to share the source of our life, the source of all life with someone else. Since we are poets, lifted up by the living water, we can all listen to and tell stories. And this is what we sought to do as we visited places all across North America. Our hope is that by reading these stories you can see how church communities have found, grasped, and used the keys to the kingdom to unlock the pain and loneliness, the aching and longing so many have experienced and from there let God do the work so necessary to sustain the new world that is coming from the many effects of the virus that we can't see. We offer you, the reader, a litany of stories that can help those of us who are tangled in a mess and are desperately seeking for God's kingdom to come right now just as it is in heaven. We offer, we hope, the poetry of everyday life with God as our maker, sustainer, and the living water for a new life.

# Part One

## Traveling Lightly and Following Jesus into the Neighborhood

"Go! I am sending you out like lambs among wolves.
Do not take a purse or bag or sandals . . ." —Luke 10:3–4

# 1

# "To Every Town and Place"

[or]

## Ministering on the Crack Corner and Loving Kids in North Philadelphia

"After this the Lord appointed seventy others and sent them two by two ahead of him to every town and place where he was about to go." —Luke 10:1

*A full-fledged Luke 10 congregation, Spirit and Truth Fellowship, was begun more than two decades ago by Manny Ortiz and Sue Baker, who were appointed by the Lord to go two by two to North Philadelphia—a place that is one of the poorest communities in the US. In this chapter, we meet people such as Taehoo Lee, who exemplifies being the stranger and receiving hospitality rather than being in control of all the resources. This is a major theme in Luke 10: living as a patient recipient—learning from what is in front of you, from your neighbor and neighborhood. The Spirit of God has been at work and remains alive in this area of Philadelphia. Besides a church, the ministry features a legal clinic, an arts program, a Christian school, church plants, a job training institute, and a health clinic. All of these grew out of faithfully responding to what God was already doing and joining God's mission in their neighborhood. Neither Ortiz nor Baker came in with a preconceived vision of how their ministry would go; there was no packaged, how-to-do-it formula in their minds. Simply, they paid attention to ways they could respond and help their community become one that reflected God's shalom—God's peace.*

*In this chapter, we sketch a fairly complete Luke 10 vision. Subsequent chapters will focus more narrowly on verses in the story.*

## Spirit and Truth

We pulled into the North Philadelphia neighborhood around 6 PM and parked in front of a former factory being slowly transformed into a church; we would learn more about this later. For now we looked out at one of the neighborhoods in which we would be meeting and interviewing people over the next four days. A liquor store stood on one corner, a couple of men came out laughing and carrying paper bags. Swirls of graffiti decorated the facing of a nearby viaduct. Row houses stretched for blocks on our left. Above them, flanked by gray clouds, an orange sunset of soft beauty was slowly disappearing in the west. Looking at it, we thought of this being a transitional time—the time when day is turning to night, the dusk-draped period when one thing is ending and another is beginning. Given the focus of why we were here, we thought of this as the liminal time that, as stories in this book illustrate, older forms of church are dying and new ones emerging. This is a time of shift and change; it is a time of transition like that of Luke 10, when Jesus sent his disciples two by two from their familiar surroundings into an uncertain world to live out and proclaim the gospel in new ways.

## Some history

A soft breeze moved in the air as we got out of the car. We were here to meet with Taehoo Lee, an assistant pastor at Spirit and Truth Fellowship, which has over the years made this part of Philadelphia home for ministry; this is a church led by Luke 10 people who came and stayed and have become a strong influence on their part of the city. On the way here, I (Moses) sketched part of the ministry's history. From its start, the goal was to invite and make room for everyone in this mixed Puerto Rican/African American neighborhood. This was a congregation whose people have been touched and shaped by the gospel and which, supported by its leaders, have paid attention to the people of its struggling North Philadelphia community and found ways to respond to their needs. And without any in-depth strategic plan, it has intuitively grown in the power of prayer and simply tried to do the next right thing for those in this area known as Hunting Park. This is a congregation that reflects the move of the Holy Spirit in compelling, informative, and yet mysterious ways—and we wanted to know more, working as two ethnographers, to uncover how the Spirit is forming and reforming this place.

4

## Meeting with Taehoo

Taehoo Lee held out a hand as we approached. A brush cut framing his strong, square-jawed face, Taehoo wore a T-shirt and jeans. Even in the dimming light, it was easy to see his smile. Over the next three busy days, we would meet many ministry leaders and church members and others who, like Taehoo, are part of Spirit and Truth Fellowship. Taehoo was the first person we met. As we stood outside Taehoo's row house on Uber Street, he talked about Manny Ortiz, the church's founding pastor who had died only a few weeks before, leaving many people feeling bereft. As Taehoo spoke, we looked up and down the street, comfortable and quiet on a Saturday evening. By now, the sun had gone down. Cars were parked along the curb; lights shone here and there in the row houses across Uber. Traffic hummed in the distance. But we knew this was a rough neighborhood in one of the poorest parts of Philadelphia, which was in 2017 the poorest large city in the United States. Unemployment is high, use of drugs is a problem, and crime is a constant issue. One night a year or so before, Taehoo heard gunshots and came out to find police swarming the neighborhood. At least thirty-two shots were fired in an execution-style shooting that left a man dead and sent a woman to the hospital. Also scary, and more personal, Taehoo had been robbed at gunpoint not long before in the neighborhood. Incidents of violence come with the territory and, although they shake you up, Taehoo has stayed here—he has dwelled in this neighborhood—for going on twenty years. Without a church, he serves as the neighborhood pastor. He sees his role as being a persistent presence. Not always evident, but always there, the Spirit has kept him where he is; commitment to a place and being known by the people is important. Manny Ortiz was the one who brought him there and told him this is where he should work. "He saw something in me that meant I needed to be here and work with the poor and the children," said Taehoo, gesturing around the neighborhood with his hand.

## Moving to Philadelphia

After Taehoo earned his Master of Divinity degree at a seminary in Korea, he came to Philadelphia and enrolled in classes in Westminster Theological Seminary, where he met Ortiz, who was professor of ministry and urban missions. Ortiz was a teacher and leader with a keen eye attuned to the capabilities and gifts of those he mentored. He encouraged them to follow the call God had given them and to serve and live among those who have very little and to be there to offer hope. He saw something in Taehoo—perhaps his reserved, monastic quality and his intelligence and passion for social justice—that inspired him to place him here. And Taehoo is grateful to Manny. As time has gone on, Taehoo has come to see the area and the people as his parish. "By being here," he said, "I can truly be light and salt to the people."

# The Summer Camp

Being light and salt, elements needed to produce life, is what it is all about. And an example of this is the free Uber Street Summer Camp Taehoo has held nearly every year since 2006. The city blocks off the streets for three weeks and one hundred neighborhood kids or more come for games, races, painting, music, Bible study, lively worship, and other activities.

Taehoo sees his role as helping to bring hope and healing to part of Philadelphia. As a Luke 10 person, he pitches in, working to move the area forward. He shovels snow for the elderly in the winter, goes to court with those who need his support, prays in homes when asked, mentors students after school, and has helped turn graffiti on buildings into decorative art. With his own money, he purchased the nearby abandoned building, in front of which our car now sat, and plans to renovate and turn it into a community center for the children. It will also serve as a place for worship. "I had no idea what I was going to do when I came here. One thing led to another and things kept evolving. I've seen things happening, so many small things have gotten big. God has sure been up to something out here," he said. The qualities we saw in Taehoo—good-natured humility, commitment to God and to the people on Uber Street—are those Jesus sought to shape and inspire in his disciples. He wanted them to pay attention to the small things, the ordinary stuff of life, that may or may not turn into something big.

Shane Claiborne, the social activist, author, and leader of a movement called the Red Letter Christians, lives in a community called the Simple Way, located about four miles from Taehoo's home. The two are friends and Claiborne is familiar with the work of Spirit and Truth—the way it has planted itself in the neighborhood. "The tree is known for its fruit and you see beautiful fruit that smells and tastes like Jesus flowing out of Spirit and Truth," he said in a phone conversation. "I've been there several times.

They have an important theology of place." Intentionally or not, Claiborne touched on an important Luke 10 theme—the practical theology of joining God at work in down-to-earth, defined places with ordinary people. Jesus sent his disciples two by two to every town and place. Place matters. Why does it matter? Because that is the context in which ministry is rooted. Place defines what is to happen as people like Taehoo demonstrate the dependable, ongoing love of Christ. It is in particular places that peace, shalom, can occur—a peace and shalom that the disciples of Jesus demonstrated by how they lived and showed love. And they must, as members of God's church, always do this in a particular place or context. "To be faithful to its calling, the church must be contextual, that it is multiculturally relevant within a specific setting," writes Craig Van Gelder in *Missional Church*. So instead of seeking to serve a large, prosperous church outside the gritty poverty of North Philadelphia, Taehoo has chosen to be God's emissary right where he is—in a place where he knows the people and they know him. A place far from the American dream where comfort and affluence go hand in hand, this is the place to which Manny Ortiz appointed him to go. This is a *practical* theology, meaning it adapts and evolves, while staying true to the gospel, wherever it exists. It is a tool, a practice of bringing the things of God out from the temple and the church right into where people live—and finding creative methods to share the truth of Christ's love with whomever you meet. It is not a theology emerging from brittle and dying institutions: it is a theology of purpose, of showing God in the flesh—a solid and persistent theology of incarnation.

## Sent Two by Two to North Philly

Manny Ortiz was a compact man with a close-cropped white beard who loved riding his bike on the streets of the neighborhoods around his church. As he rode, he often got off to talk to people he came across. He had bright eyes, an easy smile, and a steady but commanding voice. His prayerful love for Christ, and his lively imagination for ministry in the city still lived in the ways in which people at Spirit and Truth spoke about him—but especially how they are serving in roles into which Ortiz placed them.

The next day, following our visit with Taehoo, was Sunday and time for weekly worship. As the sanctuary started to fill up, Sue Baker stood in the back. A small, gentle woman with gray hair and glasses, she greeted people, smiling softly, but she was subdued. It wasn't hard to imagine how the death of Manny weighed heavily on her. Both she and her husband, Randy, had been a part of much of what Manny and his wife, Blanca, had done over the years, not just in church work but as friends who frequently visited one another's homes and went to conventions and on vacations with each other. They were neighbors and close friends. Manny and Sue went two by two. "Losing Manny has been difficult. We're all grieving in different ways," she said. But trained by Ortiz, church leaders were moving on. Always, Ortiz made it clear a church cannot survive if it relies on one pastor, however capable that person is. At Spirit and Truth, working together was key: big egos had no place here. Despite the death of Manny, Sue's attention was turned to today with an eye on tomorrow. "Our elders have stepped up and are offering the church, which deeply misses the pastor they loved, wisdom and leadership," said Baker.

Ortiz was born in Puerto Rico and then moved with his family to Harlem. Other than occasionally attending a Catholic church, God wasn't part of his family's life. As a boy, he wanted to be a baseball player. He joined the Marines in his early twenties and then ran a bar and supper club in Harlem until he got into some unspecified trouble and had to skip town. His father sent him to Long Island and told his son to look up a pastor who helped Ortiz catch a glimpse of the light he would follow forever after. It is unclear exactly what happened, but something changed. Bolstered by his new faith, Manny moved himself and his growing family to Philadelphia so he could go to Bible school. Living in an African American housing project, Ortiz read widely and voraciously, learning as much as he could about this new life of Christianity as he attended Philadelphia College of Bible. Soon after he graduated, he was ordained in a Baptist church and received a call to serve a large Norwegian church in Chicago—an area quickly becoming Puerto Rican. From there, he didn't turn back; church planting and seminary teaching became his focus. For a decade, Ortiz pastored and planted churches in Chicago, helped to start a school and other ministries, and joined the Christian Reformed Church. He and his wife also met and began working with the Bakers there.

In 1988, Manny moved with his family, along with the Bakers, to Philadelphia so he could finish his doctorate at Westminster Seminary. Starting a church in this new place was not in his plans. But it wasn't long before he stepped in to help run a house church that had been organized by seminary students but kept struggling when the students moved on. Located in the home of the Bakers, this house church saw the need to connect with young people in the neighborhood and began the Reese Street Community Center. Started in a grassroots, low-key way, the ministry grew. Within a few years, Ortiz and others launched Spirit and Truth in a church building that had been donated to them. Surrounded by closed factories and buildings scarred by graffiti, the church building was nonetheless in decent enough shape. In 1997, they moved in; the Reese Street Community Center came with them and was located in a nearby home. With only a handful of members, they worked hard not only to make the church their home but to beautify the neighborhood, scrubbing graffiti from buildings, picking up trash, and even rehabilitating homes into which members moved. They were Luke 10 people, laying down a firm foundation from which to speak and live out the gospel. They paid attention to where they found themselves, the place; they listened to what people in the neighborhood needed; they became sacred poets, using their imaginations to fill in the gaps in the social fabric, to help make their neighborhood whole. In 1999, Spirit and Truth became an organized Christian Reformed Church congregation.

From the beginning, this has been a ministry that went beyond being defined by a church building. As a church family, they sought to become an integral part of the neighborhood. As Luke 10 people, they were called to settle and dwell in the place to which God sent them. And this is what being a local church connected closely to its neighborhood means. They knew that making disciples—in ways we will be talking about in this book—is what matters. One changed heart to serve God, Luke 10 people believe, is better than having a long list of members on your rolls.

## Evolving as a Ministry

Letting your abundance grow, as you stay rooted in place, it becomes crucial to share the harvest, to let God's grace flow like a life-giving spirit to everyone around you. While the original building still serves as the church for Spirit and Truth, other smaller neighborhood churches have been planted over time, often with members from the main congregation. This is because, said Sue Baker, Manny Ortiz believed it was important for pastors to reach their communities "through the planting of small churches rather than building one big church, as he always believed that, especially in a city made up of relatively small neighborhoods, smaller churches have a larger impact." With being big comes a lack of intimacy. Just as Jesus sent the disciples out in Luke 10, Manny sent young pastors to get busy in the neighborhood. Today, Spirit and Truth has fostered other churches spread through Hunting Park and beyond; some have flourished, while others have struggled. Always important has been to have patience so God could lead the way. Besides the stand-alone churches, Spirit and Truth now has a Christian school, which is in the church building, and through a ministry called Joy in the City offers seminary courses, trains young people to repair their bikes, and offers a legal clinic. It is also closely involved in the Esperanza Community Health Center, just across the street from the church. These ministries came out of a community-needs survey the church did when it first began. Ortiz believed that a church must know its community and by doing so it needed to do what it could to serve its needs. Listening carefully to those around you gives you the chance to glimpse the Spirit at work in others. Ortiz believed that bringing lasting peace and hope to a community took dedication. "When we started here, we already had a vision—and that vision was to let the community direct that vision," said Sue Baker.

In the end, all ministry—and especially in urban areas—is addressing the social and personal consequences of sin, Ortiz writes in his book, co-written with Harvey Conn, *Urban Ministry: The Kingdom, the City and the People of God* (2001). In North Philadelphia, sin was everywhere, he writes, in lives but in the debilitating landscape as well. "The buildings are collapsing from lack of care, absentee landlords, and the systemic evil that has redlined the community so home improvement loans are not available. The streets are filled with garbage that should have been picked up by the sanitation department. No one cares. This is the environment in which many inner-city children live." The violence and hate engendered by sin too often trump love—and shalom. The only way to address sin, in Philadelphia and elsewhere, is through the liberation of the gospel. Manny believed this in his marrow; the devil was busy everywhere and only the power of God's Spirit could capture Satan and wipe away sin. He knew churches needed to be realistic about the world in which they find themselves; often they must, whether they know it or not, do ministry "as lambs among wolves," as it states in Luke 10:3. This is how Jesus describes the seventy as he sent them out. They were sent into a world defined by inequality and brokenness, by cynicism masquerading as joy, by a deep sadness born out of sin. "Nothing else (other than God's fellowship of believers) can address the enormity of sin," writes Ortiz. "The task of the church is to preach the kingdom of Christ in a way that effectively reverses the Fall and brings wholeness and peace to individuals and community." Always central to any ministry, he believed, was both speaking out and working hard on behalf of God's kingdom wherever you go.

## Opening House Churches

A few years ago, Manny strolled into a local mom-and-pop grocery store a few blocks from the church and got to know the owners, Catalina and George Hunter. Manny did this often, stopping in to talk with people in businesses and in the area. Although the scope and shape of God's kingdom remains uncertain until the Lord's return, Manny believed we are also living in the kingdom today, its sweet taste is in the air we breathe, and it is important to let others know about it. As a Luke 10 disciple called to "enter a house" sharing shalom, Manny wanted to spread the joy everywhere he went. And hence, the visit to the mom-and-pop grocery store.

Smiling and outgoing, Catilina is from the Dominican Republic and, as her store has prospered, has done her best to send clothes and other items back to the town where she was born. Sometimes she travels there to help wherever she can. George was a former Marine, which meant he and the local pastor could share stories about life in the military. "Manny was a brother in arms," said George. "He was a great man. If you didn't love him, there was something wrong with you." As owners of the store, they have had to deal with crime and trouble in the neighborhood. They came in some mornings to find bullet holes in their windows. They had been robbed. Even so, they made room in their store for Bible studies for people in the area. As they got to know Ortiz and others from Spirit and Truth, someone asked if they would be interested in being part of an outreach to see what they could do to help fight drugs and shootings in the area. "They asked if we wanted to be good neighbors to prevent crime—and that was fine with us," said Catilina. So a few Spirit and Truth members began gathering in the store amid the cases of liquor and soda, the rows of candy bars and cookies, the racks of chips and cheese snacks, to pray and talk. Outside, they walked the area and spoke to those they met. One experience led to another and in 2011 One Hope Community Church began, first as services in a tent outside the store and then in a former vending machine company and home they rehabilitated behind the store. "God connected us all together," said Catilina. "We knew that those who pray together stay together and that is what we did."

With assistance from about seventy people, they eventually bought and renovated a larger building down the street for their first site. "It all began because of Manny," said George. "He was definitely a man of the Lord who worked hard to do God's business here in North Philly."

## One Hope

On the same Sunday we attended morning worship, we had a chance to eat dinner in the home of Mat Lin, the Chinese-American pastor of One Hope. I (Chris) can't speak for everyone, but the lively conversation mixed with a meal of wonderful Korean food made by Matt's wife, who is Korean-American, nourished my body and fed my soul.

After dinner, we sat in the living room as Matt's children played and we had a chance to talk with one of the church members, Joe Sanderlin. Because of a friendship that has grown between him and Matt Lin, Joe has become devoted to this place and its people. A while before, he decided to make the move from Spirit and Truth to help out at One Hope. A slender man with a worn face and piercing eyes, he talked of the thirty-five years he spent hooked on alcohol and drugs, including heroin during the last ten years of that span. Struggling with his addiction, he was battered and beaten and driven to despair many times. He worked in factories and did roofing and other jobs. And somehow, through the blur and haze of the drinking and drugging, God seemed to be there, trying to get his attention. A sense of the Lord hovered, but he kept driving it away with drink and shooting dope. As he talked, Joe related these events in a low but steady voice; giving his testimony was never easy.

Finally, he couldn't take the drugs and drinking anymore and his body collapsed, like a building falling in on itself; he couldn't walk and ended up in the hospital. When he started to feel a bit better, someone suggested he try attending Spirit and Truth, a place that opened its arms to everyone and especially to those who are suffering. No one is excluded. A thousand times Joe had heard this kind of advice; try God, see if that worked. But this time—and he has no idea why—he gave it a shot. It was like shooting blindly at the moon, but he showed up in church. Maybe it was the Spirit touching and moving him. Always before when he went to a church, the people judged him. They seemed to be too upright, too together, for him. But from the start, no one at Spirit and Truth hassled or gave him a hard time. He liked listening to Manny preach. They were like angels helping him climb out of hell.

And that help kept coming for him: a doctor at the Esperanza Health Clinic fixed his teeth. Carrying his Bible, he went regularly to the methadone clinic. Things didn't always go great. Given life's demands and the siren call of addiction, he sometimes questioned his faith and thought darned seriously about having a drink or a drug. But then, at one point, Matt Lin grabbed onto him and brought him into the fellowship of One Hope. When he first met Joe, Matt Lin had no idea they would become good friends—or how valuable he would be in this ministry. But Joe's rough-and-tumble life taught him things—the kind of things Jesus talked about all of the time. Through Joe, Matt was reminded of an important truth: "Man looks at the outside of things, but God looks at the heart."

Once he was at One Hope, Joe became an all-purpose deacon, helping roof houses, giving rides, no longer working for money but for God. His life had been so bizarre, so confusing, his brain filled with the rush and fall of drugs, that his memory is filled with gaps and black holes. So he mostly stays in the moment, letting God take the worry and just keeping busy. He helped clear a couple vacant lots near the church of trash, hauling out rusty mufflers, tires, the urban debris that had accumulated over many years. After filling more than a thousand garbage bags with trash, he helped others from One Hope turn the space into a garden—bringing new life out of the rot and ruin of discarded things. "It's like being the persistent widow [Luke 18]. Our job is to keep at it and God will provide the increase," said Joe.

Joe's story of falling far and then rising up is common at Spirit and Truth. Also common here and in other places as well is an awareness of God "is with us . . . (and) truly cares about our whole lives—mental, physical, and spiritual. And if that is the case, then so should the church," writes Jonathan Brooks, a Chicago pastor, in his book *Church Forsaken: Practicing Presence in Neglected Neighborhoods* (2018). Church should never be treated as if it was some kind of special club; you are in or you are out. A vibrant church needs to be right there living in the messiness of life. And doing this doesn't really take a college degree or seminary education. What it takes, as we learn from Spirit and Truth, is all about presence, about listening to stories such as Joe's and helping him, as has Matt Lin, to find his way out of the swamp and onto dry land. It is all about partnering and starting small, leaving the rest to God. Scary? Of course. But necessary in our world where most maps lead to nowhere. Digging out and moving on, with people of faith striding along and learning together, is the key. Staying local and letting your mind and heart be touched and moved by your neighbors, with whomever you interact with the most, sounds almost too simple. And it is simple and yet goes thoroughly against the grain of our culture that always points to the next best place and next best thing. Needed is to slow down and at the same time allow the grace of God to flow. This is a countercultural way of being a church. But in doing this, we can become witnesses to the ordinary work of God. We become poets and prophets attesting to the holiness of life wherever we are placed. We need no grand plan because it is right in front of us. "As we enter the local . . . [w]e find ourselves entering the stories and hearing the music of the other in ways we could never do if we relied on programs or the calculation of where someone is on a scale of readiness for the gospel," writes Alan Roxburgh in his book *Missional: Joining God in the Neighborhood.* Ultimately, we come not to save but to be changed; we come carrying love and try sharing it wherever we are.

Joe Sanderlin has felt this love and has been busy sharing that love with others. Life has been a rugged journey for him and being saved from himself and his addictions is never a sure thing. But he is holding on, planting flowers in dirt that was once covered with trash and watching those flowers bloom.

## Facing Down the Wolves

About two miles from Spirit and Truth, within the Hunting Park parish and located in a bustling, diverse neighborhood, is Eighth Street Community Church. Planted by Spirit and Truth in 2007, it is located at Eighth and Butler, once a well-known corner for selling crack. A place often filled with cops and dealers playing cat and mouse. But that corner is being transformed by Pastor Andy Lee and elder Mario Pagan. On a brisk Monday morning, they were walking down the sidewalk toward church. Plaster and pieces of drywall powdered their hair and clothes. They had spent time tearing out the ceiling of a church member's home. It was waterlogged and sagging and there was little money to make the repairs.

Once inside the church, a former bar, Andy and Mario sat at a table and talked of the ministry—the arts and after-school programs, playing flag football on a closed-off street, the parties, the services, the meals. This building, although in need of some fixing up, serves as a community center, especially after school when the kids show up, drop their books out on tables, and do homework. At one point, Mario Pagan spoke about growing up just down the street and joining a gang that sold crack cocaine on that "hot corner" outside the church. A stocky man whose face was framed by beard stubble, his voice had a streetwise directness to it. He knew this place, its secrets, its tragedies, and its longings. Selling crack just outside what is now the church landed him in prison, where he felt himself break down. He hated the place and felt trapped. But talking with others, he began to experience something working on him. He later realized it was the Holy Spirit seeking to get in and change him. It took time; he is cynical and not quick to fall for easy emotion. But this was different and persistent; God was moving into him. The more he felt it, the more certain he became that the Spirit was moving into him like a special wind inside those prison walls. It felt like a higher power had taken over his soul. When he was released, he returned to live with his mother in a flat a few doors from the church.

Back living in the neighborhood where crack made him lots of money and put him in prison, he wanted a different life. He was hungry for the Bible and, since he didn't want to take the bus somewhere, started going to the church that Andy Lee pastored and that sat on the very corner where he once dealt drugs. For that matter, his father used to drink in the building when it was a bar. And upstairs, Mario Pagan and others once prepared crack for sale.

Two by two, Mario and Andy now work together, walking through the neighborhood and handing out sandwiches to the hungry and homeless, praying with people in the alleys and on the street corners. Knowing what it's like for young people to get a job, Mario has dedicated himself to working with youth and teaching them some of the skills he has—fixing cars, doing electrical work. In the process, he and Andy have joined with others to lay the groundwork for an alternative high school, Vocatio, which offers a few classes in the summer—math, English, welding, computer programming—for students, many of them ex-addicts. Mario is the vocational director. He and Andy hope to open the school full time. They have a board and teachers lined up. "We're always targeting the broken," said Mario. "It is a ministry. It can get hard, but it is awesome. We are a small church, but it is amazing how God is using weak vessels like us and is glorifying himself down here."

Mario hit the nail on the head. They are weak vessels being filled; they are like new wineskins full of fresh, new wine. Right there in the heart of the city, the two were pouring out all they had been given by God and, staying fixed right where they are, Pastor Andy and Mario Pagan are instruments of grace, an amazing grace that saves us all, whether we are wretched and fallen, crying out behind bars or simply cut off from the dazzling, sustaining current of communion with God. As Luke 10 people, they are like modern-day prophets who have eyes to see the things God wants them to see. "Blessed are the eyes that see what you see," says Jesus in Luke 10: 23–24. "For I tell you that many prophets and kings wanted to see what you see but did not see it, and to hear what you hear but do not hear it." Thus, ministry goes both ways: you give and get back; it is a holy cycle of joy and forgiveness.

## "Heal the Sick Who are There"

When he walked the dusty roads of Galilee and environs, healing was an important aspect of Christ's ministry. In that time before doctors and hospitals and high-tech medicine, Jesus used his divine power to restore sight to the blind, to help the lame walk, to cast out demons, and even to raise the dead. These were miracles that helped attest to his divinity, but they were even more than that. They were signs and examples of Christ's deep caring for the ill, the broken, and the possessed. He came to save souls but also to heal bodies. Healing was central to his work. So it is no surprise that in Luke 10 Christ instructs his disciples, as part of their work to spread the gospel far and wide, to "heal the sick and to tell them, 'The kingdom of God has come near to you.'" For many people of faith, healing has been a core of the work that they do, at home or many miles away. Although Spirit and Truth has many programs, most geared to elicit some type of healing, the church played a big role in bringing the Esperanza Health Center to Hunting Park. Today, the health center is a concrete example of the love and care people of the church feel for their brothers and sisters.

And one of these is Janet King, who arrived in Philadelphia from Jamaica in 2015 to live with friends. Soon, however, she started to experience vaginal bleeding and went from emergency room to emergency room trying to find out what was wrong. Then her sister, who knew an Esperanza doctor, suggested she go there. Almost immediately, Dr. Pam Garcia diagnosed cancer but needed to perform tests to be certain. Since Janet had no insurance, the doctor connected her to an Esperanza social worker who navigated the system so Janet could get the proper tests and see a cancer doctor who recommended surgery, radiation, and chemo. Esperanza nurses stayed close and one took her to the hospital when Janet got a blood clot in her lung. During all of this, Janet's roommates one day told her she had to leave—one more setback in a life of setbacks. But Andres Fajaro, the health center's chaplain, and pastor of the Hunting Park House Church, told her she could stay in an apartment near where he and his family live. "I moved my things in and started going to Spirit and Truth and it felt like I was home," she said. "Everyone embraced me, especially Blanca [Ortiz], and wanted to know about me. I thank God for life."

Another person for whom healing has come is Wally Hill. Without the people from Spirit and Truth and healthcare he receives from Esperanza, Hill would be in a bad way, maybe even dead. As is the case with so many others, his is a story of God seeping into his life. His story reinforces the truth, forever fresh, of things spiritual and unseen touching and shaping a life. He went to a Catholic grade school and worshipped for a time at a Baptist church with his dad. Running the streets as a teen, he picked up Spanish and worked as a translator during city elections. In the early 2000s, he owned a retail clothing store in an area mall. One night on the way home, he parked by a grocery store, planning to go in to get something. A gang of teens approached his car and told him to move; he was parking in the spot where they sold drugs. When he refused, they dragged him from his car and beat him badly. Nine days later he woke up in the hospital with a broken jaw, shattered cheekbone, and massive head injury. Out of the hospital, he moved back with his mother, who cared for him. Nurses and doctors from Esperanza tended to him, in office visits and at home. But recovery came slowly. With a swollen, bloated face, he said he looked like the movie character the Elephant Man. Despair began to settle in and he was about to give up hope when a group of Spirit and Truth members, going door-to-door and praying for people, showed up in his bedroom. These were Luke 10 people, answering Christ's call to bring healing to the sick. Wally's mother had let them in. An elder stood him up and everyone gathered in a circle around him. Powerful prayers made the room feel like it was vibrating. A spirit seemed to be alive and shaking his beat-up body. Those feelings left when they left. But he remembered them and the prayers. Even in his suffering, he started to sense a sliver of hope. And then one Sunday, he got out of bed, though he isn't sure why he got out of bed. On shaking legs, he made it the few blocks to Spirit and Truth, where he stumbled in the front doors and fell on his knees. He was again surrounded by praying hands. When he settled, he sat up front. He liked the service and, as he kept coming, he liked learning about the Christian Reformed Church and its strong, Bible-based teachings. He found a firm foundation of theology and teaching in the CRC that he hadn't even known he was hungry for. But he fell away, drinking and partying, and yet only for a time. He came back and is now a member of one of the church plants at the nearby Joy in the City building. "God has a way of knocking you down like Job," said Wally Hill. "People at Spirit and Truth pulled me up."

## Directing the Clinic with Great Joy

Susan Post can see the Esperanza Health Center from a window in her home. Every time she looks she is filled with gratitude as she thinks of all the work it took for it to happen. It is a special place of healing in a part of Philadelphia that has had to cope with all the brutality urban life can throw at people. As executive director of the center, she is grateful to be part of a work that can provide healthcare to people such as Janet and Wally. Each of them is a child of God, a child who had been rejected and needed help and couldn't find it until arriving at the health center. Thinking of Jesus, the greatest healer of all, Post is certain he would approve of what they are doing—bringing health to the lowly, to those forgotten by a system that sets things up for itself, to those who don't have the resources to go to doctors in upscale offices with fountains flowing in the lobby and expensive artwork on the walls, to those who can't simply slap down an insurance card and receive the care they need. At the same time, she sees that treating what's wrong with the body is only part of it. All dimensions of a person, whether curing cancer or helping someone cope with cancer, or offer dental care and follow up after a beating, are crucial. And at the top of the list has to be faith in Christ; it is all about finding and sharing the power to soothe souls in sorrow. Post keeps coming back to this. Real healthcare—the kind referred to in the story of the Good Samaritan in Luke 10—is about binding up wounds and bringing those afflicted with addiction into a new life of being clean and sober and staying with them as they grow in that journey. And it is about helping people, suffering from domestic violence or the dozens of diseases that come with poverty, climb out of the wreckage of their lives. Susan Post, an elder at Spirit and Truth, is fine with practitioners praying with patients right in the treatment rooms. In fact, the whole clinic is bathed in prayer; it flows from room to room, shifting and sorting and reaching people who have come here for help they can't get anywhere else. The job, whether casting an arm, stitching a cut, or diagnosing a disease, is always showing the love of God in what you do. And, when possible, it is bringing a person in pain one step closer to God. Jesus healed lepers, made the blind see; he used his own form of miraculous healthcare to share the good news. And that's what Susan Post is all about. Looking out her window, she has seen the needs of her community and played a part in addressing them. Oddly enough, it's simple: just follow what is in your front yard and use the skills God gives you to make a difference.

## Reforming the Vision

In *Stay in the City* (2019), Mark Gornik and Maria Leu Wong write that Spirit and Truth has an unusual vision of wrapping all of their neighbors in love. The nexus of their work is offered across the street and right around the corner. You need only to open your eyes to how you can help and open yourself to the Spirit that is always but a breath or two away. "Grounded in Scripture, they (Spirit and Truth) concentrated on their neighborhood and its experiences. They worked for God's peace and reconciliation amidst the divisions of their city. They committed themselves to the next generation of leaders. They shared the life-changing power of Jesus with everyone they met in the city. They trusted in a sovereign God." In his comments, referring to the sovereignty of God, Gornik touches on a key teaching of the Reformed faith—and a teaching he believes is being lived out in North Philadelphia. It is a system of thought that makes what Spirit and Truth is doing, as well as what other ministries are doing, strong examples of following Reformed thinking and translating it into all areas of life.

Reformed Christians teach that God is over everything and God's presence is in all places. In essence, this approach can be traced back to the early reformers such as John Calvin, who believed that the Christian faith should be woven into the entire social fabric of Geneva, where he made his home. At work in many Presbyterian denominations, it evolved over the centuries and we see it expressed in the early twentieth century by Dutch writer and theologian Abraham Kuyper, who held a worldview that taught our faith should be active in all places and we should keep in the forefront our minds, especially when we are involved in missions, that "every square inch" of God's world is worthy of our attention. It is an approach and theology that is practical and wide-ranging. It is about redemption of everyone and of the world. In his book *Engaging God's World* (2002), as he speaks about the role of the church, Cornelius Plantinga, Jr. writes: "Everything corrupt needs to be redeemed, and that includes the whole natural world, which both sings and groans. The whole natural world, in all its glory and pain, needs the redemption that will bring shalom."

CRC congregations have for many years spoken about how we need to be deeply involved in all aspects of culture. Still, there has remained a tribal aspect in which we acknowledge the need to expand our view of the world. But that is changing across the religious landscape. In recent years, this approach and all that it means has started to grab hold; people in churches are seeing it has deeper meaning. Students studying in seminaries are coming to see that the churches they will serve after graduation are beginning to live out life and ministry in different ways. They are starting to see that there is a spiritual hunger among the people and there is a need to move from being a big church and asking people to make Jesus their friend and all will be well, to a way of thinking that takes very seriously the place, the context, the locale in which each church finds itself. Spirit and Truth is a church that is taking very seriously the Reformed call for reformation of everything and everyone and in all places. Instead of offering Christ as something to be purchased through our good intentions and accepted; instead of making religion a commodity; instead of being a decision to make one soul at a time, it is much wider. It is a theology that is as much about the place as it is about the community that lives there. It is about the gritty world in all of its madness and joy. It is about growing a church, like a garden, in a particular setting—for instance in North Philadelphia—and adapting the practices and approaches to that world. It is a movement coming out of our souls and is willing to engage the world in experimental and creative ways. Emerging is a new language and new messages posed in ways that people can hear. At work is paying attention in new ways; we need to do it differently. "It requires paying critical attention to the cultural context and the faithful translation of the gospel to speak meaningfully in the vernacular of the context," writes Craig Van Gelder and Dwight J. Zscheile in *Participating in God's Mission: A Theological Missiology for the Church in America* (2018).

## Loving the Kids in the Neighborhood

Not long before Taehoo Lee's monthlong annual summer camp began in July 2018 in North Philadelphia, two people were shot in a nearby neighborhood. Then, just after midnight on a Tuesday morning, two shooters killed a fourteen-year-old boy and wounded three other boys in a neighborhood several blocks away. Fueled by gang violence, North

Philadelphia is probably the most dangerous neighborhood in the city, say police. But Taehoo Lee has been through it all, since 2003, living and ministering in one of the row houses on Uber Street and getting to know the local people—drug dealers, homeless squatters, families, business people, and especially the children.

When we met with him that Friday night in early spring, he mentioned briefly that he holds the summer camp for the local kids. But we wanted to know more and, just as the annual summer camp was starting, we talked with him on the phone about it. Taehoo was busy. Even so, he took time to talk. And he reiterated that a main focus of his ministry are the children he sees coming and going and helps to mentor during the school year, and they often simply hang around with little to do in the summer. They are the ones for whom he began the camp. "Kids around here are poor, and there isn't much for them to do during the summer," he said. "We had maybe forty kids that first summer, but this year there are about 120—and now they are coming from six or seven blocks away."

More so than in other years, the mothers and the grandmothers in the area this year have supported the effort and spread the word about the summer camp. Many have also shown up to help out. Others gather at a picnic table to watch. "One of them just asked me how I got this going because she wants to start a camp on her block," said Lee. Begun in 2006, the monthlong camp celebrated its tenth anniversary in 2018 because Lee had to return to Korea for two years as part of the process of becoming a US citizen, which was finalized in 2017.

Especially gratifying for Taehoo that year was to have two young men, Brian and Messiah, and one young woman, Ayasha, working as volunteers. They attended the camp regularly while they were growing up. "We have many other volunteers, but these three are special. The kids look up to them because they are role models," said Taehoo. Grant Hofman, pastor of youth at Spirit and Truth and also a camp volunteer, added, "Through them, our kids get to see young leaders who share their same skin color, grew up down the block from them, and have gone through the same joys and struggles. This is tremendously exciting because these three are ministering to their peers and serving as an example of hope to them in a way that those of us who are not native to North Philly will never fully be able to."

Only in 2018 did Lee incorporate his neighborhood ministry into a Christian Reformed church plant, which is called North Philly Community Church. He was in the process of raising funds to rehabilitate that empty building at the end of Uber Street—the one in front of which we parked the night we talked to Taehoo—and turn it into a community center and as a place for worship. "The main reason I'm doing this now is that it makes more sense to proceed with the building project as a church, even though, in a way, I already have a church in my neighborhood," he said. "It will take some time to meet regularly but what is already going on in my community is a part of the life of a local church."

City workers block off either end of Uber Street every morning for the camp. Volunteers arrive about 9 AM to clean the street, and kids start showing up about 9:30. Camp opens at 10 with the singing of a few praise songs, after which Lee offers a short message based on a theme. In 2018, that theme was "Our Children Matter," based on the story of the exodus. Taehoo used Exodus, the book in which the Israelites were slaves in Egypt for many years before God led them out, because it applies to racism and African Americans in the past and today. It is about God's special love and saving grace for a people that had been enslaved. After he gives that day's lesson to the children—most of whom are African American and some of whom are Hispanic—they have a chance to talk about the message, and from there the day unfolds with crafts and games, lunch, and more activities. Then the day wraps up with a short time of praise.

On Wednesdays, they spend the day swimming in a pool outside the city. And on Fridays they gather for a picnic and activities in a park, also outside of town. "Many of these kids otherwise never leave the city. We want to show them some places where they can see and experience nature" and some other surroundings, Lee said.

Hofman has volunteered at the camp several times—the first year as an intern while at Calvin Theological Seminary. It was one of the main factors that led him to move to North Philadelphia upon graduating. "What I love about Pastor Taehoo is that he sees his entire life's call being to love God and love his neighbor. He sincerely loves his neighbors, and most especially their children," said Hofman. Every time he has heard Taehoo pray before a meal, Taehoo has asked that God provide daily bread for his neighbors. But he isn't just praying; Taehoo has put his convictions into action by moving into this neighborhood. "Knowing the tense history between black individuals and Asians in the 'hood, his moving into the neighborhood as a Korean and truly seeking the well-being of North Philly has a prophetic quality to it," said Hofman. What he has found so compelling about Uber Street Camp is that he has witnessed God's kingdom in North Philly, as it is in heaven, in a way he had never seen before. Being there with Taehoo often makes him think of Zechariah's vision, says Hofman, in which the prophet says that the land of Judah was "so desolate that no one traveled through it" (Zech 7:14) and "no one could go about their business safely because of their enemies" (8:10). But through Zechariah the Lord said, "Once again men and women of ripe old age will sit in the streets of Jerusalem, each of them with cane in hand because of their age. The city streets will be filled with boys and girls playing there" (8:4–5).

This might as well be a literal portrait of the street camp. Though North Philly has gained a reputation as one of the "bad" parts of town, there is a different picture you see during July: boys and girls playing safely on the closed-off streets that would otherwise be covered in shattered glass and burdened by violence. Grandparents sit on their stoops, some actually with canes in hand, watching the children and enjoying the chorus of their joy and laughter. Hofman said he also thinks of the final vision of the wedding feast of the Lamb, of the great multitude from every nation, tribe, people, and language joined together in Revelation 7. "The camp has served as a foretaste of this banquet. For our final event, we have a block party in which our neighbors, mostly black with some Latino and other ethnic populations, and Korean congregations from around the area bring in their favorite dishes to dine together on a feast that feeds the entire neighborhood," he said. "It is the only place where I have eaten soul food with chopsticks. And I imagine Jesus' table won't be too distant from that experience." The camp is also a place where city workers turn on a fire hydrant for the kids to run through the spewing water. They shiver when it falls on them, and yet some shout for joy before going back to get drenched again. Watching them, Taehoo grins. That water, pouring from the fire hydrant, is like the water of life, falling with a shower of grace on these kids running through it.

That street fair is only one of the ways that the Luke 10 people of Spirit and Truth present the gospel in a concrete fashion through words and deeds. We see how Luke 10 leaders such as Taehoo Lee carry with them the bedrock belief that everyone in this community deserves to be part of God's kingdom. We see how everyone, especially the children, deserve to be refreshed by the water of life. We see how water gushing from a fire hydrant, in the midst of this community on Uber Street on a hot July day, is a symbol of joy—a symbol of the new life that is being preached and lived out every day in this specific place called North Philadelphia. In the end, we see how two people, Manny Ortiz and Sue Baker, went two by two and joined with others to live out a Luke 10 theology that sees God everywhere and works to open everyone's eyes to this truth. The Spirit is always at work in this community in whatever it does. In the end, the harvest is plentiful and no one is excluded.

# 2

# "Like Lambs Among Wolves"

[or]

## Coffee, Football, and Embracing
## the Homeless in Seattle

"Go! I am sending you out like lambs among wolves. Do not take a purse or bag or sandals." —Luke 10:3–4

*This is about going and being sent, and living there, and staying put, regardless of the danger, challenges, or disappointments of a place. It is about leaving behind those practices and approaches that no longer work or matter. It is being and living in the real, tough, no-sugar-coated world compared to living in the confines of a like-minded affinity group. In Seattle, Aurora Commons opens itself to the homeless, the broken and forgotten, who face their own share of wolves—those that are fierce and others that are subtle. We meet a woman who was beaten badly by a man and the police refuse to arrest her assailant and then a woman who speaks of sexual predators who she has to deal with in homeless shelters. A ministry following the Luke 10 path of seeking welcome in a new place, Aurora Commons steps into the world of the homeless with fresh eyes and open hearts. Also in Seattle is a ministry shaped around a weekend football league overseen by Pastor Clarence Presley. We meet one of the coaches whose father killed his mother and who has turned to God for solace. Coffee shop ministries are important here as church planters seek to listen to and discern what people long for in a ministry that touches their lives.*

## Aurora Commons: Dealing with
## the Wolves of Sin and Sorrow

B acon, eggs, pancakes, and potatoes were cooking in the People's Kitchen at Aurora Commons in Seattle, Washington, on a chilly Monday morning in November. As people lined up for breakfast, a man and woman sat and dozed, heads tilted toward each other, and another man was paging through a magazine on the large couch of this shelter that bills itself as a "community living room." Basically, a large, open room painted soft yellow with art on the walls, it is a comfortable and safe place to stay for a few hours three days a week. Always a busy space, a mix of volunteers and visitors from off the street chatted and laughed as they broke eggs and flipped pancakes and bacon in the kitchen. Meanwhile, coming in the front door, Gene Northrope smelled the food cooking; he was hungry and wanted to eat. But first he set down his bulky duffle bag, stripped off his coat and the two sweatshirts he wore to keep him warm the night before in a nearby park. Rubbing his hands together, Northrope said that although he was famished, he planned to eat after he dug his dirty clothes out of his duffle bag to put in the free washer in the back room.

Allowing people to wash and dry their clothes for free, to take a shower, and to get socks and other items, Aurora Commons is located on a stretch of Aurora Avenue not far from downtown Seattle. This area is known for its active sex industry, drug dealing, violence, and homelessness.

Founded by church planter Ben Katt and a few others, Aurora Commons opened in 2011. Staffed by volunteers from nearby Awake Church and elsewhere, it has made itself a community home for those who live on or work on or near Aurora Avenue. "The vision for the Commons grew out of the ministry of presence and neighborhood rootedness along Aurora Avenue of Awake's founding members, particularly the relationship-building and community development work that we did along Aurora and in the motels," said Katt.

This morning, as the shelter buzzed with a mix of sounds, Robert came up to a visitor to show an envelope on which he had scrawled several phone numbers, one apparently to the local FBI office. A slender man with sad eyes and a lined, drawn face, he talked for a few minutes, bouncing from topic to topic—a gas station clerk he had a crush on, a judge somewhere whom he didn't like, his Uncle Ray to whom he owed money, how he'd like to go overseas to France for vacation, and then something about George Washington

26

having come to town. Though dealing with some cognitive challenges, Robert was nonetheless very clear when asked how he liked coming to Aurora Commons: "They are good to us. When you walk in, they give you a smile. You know, they are real soft-hearted people."

## Greeting Visitors

Volunteers say kindness and a smile go a long way at this low-barrier shelter, meaning it is open to everyone and has few rules people have to follow. At the heart of this place is a mission to create relationships.

"We want to have a face that people can recognize, and we want to be here to show hospitality that they can experience," said Hayden Wartes, who was serving as a host today, circulating the room, greeting and checking in with people. Taking a break, Wartes sat in a chair by the big picture window looking out on Aurora Avenue. At the Commons, she said, they seek to model the incarnational ministry of Christ, trying to show love, acceptance, patience, and compassion. This is not a church, and yet it is a community that gathers around a liturgy of conversation, meals, and cups of coffee. This is a place where the Luke 10 people say "Peace to this house." Many who come here have been hurt in some way by organized religion, or they have never been connected to a church. "Many of them would face barriers if they stepped into a church community of people who looked healthy and fine," said Wartes, who has been connected to Aurora Commons since it opened. "Many of the people who come here are estranged from their families. They feel ashamed about their lifestyle." These are definitely people sorely seeking peace that comes from an incarnational theology putting relationships first. The ministry at the Commons is filled out with such things as a wound clinic held every week, an art program, a risk-reduction program for drug users, a support group for women, and a Monday-night gathering for men who at this time of year usually watch Monday Night Football on TV. On serving at Aurora Commons as a host and in other ways, Wartes said, "Doing this is important to my own spiritual journey. I do a lot of listening to people who are suffering and don't have someone who can listen to them talk about their trauma."

## Helping a Battered Woman

Outside after breakfast, Gene Northrope lit a cigarette and looked at a woman who, arms folded across her chest, was pacing back and forth on the sidewalk. Clearly agitated, she had two black eyes and bruises on her swollen face. Her blonde hair was disheveled. Northrope said the man who recently beat her so badly has not been arrested by the police. But that didn't surprise him. "Lots of times women will tell the police they've been beat up and who it is was . . . but the cops won't believe them. The guys get away." Overhearing him, the woman shouted: "Why don't you believe me?!" Then she stormed off down the sidewalk. Later, once Aurora Commons was closed for the day, she would return, and Sparrow Carlson, a founder of Aurora Commons, would sit and talk with her for a long time. For now, Northrope shrugged, stubbing out his cigarette after the woman stomped away. "I didn't say I didn't believe her. . . . Man, life is tough out here. You have to watch out all the time."

Going back inside and sitting at a table, Northrope didn't talk about what he had to watch out for, but he did say he grew up in Lynnwood, a city outside Seattle, and that he has been homeless for a long time. He has a sketchy past, his life motivated by the need to simply get by. He looked like a man driven and dogged by memories and experiences too hard to address. "I like it in here," he said of the Commons. "People can come in to get real food. There is a computer available for anyone who asks. They meet us at our level. These are good people with good intentions who work here." Asked if he went to church or prayed, he shook his head. "I think sometimes God walked away from us when he wiped most of the people out with the water" (referring to the great flood in Genesis 7). As for prayer, he offered what sounded like an assessment from a street theologian, hardened by experience, devoid of any sentimentality. "I think sometimes God answers prayer. So I guess I think he's there. But I don't believe he interferes with us. I don't believe in divine intervention. I think he just leaves us to live with the consequences of our choices."

## Sorting through Harsh Memories

Since she moved into one of the nearby tiny homes—simple structures built to accommodate the homeless—a couple blocks from the Commons, Marlys Anderson sleeps on a pad on the floor by the door. A man named

Joe sleeps in the small bed. While Joe spends much of the day watching TV, she likes to walk over to Aurora Commons. Sitting at a long table, Marlys said she enjoys the food and the chance to talk to others: "I like to talk a lot. It helps to calm my anxiety. It feels good to be here. It makes me feel good when people are nice to me, especially when you have health problems like I do." Marlys's heart acts up and her legs hurt. She is prediabetic and has high blood pressure. Lately, she has had a hard time eating because she lost her dentures. She has been homeless for a long time, and she shared stories of staying on shelter mattresses that had bedbugs and lice. But she keeps moving on in a life that has taken her to places she never imagined, like homeless camps where she had to be on the lookout for sexual predators. "Really, Seattle can be a wild place," she said. Still, she has hope. The day before, Sunday, she stopped in for the service at Awake Church. "I want to pray and read the Bible," she said. "I'm trying to change; it is so hard. But anything is possible with God."

## The Tattooed Man

Over by the coffee machine, Nick Bunning stood with his small pet bull-dog, Lulu. Bunning is a mysterious guy. He has been featured in news articles as a highly successful architect in New York City. One story said he worked on Trump Towers. Another story called him "the most tat-tooed man in New York City." Bunning's entire face and head are filled with ink drawings, and so are his back and his arms and legs. He is said to own property in Seattle. He was here that day, he said, because a friend who comes here often invited him. Bunning smiled as he looked around the big room with its long dining table, the colorful walls and paintings, and a large bookshelf, serving as a lending library. "I adore it here. It is a great place," he said. "I've seen missions where they bang religion at you. This is a simple place, sunny and warm."

## A Volunteer

By 1 PM, the day began winding down, although many of the men would be back at 6 PM to watch football. Zach Jenkins, an IT worker who lives nearby, said he planned to be there. For now, though, he was chatting with visitors and helping to clean up after people had eaten. As a volunteer, he has some-times had to separate people fighting outside, or calm down someone who was out of control, likely caused by drugs or alcohol. "It can get messy," he said. "But I think this is something that Jesus would do—to be with those who are struggling—and we're called to do it."

## Football, Pizza, and Fellowship

Andy Carlson, pastor of nearby Awake Church, bustled around in the People's Kitchen, unpacking ingredients for pizza for the Monday night men's group. Earlier, this spacious shelter was brightly lit from the sun and lights. Now, it is dim; there is a less hectic feel. Outside, a bitter wind was blowing and men were huddled at the door, peering in, ready for some warmth, pizza, and football. In a few minutes, Zach Jenkins, who was volunteering earlier, opened the door and let the men in for Monday Night Football, which featured the Miami Dolphins against the Carolina Panthers. The men milled around, speaking quietly, and some sat on the couch and chairs. Meanwhile, players were warming up on the big TV screen. One of the men who was here tonight was Vince, a jack of all trades who likes to pitch in when he's at the Commons. Before helping Andy get things ready, he recalled how he walked by the Commons about three years ago and on impulse decided to stop in. Since then, he has kept dropping in when he's on this side of town. Right now, he comes in often, since he lives in one of the nearby tiny homes. Reflecting on his wandering, homeless lifestyle, Vince said it isn't so bad. It could be worse. Now he has a place to sleep at least. Plus, he said, having the Commons is good: "Without it, we'd be in trouble."

Nearby was Casey, who is sixty-two and grew up in St. Louis. He has been a regular ever since the Commons opened. He also has attended Awake Church—and rarely misses a Monday night meeting for pizza and football. Life on the streets can get tough, but he is grateful he has an antidote to the chaos he so frequently encounters. "I love Awake Church. They are beautiful people who go there—man oh man, they help you out."

After getting the food ready and the game started, Andy Carlson sat down. Looking around, he reflected a bit on the practical theology that motivates him and others in Awake Church. Mirrored by the other ministries begun since the late 1990s in Seattle, it's a Reformed theology that teaches that everything in the world is under God's domain—and Christians are called to be part of it. Every part of it. They are called to leave their places of comfort and go out to be with people in their homes, neighborhoods, jobs, schools—in every place. It is a theology, arising out of Christ, that makes wide room for others. A Luke 10 theology in which you are asked to "Heal the sick who are there and tell them, 'The kingdom of God has come near to you.'" And those with whom they work are ailing and alienated in a number of ways. "A large number of the people we serve wouldn't be part of a church if it weren't for Awake," said Carlson. "Many of them have found themselves on the fringes of Christianity. Some have been abused and hurt deeply." As a result, Carlson said, Awake is part of a movement of church communities that believe making the gospel tangible is important. Take the message out from the church building and find ways to make it the lifeblood, the blood of Jesus, in all aspects of your neighborhood and of society itself. A big task, and one many may find impossible or simply ridiculous, to be sure, but it is a job that those who have been welcomed into God's community must carry. It is a burden that is heavy and one under which you can stumble, but it becomes much lighter when you carry it along with others. The Bible, of course, is key, but revealing Christ by your actions also matters. Having a strong and ongoing relationship with Jesus and then acting out his message of love, in all of its facets, is what members of Awake try to do—and Aurora Commons is a living example of that.

"We don't see the Commons as an evangelistic tool," said Carlson, a mild-mannered man whose hands are rough and calloused from making a living as a woodworker. "What we do here is very much an expression of our faith."

## The Green Bean Coffee Shop Ministry

Randy Rowland had spent a long day meeting with Seattle-area church leaders to discuss ways the Christian Reformed Church might consider adapting to meet the fracturing reality of congregations across the denomination facing the need to change—and, in many cases, they were hard-pressed how to do so. Communities were breaking apart; membership in many churches was dropping. And there were no magic fixes for the CRC. A denomination once defined by one ethnic group—the church has its roots in the Netherlands—was grappling with what the Spirit was saying as it tried to open itself to a wider range of groups for whom the Reformed faith meant little. Other churches and denominations were also in this fix. Lots of books described the problem and offered so-called missional solutions. At the meeting held earlier at Bellevue CRC in Bellevue, Washington, south of Seattle, Rowland had shared some of his thoughts and offered a few solutions out of his own experiences. He had a fair amount to share, but he had to leave the meeting and rush back on this Saturday night to the Green Bean, a coffee shop and ministry center that he founded in 2005. He had to conduct a memorial service for a homeless man who had died in his car.

When Rowland arrived, the lights in the Green Bean were on. Earlier, a fierce windstorm had killed the electricity and no one knew if the memorial service would take place. But the power was back, the lights blazing from within this place that was in many ways a seminal ministry in the start of new forms of outreach in Seattle—church work that went beyond the normal Sunday service. Connecting in places such as the coffee shop that was itself a form of worship, a kind of prayer lived out in the places where people spent much of their time beyond the weekends. Friends and family of the man being eulogized had started filing into the coffee shop. With everything in place and several minutes to go before the service, Rowland stepped next door to a pizza place.

## Taking a Break

A former radio disc jockey and a longtime stadium announcer for the Seattle Seahawks football team, Rowland sipped a drink and spoke of how he had worked for many years as a church planter in the Presbyterian Church (USA) before joining the CRC. Serving on the front lines of church growth, he learned firsthand what it takes to begin new congregations, the lifeblood of any denomination. A church planter must be flexible and find creative ways to gather a core group of people who can live out the gospel message in a local context. He tried to do this with his church, Sanctuary CRC, formally organized in 2007, seeking to weave it into the life of the Greenwood neighborhood. And one important part of the ministry has been the Green Bean. In 2011, it was destroyed by a fire; but it had reopened in its new location. It is a money maker, serving coffee to customers, as well as a venue for gatherings such as the memorial service. Sanctuary meets for services in the nearby Taproot Theatre, a local theater with a national reputation for fostering the arts. Every Sunday, about one hundred people, many in their twenties and thirties, attend the service. To a large extent, it has been a refuge and way station. Some 800 or so people have come through the church over the years and, hopefully, says Rowland, moved on to other churches. On the same Saturday morning of the memorial service, Sanctuary had invited members to take a morning stroll through their neighborhood. This was a good way to familiarize people with the surroundings, as well as help them get to know each other, forming bonds the church can nurture. As they walked, they chatted and prayed. They did this regularly, these walks through the area, to get to know and befriend this community and all of the people, said Rowland, waving a hand out the window at people passing on the crowded sidewalk.

Church members say they are drawn to Sanctuary because it is an urban church with a "vibrant mission, strong leaders, and a coherent . Reformed vision." Sanctuary puts into practice living out the grace of God. Heather Whitney has been attending Sanctuary with her family for several years. "We were drawn to Sanctuary because of the community of people we found here."

Alyssa Groenwold said feeling loved is important, but so is the fact that Sanctuary works, as Rowland had said, "to have a presence in the community." Creating community, said Rowland, is having a tolerant, open-minded approach that fosters ministry to all people in the area. The man for whom the memorial service would be held was a church member who died drunk in a parked car. A significant portion of the population to whom they minister, said Rowland, are the "nones"—those young people without a church. And this has meant gearing messages and ministry to the needs of Seattle's young, often highly educated, exceptionally mobile, electronically sophisticated, and skeptical population. And sometimes these young people come and quickly move on; even Sanctuary with its more open approach is too confining. For them, spirituality means hiking on Sunday mornings, going kayaking on a local river or out in Puget Sound. For many of these folks, Jesus was a good teacher, but so was Buddha. Trying to help them see the divinity of Christ and what that means is a major challenge. Nate and his girlfriend Kate are two of these nones; they attended Sanctuary for quite awhile. Nate helped on the praise team. But after a time, they began to drift away, preferring to connect with a multifaith group that didn't limit itself to the Christian message. For that matter, they missed having the time on Sunday mornings to be outdoors and spend time with their friends. "I guess," said Nate, "the traditional Sunday thing just became less of a big deal to us."

## Laying a Friend to Rest

Trying to meet the needs of young people such as Nate and his girlfriend is a tough business. In a culture with so many choices, and in a secular city such as Seattle, it can be hard for people to hear the voice of God—if they are even trying to listen for it. "We have to be constantly asking, 'How do we make serious contact with the next generation?' We want to be hospitable," said Rowland. Yet, even being hospitable isn't always enough in a time when people seem to have little hunger for faith. God is at best a good idea; but mostly a distraction for many. Church is simply a place with too many rules and restrictions; it is not in tune with the issues and experiences of people in their twenties, thirties, and even forties. But Rowland keeps trying, touching and turning the knobs of innovation, always hoping the Spirit will touch and infuse lives.

It was nearly 7 PM and people had assembled for the service next door. Rowland got up, checked his phone for messages, and went into the Green Bean. He was ready to pray a Psalm and speak "of a man we loved and who just kept going back time and again to drinking." Surrounded by friends at the service inside the coffee shop, Rowland was continuing to do, he believed, what God asks: Don't give up; keep at it. People will find their way to the solace that solid faith, supported and defined by the fellowship and love that a community can offer.

# Word of Truth International Ministries: Playing Football for the Lord

A soft, chilly drizzle was falling in the football stadium in Renton, south of Seattle, as Pastor Clarence Presley strolled from the sidelines to place his hands on the shoulder pads of one of the Auburn Panthers and of an opponent playing for the Five Star Cougars. Kneeling on the green turf, the two young players and their teammates listened while Presley prayed, thanking God for the day and for the ways in which the Panthers and Cougars played their hearts out in the championship game, which the Panthers won 26–13. All morning and into the afternoon, Presley helped to oversee the games and took time to pray with and pray over the teams, whether they won or lost in the various divisions of the Northwest Premier Junior Football league. The Spirit of God is alive on the football field and especially in the lives of these mostly African American youngsters coming

from various backgrounds, some shaky while others feature sturdy one-
or two-parent homes. It's a mix that Presley—as a Luke 10 person seeking to enter into and bless various communities—wants to touch; God is
everywhere and cares for us all, whether or not we call ourselves members
of a church. Presley knows this and wanted these young men to know it as
well. And this is especially important at a time when Christianity faces a
new world with new questions. Presley once had many questions and he
believes it is crucial for those in ministry to go where the people are, just
as Jesus did, and share the message in all ways possible—and to answer
questions, if not just in words.

For Presley, this means serving as commissioner of the football league
and as pastor of Word of Truth International Ministries, a Christian Reformed Church outreach that includes churches and ministries in Seattle-
area neighborhoods, a discipleship center, and a network of other urban
missions and ministries. "The Holy Spirit has been working through us in
so many ways," said Presley during a break between games. They have pat-
terned their ministry after that of the early church in Acts and in Luke 10,
he explained, when Jesus followers went out "to preach the Word wherever
they went." It is a Word deeply embedded and ever-expanding in a person
such as Presley who carries the Word, often in creative and imaginative
ways, with him into the world of everyday life.

## A Hard Childhood

Growing up in Little Rock, Arkansas, Presely faced poverty, joined gangs,
and sold drugs. Looking back, he sees himself as a wandering soul. Lacking stability, he felt lost and without hope. Things were forever fragile; he
was consumed by confusion and fear. But when he got married and his
daughter was born, a shift in his life occurred. Looking at his daughter's
face, and experiencing the love and support of his wife, Athena, he knew
he needed something solid, something that didn't threaten to break. By
that time, he was living in Seattle. After his marriage, he met people who
believed in God and he saw and sensed a humility and serenity in them, a
soft security in their eyes, that he found attractive. Slowly, his perspective
shifted and he sought God. As if caught at the end of a dead-end street and
with no other place to turn, he called out for help. A sliver of willingness
to change, what he now sees as that humility he saw in others, emerged
from deep in the soul he thought was lost. It took awhile, but one step at

a time, his life began to turn around. That was several years ago. Once he felt the power of God begin to undergird him, he knew he wanted to share with others what the Lord had done for him.

## Turning to God for Relief

More than twenty years ago, Presley started a nondenominational worship community among homeless people living at the Seattle Union Gospel Mission. This was a population he knew; these were desperate people and he knew how they felt. He met with them and invited them to pray, to seek the same turnaround he experienced. He told them not to give up; to keep with it. And his church grew, not connected to any broader ministry. Then, going on fifteen years ago, he met Randy Rowland. The two hit it off; Randy saw something in him and he in Randy; they became friends. Through conversations with Rowland and another pastor, Presley began to learn and deeply appreciate the basics of the Reformed faith. He especially resonated with the teaching that all of the world is filled with the glory of God and is ripe for the blessings of the Holy Spirit. After a time, Presley proposed to his church that it join the CRC. That didn't go real well. He lost half of his church membership; the people preferred remaining independent and were wary of this church denomination that they feared might want to gobble them up. But the other half agreed to join the CRC.

Especially at the start, and occasionally since, things have been a challenge for Presley, an African American man who is a minister in a primarily white denomination. Fitting in has been hard at times. But providing balance and ongoing connection was linking with Rowland and a cluster of Seattle-area churches, most of them church plants supported by the CRC that were trying to do ministry in urban settings in creative ways. "The cluster became my family," said Presley. "As we met, God began to focus me on discipleship, and training leaders became the entire DNA of what we have been doing."

## Training and Sending

Word of Truth International Ministries is based in Tukwila, a community bordering Seattle that is known for a high crime rate. Church members come from the neighborhood, are taught how to grow in Christ, to "find their sweet spot"—what they most love to do—and to use whatever talents they have to help others and participate in God's ever-evolving kingdom. Once they have been trained and are ready, they are sent out. "We are about helping people establish a relationship with Christ and become leaders," said Presley. Today, these leaders—as modern-day Luke 10 people—do ministry in their neighborhoods, their workplaces, and wherever else they find themselves. For instance, one man has become familiar with residents of an area nursing home and has started a Bible study there. Another woman has become a business consultant and weaves her faith throughout all she does. Another man owns a water treatment company and uses it to disciple his employees—at least those who are responsive—in the faith. Others have begun a catering company that has at its core the desire and hope to provide good food while at the same time connecting and sharing with customers, as much in words as in their hospitality, about what God has meant to them. The church also conducts job training, parenting classes, and tutoring for students. It began a baseball ministry for area youth a few years ago, believing that young African American boys and girls, especially in the city, have few chances and few spaces in which to learn to play the sport. "We are in this as brothers and sisters who want to help others walk in freedom," said Presley. "We follow wherever the Spirit leads and get involved in many ways. We try new things. You can't be afraid to break some eggs."

Matthew Wayman is a longtime member of the church and credits Presley's ministry with helping to keep his family together after his father murdered his mother. The death devastated his family, plunging it into chaos, causing deep separation, especially when their father went to prison and they weren't sure how to deal with him. The family tried everything—from hard discussions to, in some cases, trying to find relief in alcohol or drugs—but nothing worked. At their wit's end, they sought help in religion, said Wayman, a pipe fitter whose sister, Athena, is Presley's wife. "All of my siblings started going there, and we are all still there," he said. "Clarence teaches; he really teaches the core values of the church. His heart is for the community."

## Taking Church into the Stadium

The idea for the football ministry came about seven years ago when Presley's sons were playing in a league. On the one hand, he was disheartened by the win-at-all-costs approach of the coaches and unsportsmanlike conduct he saw at games.

But then one Sunday the league in which his sons were playing held a big event called a Jamboree, in which teams held brief scrimmages against one another. Presley was torn; he couldn't imagine missing church to watch his boys play football. But these were his sons—and they wanted him there.

He found someone to fill in for him at church, and he went. Entering the stadium, he was shocked. There were maybe 5,000 people in the stands, shouting and cheering, a huge community brought together by this game. As he took a seat and looked around, Presely asked himself: How many people across Seattle were in churches on that Sunday? Sitting there, he reminded himself he was serving as a preacher during a time when membership, nearly across the board, is declining. People, especially young people, aren't interested in formal worship. They prefer shooting messages back and forth on social media, maybe going shopping, hanging out with friends— or, and here he was, scrimmaging against one another on the football field on a Sunday. Maybe, he thought, this is where the people were, and this is where God wanted him to go. It was an odd but eye-opening realization for a preacher who defined the church in pretty traditional ways. He started to see what some theologians meant about being missional: God is already at work in the world ahead of us and we need to follow God there and join in what God is doing, whether that is outside the Seattle Union Gospel Mission or on the playing fields where kids make tackles or hit home runs.

Not long after watching his boys play football that Sunday, the league they were in fell apart and some concerned leaders asked to meet with Clarence to consider how to resurrect a new league—and to do so by asking him to be commissioner of the league, offering a different direction in ministry with a God-given emphasis on players, coaches, and fans. Clarence agreed to give it a try and recruited several men, who he knew were strong Christians, to step in and become coaches. This was key because Presley believed good coaches could reach youth in grade school and help prepare them for what life would deal out as they grew. Eventually, he became the commissioner, convinced his ministry was both in the formal church but also working with young people, praying with them after wins or losses, showing them that it takes persistence and a willingness to accept hard knocks and unexpected setbacks if you are going to play sports—and life is like that as well.

## Playing the Game

On the Saturday morning in the drizzle and under the gray skies at Renton Stadium, the Rainier Ravens, who were in the early elementary league, faced off against the Puget Sound Lancers. Soon after the opening kickoff, the Ravens' J'Shaun Wilson burst out around the left end and ran forty-four yards for a touchdown. Led by cheerleaders who are also part of the elementary and middle school football league as well as the ministry, the fans erupted in the stands. The Ravens eventually won the game, and the division championship, by a score of 31–0.

After the game, the Ravens' assistant coach, Demetrius Dickerson, who works for the local power company, had a big smile on his face. Thirteen weeks of practice nearly every day and a series of games had led up to that day's championship trophy. Taking a break, he sat in a small room just off one of the end zones and said he had met Presley a few years ago. He and his wife, looking for a place to worship, attended Presley's church. Although they now go to another church, they have remained friends, and he was happy to be recruited as a coach.

"I see this as a ministry. I believe the players see coaches in a different way," said Dickerson. "We love on them, pray for them, help them out." Sometimes he has needed to push the players and get after them for the way they act. But he always does so in a spirit of love. He believes it is important to provide kids in sports with godly leading and direction.

Also sitting in the room was Bookie Gates, who grew up in the area and played professional baseball for the Arizona Diamondbacks. He connected with Presley after he left baseball several years ago.

Although he is now involved in the sports ministries at Word of Truth, he was drifting and had no sense of God in his life when he met Presley, who told him they needed a quarterback for a men's flag football team sponsored by the church. So he joined up. When Presley invited him to church, he came. Hearing the music, listening to Presely preach, talking and getting to know the people in the church had an effect on him. He came from a secular life, playing baseball under the bright lights, but now he experienced a different light. It only took him a few weeks to realize, as he put it, that "the hand of God was on me"—and he joined up.

Eventually, Gates began the church's baseball ministry and is now actively involved in the youth football league. And he knows these kids; they suffer many hard knocks. He grew up in this area, scrambling his way on the streets, seeing his friends fail and fall. Baseball brought him out of it for a time and now he was back. His heart ached to reach the young people who faced so many struggles, ranging from dire poverty to child abuse and addiction. "We want these kids to have a platform to build on, not just in sports but in life. Seeds are being planted."

## Football as a Way to God

Clarence Presley has come to see the football league, with its forty-eight teams and nearly 1,600 players and cheerleaders, plus their family members, as part of his parish.

By connecting through the sport, he can meet families and talk to them about their challenges, as he did once when the babysitter of one of the players in the league was shot. He was able to stand with and show care and concern to the family following the tragedy. He has also, with the help of others, joined with the local police and a range of local groups to start a flag football league that brings underserved communities and local law enforcement together to establish positive relationships and reduce the tension between the police and communities of color. "We don't compartmentalize our ministry," said Presley. "God is sovereign and in control, and we go where God leads us."

## Walking the Emmaus Road

One of the people who have been lifted by the Spirit of God and the work of church planters in Seattle is Biff Gaitan. On Sunday mornings, he stands by the front door of Emmaus Road Church in the Maple Leaf neighborhood and he shakes the hand of everyone coming in for worship. But being the greeter is only one of several roles that the man who was once homeless in Seattle holds at the church that has itself had a few homes before settling into its facility and joining with a local CRC couple to do ministry. "I've been at Emmaus Road for fifteen years and served in a lot of capacities," said Gaitan one Saturday afternoon as he cleaned the church before the next day's service. Sporting a purple beard and tattoos, he is an elder, has worked with the homeless and youth, and offers support in many other ways to the ministry that has meant so much to him. "Boy, I was your basic mess. I couldn't get a handle on my problems and couldn't get right with God until I started coming here," said Gaitan, who landed in Seattle after leaving Jackson, Michigan several years ago. He connected with Emmaus Road while living and then working at the downtown Seattle Union Gospel Mission. "When I came in, Emmaus Road was welcoming, nonjudgmental, not self-righteous. People were happy to see me," he said.

Started by Eric Likkel in the late 1990s, Emmaus Road is one of the oldest of the CRC church plants that began to work in creative ways with people in the city. This urban ministry has worshipped in homes, coffee shops, and a homeless youth drop-in center near the Space Needle in downtown Seattle. After earning degrees as music majors in college, both Eric and his wife, Alicia, felt the call to ministry. A compelling need for innovative ministries, along with the lure of Cascadia (Eric grew up in British Columbia), led the Likkels to move to Seattle and be part of the church planting movement. Like a handful of others, Eric wanted to reach young people in an area that was known for young people who wanted no part of organized religion. And his experience has only confirmed that they work in a blatantly secular city, in a place that spawned the likes of Amazon and Starbucks and has been for many years the home to Boeing, the international aircraft manufacturer. Culturally, it has also been a hub of grunge, also known as the Seattle sound, a genre of alternative music made popular by bands such as Pearl Jam and Nirvana. "I wanted to speak the gospel in a language our peers could hear and listen to," said Likkel of why he came here. "People of my generation weren't being reached."

Likkel had—and continues to have—a passion to pass along the message of Christ in ways that harken back to the era after Christ walked along the Emmaus Road with two people who were shattered by Christ's death and yet had their faith renewed in a powerful way when they saw that the resurrected Jesus ate and broke bread with them. Likkel has wanted to find ways to reveal the sacred on roads that might seem impassive and at meals that can reveal much more than one might suspect.

The church found a home for years in the downtown area, where it built connections to the Seattle Union Gospel Mission and New Horizons, which works with homeless youths who sleep in doorways, in tents along the freeway, in alleys, and in encampments created in empty spaces around the heart of the city. "We wanted to help young people. We wanted to be in their territory. We wanted to find ways to help them deal with the brokenness and sin that leads to homelessness," he said. But by 2016, the area in which they worshipped faced problems. Upscale housing and high-tech business began displacing the poor and the needy. Rents soared for longtime residents and businesses. Gentrification took hold, forcing out anyone but the wealthy, a process buoyed by a booming economy and yet marred by greed and mixed motivations. And then, as if serving a knock-out body blow, a beloved worship leader died—and Emmaus Road began searching for what God wanted the ministry to do next.

## Ministry in the Playground

Brian and Betsy Turnbull, church planters with a particular and yet, at least initially, traditional vision, came to work in Seattle, having moved here several years ago with hopes of launching a large, successful church with an emphasis on people who didn't attend church. Like many church planters, they had a strategy with the goal of building membership and starting programs to reach out to the community. To do this, they followed a traditional church-planting model, taking time to develop a core group and to build from there. They rented a community center, loaded up their van every Sunday with food, signs, and musical instruments, and then set it all up in the community center. "It was a lot of work. We did it every Sunday and we waited for people to show up," said Betsy Turnbull. But that effort never took off; the people never came. So they tried different ways—such as holding special events for the community. But nothing worked; they "hit a wall." Still convinced, though, that God had called them into ministry, that they had been sent to Seattle for a purpose, they connected with mentors who helped to guide them in a different direction.

Give up the model of building a Sunday-based attractional church, they were told. Think differently; pay attention to what is going on in the world around them and see how they might respond. Join in an organic, grassroots process, less one arising out of a church-growth axioms and more out of their own experiences, out of their lives, their hearts, hopes, and dreams—and especially out of self-assessment that allowed them to see who they were as pastors and what gifts they had that could be used. Out of this evolved The House, a much more low-key, one-on-one outreach that takes place with people they meet in their daily lives, said Betsy Turnbull. In essence, they became chaplains to their northeast Seattle neighborhood called Maple Leaf. This has meant they have needed to find other work to help pay their bills. And, as they have done this, they began to share their faith by how they lived their lives and interacted in those normal places where people gather. "I found myself translating God to people I met on my child's preschool playground," said Betsy, who works as a fitness coach. "These connections and conversations, and chances for discipleship, happened in random places." Dreams for ministry have narrowed and, as a result, stronger connections have formed.

They have held Bible studies, book discussions, game nights, met with neighbors over meals. They have built close relationships and served as spiritual directors for people. In doing this, in various circumstances, said Betsy, "I have experienced Jesus in deep ways and realized we want to be the church that is out there on the fringes. We want to find the places where the Spirit is at work." This takes time. While the Spirit never hides itself, finding it can be tricky. But it is satisfying, touching and sharing faith one person, one soul at a time.

Through The House, which was basically located in their house, the Turnbulls have come to realize they are doing exactly what God wants them to do—and not to fill a community center on Sundays with worshippers. They realize how crucial it is for them, for the others with whom they work, to know that the love and "work of God is so quiet, so subtle, and so soft." This is a new theology for them; it is not a high-yield job of evangelization. Rather, it is waking every day and being able to respond to what God puts in front of them.

## Finding a Church

In 2016, Betsy and Brian, who works as a financial and spirituality consultant, found out that a church in their neighborhood, Lux Communities Church, was closing. When they learned the church was leaving, they thought of their longtime friends Eric and Alicia Likkel, who were looking for a new place for Emmaus Road. One thing led to another and late in 2016, the four of them were able to make arrangements to obtain the church from the Christian Missionary Alliance, the denomination that owned the church building, and they moved in. The Likkels and Turnbulls then became partners in ministry, combining their strengths and approaches into one ministry. As this occurred, an irony struck Eric Likkel. He never thought Emmaus Road, a sort of seat-of-the-pants ministry that had been located in and around downtown Seattle for many years, would end up in a traditional brick church building tucked away in North Seattle. "But we know Betsy and Brian and we're getting to know the neighborhood through them," he said.

Doing ministry in the Maple Leaf community, the Likkels and Turnbulls have combined their skills and visions to make a difference in the area of comfortable homes and well-tended lawns. They are trying to do this in many ways. One example: In October of 2017, they held a Halloween event outside—Trick 'r Treat Oktoberfest—at which a polka band, featuring Likkel on the clarinet, played. They drew a large neighborhood crowd. People mingled and danced and sang and ate. Staying faithful to the roots of the Emmaus Road story, church members continue to reveal the rising love of Christ in many ways. They provide meals for homeless youth, put together packs of toiletries and other items for street people, and hold various small group meetings in their neighborhood. In some ways, the two ministries that have been on a course that is outside the norm have now partnered to work in a building that has some of the trappings of a traditional place of worship. But in intent, focus, and spirit, this ministry is doing what the Likkels and Turnbulls have been doing for years—accompanying people, such as Bill Gaitan, the greeter and the elder, down a road leading to deeper faith. "Over the years, we've cultivated lots and lots of sparks. We've been a small church and these sparks have not been snuffed out yet," said Eric Likkel. "We are still seeking to be a bright light wherever we are."

## Awake Church: Supporting a Grieving Couple

Faith in God has always been important to Christy Bauman, who grew up Catholic and then attended an Assemblies of God congregation. She earned a master's degree in counseling from a Reformed seminary and also traveled the world and wrote a book about being a missionary. All of those connections helped to shape and deepen her faith. But it was the way members of Awake Church in Seattle responded after the death of her first child—Brave Bauman—in December 2011 that brought the bedrock message of Christ's love home—both to her and her husband, Andrew. "It was so hard to lose a child. I'd never had to be part of something like that before," said Bauman, a psychotherapist in Seattle. "But the people in our church stood with us, and we all went through the grief together." Ben Katt and Andy Carlson, Awake's pastors, came to the hospital and baptized the Baumans' baby. The baptism, in the hospital, helped. But it was still a time of quiet terror and disbelief, watching their child—so soft and fragile—die. Hopes for this new life withered and a painful hole opened in Christy and Andrew. But they couldn't take time to lament. In the midst of their grief, they had to make the funeral arrangements. They steeled themselves and did what they could, loaded down with the loss that came from an unexpected event. Preparing themselves as best they could, they felt alone—yet only for a time. That sense of loneliness, of being singled out by tragedy, began to ease as they walked into the crowded church with the small, white casket for the funeral service. Awake members were there, many weeping along with them. They immediately felt an amazing solidarity; they were not going through this alone. In turning to their church, they found God right there. And at the cemetery, after the parents dropped handfuls of dirt into the open grave, church members filed up and did the same. One after another, they helped to cover the casket with earth; they were part of a procession of love and lament, showing they also were cut deep by the death. Going through this made Christy realize in different ways that by being part of Awake she experienced something new. "I had never felt the kingdom of God so palpably," she said after a Sunday service at the church that meets in a Chinese restaurant in a gritty part of Seattle. "I've had the opportunity at Awake to know God and to be God's hands and feet in ways I'd never experienced before . . . I had not been involved in this kind of embedded spirituality before."

## A Church Plant in a Gritty Place

A church plant that began as a dream in 2007 and was officially started by what was then Christian Reformed Home Missions in 2008, Awake is both a place for worship and a place that lives out its beliefs in many ways—for instance, by reaching out to people experiencing homelessness, substance addiction, and sexual exploitation along Aurora Avenue through Aurora Commons, the shelter that is just across the parking lot from the church, the main street cutting through Seattle.

Seattle is a city of contrasts. It is a city of soaring high rises, bustling night spots, and condo complexes. But it also has, according to an estimate in 2020, more than 13,000 unhoused women, men, and children who seek shelter, food, and clothing along such thoroughfares as Aurora Avenue. With all of this in mind, a few young people decided in about 2007 to "step into the brokenness down here," said Jay Stringer, a mental health professional and ordained minister. Early on, they would visit seedy motels along Aurora and speak with and offer food to the people living there, many of whom were on drugs or working in the sex trade. This activity convinced them that God was calling them to plant a church there. "Working with people involved in the sex trade, I realized how important it is for us to care about some of the darkest issues in the world," said Stringer.

One Sunday, Ben Katt, founding pastor and a driving force behind Awake until he left for another position in 2016, took on the once-familiar job of preaching at Awake. In his sermon, Katt gave an overview of the things he believes churches, especially those working in cities and other densely populated areas, ought to do in following where the Holy Spirit is leading them. "We live in a world of constant change. In our lifetime, we will experience driverless cars and trucks," he said. "You have to ask, 'How much will driverless trucks affect the industry?'" Disruption, Katt added, is also happening in the American church. "Hundreds of churches are closing, seminaries are shutting down, and millennials are leaving the church in droves," said Katt, standing in an elevated area that serves as seating for diners during the week in the Chinese restaurant where the church meets. While these changes sound bad, Katt said, "I find these shifts intriguing" because they can invite "us to pay attention to how God's Spirit is on the move."

Katt was basically speaking about the mandate of Luke 10 to scatter into the world and share the gospel in every town and place. In recent years, said Katt, God has sent people into new and challenging places in urban areas, such as Aurora Avenue in Seattle, where people mix to learn about God together. "We are free to open our eyes to see and address the suffering of others, especially in our everyday lives."

## Walking the Neighborhood

Following the service, Andy Carlson, pastor of Awake, and Karen Cirulli, a co-founder of the church and director of community engagement for Aurora Commons, took us on a tour of the neighborhood.

First, we walked over to Aurora Commons—the shelter for the homeless run by Awake. Next to it is Fremont Fellowship, a building that houses Alcoholics Anonymous meetings all day. A man named Mike came out of the AA building, walked up to Karen Cirulli and talked about a spiritual experience he had recently. "I don't want to lose it," he said. "But guys on the street are picking at it, telling me it isn't real." Cirulli put a reassuring hand on his shoulder, telling him to have faith and to stop into Aurora Commons the next day if he wants to talk more.

Up and down Aurora Avenue are many motels that once served the needs of travelers driving through downtown Seattle before the coming of freeways. Also out here are glass repair and auto repair shops, a rental store, a few factories, and fast-food restaurants. In addition, there is the village of tiny houses, standing in a fenced-in gravel lot, about three blocks from the church. Built as homes for the homeless, the twenty-five or so structures each have locking doors and windows, heat, insulation, and an electricity outlet. A large restroom on the grounds is also available to the residents.

This is a solution, but a very small one, to the city's growing homelessness crisis. Modest but increasingly expensive homes are in neighborhoods along Aurora Avenue. Many Awake members bought homes in the area when they were much more affordable, and even now some church members have had to move out because of skyrocketing costs. Walking along, Cirulli said, "At Awake we have had to trust in the Holy Spirit and to use our imaginations to follow the Spirit. We know that life is messy, but we need to honor each person and to allow the Spirit to guide us." Next to her, Andy Carlson looked around, at the vehicles passing on the street, the aging motels, a scattering of homes. "My heart is really drawn to this neighborhood. I walk these streets all of the time," said Carlson, who supplements his pastor's income with his job as a woodworker. "We are in the thick of it down here." But, he added, there are times he gets weary from the work, especially with people who live on the edge and have to deal with a raft of difficult problems. A lack of money to fund the church is also hard and discouraging, sometimes making him wonder if a church such as Awake can sustain the type of ministry that it does. But worse is the despair he sees in people's lives. "I can get tired of seeing people killing themselves with drugs or being killed. You can feel the weight of evil and try to make sense of all of it," said Carlson. Yet, he doesn't feel alone: he has others with whom he works and who share his vision of joining the presence of God in this section of Seattle. "There is a life in the Spirit here, and there are others who are part of it and feel the same way that I do."

# 3

# "And Who Is My Neighbor?"

## [or]

## An Advent Neighborhood Brunch in Edmonton and Finding Friends on a Roof in Lacomb

"But he [an expert in the law] wanted to justify himself, so he asked Jesus, 'And who is my neighbor?'" —Luke 10:29

*According to Luke 10, a neighbor is someone who promotes peace and joins in learning what God is doing. This is a posture of being "with" and not doing ministry "for." It is hearing—really setting ourselves aside to listen to the stories of those with whom we are connected, essentially with our neighbors. In this chapter we feature Karen Wilk and a Christmastime worship service she had with her neighbors in her home in Edmonton, Alberta. Hers is a ministry in which members of the congregation speak about their passion, vision, failures, fears, anxieties, hopes—and through it all, they seek to hear where the work of the Spirit among and through them is unfolding. We offer mini-profiles of a few of those who attend Wilk's neighborhood church. One is a woman who uses her newfound faith to help her cope with cancer. We also drive one hundred miles south to Lacombe, Alberta to spend time with Rick Abma, who stepped down from being a youth pastor of a large church to start a ministry in which he sells coffee to people in the area he serves and holds barbeques for people who ask him to fire up the coals and put on the burgers and steaks during the gathering. As they eat, Rick is always aware that the best way for him to preach is living as a disciple of Christ, meaning God always comes first in whatever he does—and not the pastor's desire to be liked or to wield authority, however subtly, over the church.*

## Neighborhood Life: Christmas at the Wilks

T he gathering for worship began with a potluck brunch in the home of
Karen Wilk. People milled about, catching up, sharing stories. Sunlight
shone outside. It was in the middle of Advent, that time of waiting, of gathering, and looking ahead to the coming of a child whose life would change
the world. New life would be Wilk's message that day. For now, Wilk, a former established church pastor who leads a ministry called Neighbourhood
Life in her middle-class community of Edmonton, was helping to get breakfast ready in her kitchen. Once things were arranged, she offered a gracious
wave and invited everyone to join hands and pray, and then dig in. Filling
their plates, people took their food and coffee or juice and started drifting
into the dining room where they took seats and began to eat around a large
table and Wilk invited them to share stories with one another about where
they had seen God at work in their lives and neighborhoods over the last
week. As they did, a mix of voices punctuated with laughs filled the room.
Many around the table lived in this neighborhood of Laurier Heights in
west Edmonton overlooking the North Saskatchewan River.

## A Lively Faith at Home

Sitting at one end of the table was Donna McLeod, a spunky, dark-haired
woman who worked as an assistant school principal in Calgary before
moving to Edmonton four years before, so that her husband could attend
graduate school. They live around the corner and she is deeply connected to
her neighborhood. Her home is the place in which she lives out a religious
faith that these days she holds dear. But that wasn't always the case. Her
experiences in church have not been particularly pleasant. On and off over
the years she has drifted away, sometimes quite far from church. In fact, she
brought this uncertainty to this new city. But coming to Edmonton offered
a new chance to shift gears. "When we came here, I had a chance to recreate
my life." As she talked, her young son played in her lap.

McLeod had grown up attending Baptist churches, and not always
liking it. So attending a traditional church in Edmonton was not part of
what she had planned as she rearranged her life. Becoming more involved
in her neighborhood, however, was something that attracted her once
she met Karen Wilk, who cast the vision of doing ministry right where
she lived. Why not express her connection to God right on her block in

practical, day-to-day ways? It was a welcome vision that gave her the sense that who she was, right now, is all she needed to serve God. No need to be someone other than she felt she was inside; no need to struggle over doctrines and beliefs that could feel far away and not really relevant. Having what it takes as a Christian, she started to see, meant looking in the mirror and embracing your gifts because you certainly have them. Have confidence. Live out your faith right where you are. Wilk told her to take baby steps, to simply look around and get to know the people who lived next door and across the street. The rest would come after that.

Inspired, McLeod got involved and now serves as a "block connector"—someone who has the role of getting to know their neighbors and nurture, care, and connect with them on her block. She knocks on doors, sits at her kitchen table talking to neighbors about their joys and concerns.

Over time, McLeod has built relationships with her neighbors, even those who initially weren't particularly receptive. She has come to know who is sick, who has lost a job, who is getting divorced, who is celebrating the birth of a child, who has furniture to donate, who is far away from God. In various ways, she helps these neighbors, and they help her family—perhaps with a meal, a card, or especially the chance to pray and talk together. Connecting with her neighbors is a role she considers a ministry. She lends or gives them things they need. And others reciprocate: one woman gave her baby items when she learned McCleod was pregnant. It took time and commitment to build that kind of relationship with the neighbor. "You can't know when being a good neighbor is going to be critical to your life or their life. I see that loving your neighbors and learning who they are is what God wants us to do," she said.

## The Service

When people finished eating, they went into a large room that had windows at one end, showing the backyard and a park beyond in which you could see people walking their dogs. Christmas decorations were scattered around the room: angels; a manger scene with Jesus, Mary, and Joseph; lights; and an evergreen branch draped the mantel above the fireplace. The weekly worship service began as everyone took seats and most of the children sat on the carpet. The younger ones were a little noisy, but that was fine. Noise is part of worship; mess is allowed; prayer can come as much in giggles and smiles as in formal words. Later the children would go downstairs to play. Although most of those in the room lived in Laurier Heights, some had driven in from other areas across Edmonton. "We've been talking about Christmas symbols," Wilk said near the start, weaving common items of life into a discussion about something sacred. This is an underlying motif in her theology—how the glory of God is charged and shines in the ordinary and how it is crucial to view the world through eyes that show the crackling, cascading energy of creation in all things big and small and especially right next door and around the block. She wants people to recognize and tend the Lord's fire in their hearts. "The candy cane is a symbol of a shepherd's staff, and Jesus is the shepherd," said Wilk, holding up a piece of the candy. "The red symbolizes the blood of Christ, and the green symbolizes new life. As the stripes wind around, they symbolize the love of God that never ends."

## Ministry Modeled on the Early Church

Besides serving her immediate neighborhood, Wilk coordinates similar efforts in other neighborhoods in Edmonton. She is the author of books such as *Don't Invite Them to Church: Moving from a Come and See to a Go and Be Church* (2010). Discerning and joining the Spirit on God's mission in the very places in which people live is now her focus, but she started out as a youth and outreach minister at West End CRC in Edmonton before becoming part of a church plant. She loved the work. But then a few years ago she went to a conference where she learned about the missional church conversation, about God as "the sent and sending One and therefore how the church does not have a mission but the mission of God has a church." Mission, she learned, is the very nature of God and therefore the very nature of the church. "Those who have built the church over the last centuries have often failed to see this," she said. "Instead, they have built traditions, perhaps not intentionally, that kept the church 'inside,' allocated mission to a few, and focused on events or programs to attract people to come to them." This new understanding of going and being, living amongst like Jesus, was the beginning of a big change for her in terms of her understanding of who God is, what God does, and what God has called and made the church to be. She learned, she said, that mission is about "God's personal presence in the world by the Spirit." Alan Hirsch was one of the thinkers and writers who had a profound impact on her. Initially his book *The Forgotten Ways: Reactivating the Missional Church* (2009) was very significant, describing the huge paradigm shift needed for Christian churches to more faithfully reflect the movement that Christ began 2,000 years ago.

Using as a model the early Christian church before it was institutionalized in 313 AD by the Roman emperor Constantine, the neighborhood missional movement invites and challenges the church, said Wilk, to reimagine a faith that is shared and grows one person at a time in the normal places in which people live and gather. "It is a grassroots approach that is founded on discerning what the Spirit is up to out ahead of us, joining in that work, and in so doing, sharing the needs and longings, the dreams and desires, of the people with whom we live," she said.

## Moving in a New Direction

This new missional outlook shook Wilk up, inspiring her to pay more attention to her neighbors and what God was calling her to be and do. If God was truly alive in us all, if everyone is an image-bearer, then, she realized, we need not look far to find the "flesh and blood of the Lord being poured out in amazing ways nearly everywhere and at all times." Backyards became monasteries; local parks were cathedrals; meals shared at home became the best kind of communion. Additional reading, attending conferences, talking to others, and beginning to engage in new practices convinced Wilk that the Spirit was inviting her and others to reimagine church beyond its emphasis on Sunday worship in a church building, to living among and serving with her neighbors. "The Sunday gathering could become an opportunity to celebrate what God was doing in our lives and neighborhoods, lament the brokenness, encourage our daily participation in God's mission, worshipping, praying, and learning together how to continue to disciple and be discipled in incarnational, holistic mission right where we live."

A few years ago, after moving in this direction under the umbrella of a church plant, Wilk and others began Neighbourhood Life. They needed to follow the Spirit they sensed at work in their homes and in the homes of their neighbors. "As I paid attention to the neighborhood, I saw that God was at work in ways I had never noticed before," said Wilk. "I recognized the Spirit's presence in the lives of people who were disconnected from church but were clearly engaged in kingdom practices."

## Moving Beyond the Norm

It wasn't long before Wilk and others made the change from meeting in a church facility to gathering in the neighborhood. And it has repeatedly proven to have been a good idea. She sees confirmation in many ways and has learned important lessons as Neighbourhood Life has moved forward and spread into neighborhoods. In this ministry, Wilk knows the people next door; they know her; they share their lives. The Spirit is as real as any breath; it is as present and active as yeast in any dough; it is the story behind the story, uncovering mystery and pointing the Lord's people, she said, "to his mission, his love and grace at work in the world right where they live." As the pillars holding up the structures of the past begin to crumble, new blueprints are needed and the Spirit is up to something, doing a new thing (Isa 43:19). "Over and over again, God has been ahead of us," said Wilk. "God has opened doors and inspired us. We have many stories of how the Spirit has healed brokenness, nurtured a caring community and human flourishing . . . [for] the peace and well-being of the city [Jer 29:7]."

Rich Braaksma, a pastor at a church in Calgary and CRC regional leader in western Canada, said large churches such as The River, the church plant where Karen served, are thriving and will probably continue to do so. And they have an important role to play in the ongoing life of the church. "They have resources and programs that attract people." This is a model that is tried and true and still works. But not all churches have what it takes to fill this space. "Meanwhile, smaller churches, neighborhood churches like Karen is catalyzing, are growing in importance because, I think, people are looking for that kind of intimacy," said Braaksma.

## Gathering for the Advent Service

Intimacy is what it is about—ongoing communion. Sitting in the room at Karen Wilk's house that morning, along with others involved in Neighbourhood Life, were people from a range of religious backgrounds. Some had grown up in the CRC and still considered themselves members of the church; some had been active in the larger, suburban congregations as worship leaders and council members; some had drifted away from God for periods of time; some had been hurt by the church; and some had found big churches too impersonal and their programs overly theatrical; a few had little previous church experience. But a common thread tying all of these worshipers together was a hunger to discover and join the Spirit on God's mission right where they lived, including by gathering as God's people each week to connect with God and one another. They longed—and some didn't even know it—to experience the grace of God to touch and fill them, and their neighbors, in tangible ways. As Wilk put it, they want the place where they live to be their community. Many longed for, and believed God was calling them to a more local, personal, and connected way of being. They seek to be grounded and to find the sacred where they are—instead of commuting to an often distant space to find it. "Even though I'm struggling with a serious illness, God comforts me," said Julie Rohr before the service. She now sat at one end of the room with her husband, David. A silk scarf covered her head—a fashion accessory to obscure the effect of chemotherapy. "I once saw God as vengeful and angry. Now I see God as a loving creator," she said.

Julie struggled with her feelings about God after she went through a divorce. But meeting David, starting back at a small church, and then being introduced to Karen, who got her involved in her neighborhood, has brought her faith back in a new and startling way. Learning about the lives of her neighbors and having them over for meals or simply to talk has added an abiding sense of abundance to her life—especially as she has struggled with her illness. "The presence of God is so real to me now," she said. "I'm having a beautiful walk with God that I never thought I'd experience."

## Another House Church

Not present that morning were Carla and Mike Stolte. They are connected with Neighbourhood Life and have started a neighborhood church in their community of Westmount. Mike has strong roots in the CRC and was reluctant to get involved in neighborhood ministry when Carla, who also grew up in the CRC, felt a call to do so. She was inspired after volunteering time and participating in Edmonton's Abundant Community initiative, helping her neighborhood become a healthier and more connected place. She saw how the city itself wanted to make neighborhoods more liveable; to take care of the parks; keep the streets clean and safe; to encourage ways of living that found room for everyone to express their creative ideas and gifts; to share time and help out when they see needs. "I felt increasing discontented with the organized church community and was more and more intrigued by the house church," said Stolte. A turning point happened one

Advent. After meeting with like-minded Christians in the neighborhood, the group hosted a gathering in Westmount, inviting neighbors to one of their homes for an Advent service, which included reflections, Scripture, and carol singing on a Sunday evening. When more than seventy people showed up, "it felt like a Holy Spirit moment," she said. She was convinced a neighborhood church was possible—and soon Mike agreed. "When we left our old church [a CRC congregation], we left well," said Mike, a psychologist. "The church saw that we were called to this ministry."

## Abundant Community

Edmonton, a city of nearly a million people, has more than 150 designated neighborhoods and has launched the Abundant Community initiative to connect and facilitate neighborliness on every block in the city. As a city, Edmonton does this as a way to support and encourage abundant, flourishing, and vibrant neighborhoods. Serving as coordinator of the effort is Howard Lawrence, former pastor of a large Baptist church in Edmonton and a strong backer of the work Karen Wilk is doing. He still views things through the lens of his faith, though he doesn't emphasize that when working for the city. "The Bible doesn't focus on the family; it focuses on neighbors," said Lawrence. "This is about God seeking shalom in the places you live. 'Love your neighbor' is the best commandment. There is less child abuse and less violence, and people who are sick are more likely to receive help when you know your neighbor."

## Celebrating Advent

During the service at Wilk's home, one of the children lit the Advent candle for that week and recited a prayer. The group sang some familiar Christmas songs, and then Wilk led a time of teaching from Luke 2:1–7, in which Joseph and Mary travel to Bethlehem at the time of a census. While there, Mary gives birth to Jesus and wraps him in clothes and places him in a manger because "there was no guest room available for them." Wilk asked those in attendance why people in Bethlehem made it so that Jesus had to be put in a feed trough for animals. Was that a sign, on a larger scale, of the world rejecting Jesus and forcing him to be born among animals? People speculated on that, saying perhaps it was a sign of people seeking to shun Jesus. But Wilk offered a different take on it: "Think of it this way: Joseph is of royal blood, the house of David. People there knew him. This was his hometown, his neighborhood. And in that culture and time, hospitality was an essential practice. No community would allow for a woman giving birth to be left alone and uncared for!" As Kenneth Bailey in his book *Jesus Through Middle Eastern Eyes* (2009), explains, Wilk said, the typical peasant's home at that time would have had animals in a room attached to their living quarters—the animals would provide warmth for the occupants at night, and the manger would have been enclosed and part of the home. "Perhaps the town was packed with people who were there for the census. Perhaps the people of Bethlehem gave Joseph and Mary the best accommodations possible, under the circumstances. Perhaps the story is all about making room for and loving your neighbor."

Most importantly, Wilk said, "Perhaps this is about the flesh and blood of God being born in and embraced by a simple, ordinary neighborhood."

## Rick Abma: Into the Neighborhood in Lacombe

Even after graduating from Calvin Theological Seminary some twenty years ago, this unsettling sense of how he would fit in as a pastor in a traditional church dogged Rick Abma. He was familiar with the role for which he was trained: Step in as associate or senior pastor of a settled, or perhaps new, congregation and assume the responsibilities of preaching, teaching, marrying, baptizing, and tending to the sick. He would be the cog around which the church would run; his energy and commitment to God would be the fuel that kept things running. The path was clear and he had gone to school to steer a church and its people in a fairly timeworn and time-tested direction. But this just didn't jibe with how he thought he ultimately wanted to function as a pastor. To a large extent, he came out of a process that trained him to be the hero, the one who carried the flag and set out to put his stamp on the church he served. But something seemed wrong with this approach. In his opinion, it lacked connection with the people he would serve. But, as he graduated from seminary, he couldn't exactly put his finger on this; he simply had this notion that ministry for him might be too circumscribed in a normal setting. Eventually, still feeling the gnaw of questions, he decided that serving as a youth pastor might be the best fit for him. There might be more freedom in it; he might have more of a chance to engage young minds with fresh ideas and the kids might do the same for him. So he answered the call more than twenty years ago to work with the young people at Woody Nook Christian Reformed Church in Lacombe, Alberta.

## Ministering in a Home Setting

Abma came from that area a couple hours south of Edmonton and knew its people. Right off, he loved the work; young people offered challenges and often asked questions that Abma appreciated and found valuable. Answering these questions and growing close to young people helped him to grow as a pastor. But something kept nagging him—a persistent notion that he wanted to step outside the confines of an established church. Again, he saw himself as a worker, a partner, and not the guy—at least in his case—who led the charge to make the church move in one direction or another. He was touched by a Spirit, working for years in the background, that led him beyond the confines of normal ministry. Finally, a series of circumstances a few years ago led him in this direction and Rick Abma left Woody Nook.

Not sure what awaited, he nonetheless believed making the move was right and the Spirit was with him. He saw a wide open landscape of opportunity—and it didn't necessarily involve making Christian disciples in any traditional way. "I was able to open myself up to a totally different world of people who didn't even know about such things as the Holy Spirit." Paradoxically, he ended up finding God using people who may not know much about God, to show him more about God and what he ought to be doing. Taking a break from the church ministry, Abma came to realize that he wanted to become a missionary by sharing the gospel message and developing followers of Christ in his own neighborhood and community. He had read many books on missional ministry and especially linking that ministry with your community. How he was to create his own ministry, however, was an evolving process. "I left Woody Nook asking the question, 'How do I go out and make disciples?' I had a vision of how to do that, but at the same time I really wasn't sure what I should be doing."

## Reaching Out to His Neighbors

Inspired by the Neighbourhood Life ministry in Edmonton, Abma opened his imagination to the whispering lead of the Holy Spirit. He found himself on an uncertain cutting edge seeking to bring the church into all aspects of life, certainly a Reformed notion, and doing so in ways he learned from Karen

Wilk. Her focus for the last few years has been on connecting with, getting to know, and creating spaces for worship with her neighbors. Wilk has come to see the neighborhood and the people up and down her block as being the key to ministry, not necessarily a church building or an emphasis on Sunday gatherings. Given that this approach tends to be informal and unpredictable, Abma learned fairly quickly his new calling would mean setting aside agendas and "learning how to dance with the Holy Spirit." He had to leave behind a ministry defined by the church week, its services, meetings, and calendar. He saw the need to become more vulnerable to his circumstances so he could be "an incarnational presence to my neighbors."

He was reminded how Jesus brought his divine self to bear on the little places and everyday people in the world: wells, weddings, meals, walking on dusty roads. Everything became a prayer; all experiences could sing with grace.

In the process, he launched Good Neighbour Coffee, a ministry in which he sells organic, hand-roasted Honduran coffee to people and businesses in Lacombe and nearby Red Deer. It wasn't long before he also launched the Good Neighbour Coffee Shop in downtown Lacombe, with help from friends. These businesses provide him with an income as well as an opportunity to get to know people and have conversations. This allowed him to step through what felt like a veil that surrounded the traditional church, confining him by rules and worn practices, into a world with little definition other than the translucent, transformational forms offered by the Spirit. Over time, he purchased, also with the help of those supporting his ministry, a barbeque grill. He began bringing the grill to neighborhoods for people to use in gatherings, including block parties and family events. Usually he hauls in the grill, sets it up and, if needed, teaches people how to use it. Smoke billows as meat sizzles and curious people show up to eat and talk. Then there is his espresso coffee bike that, weather permitting, he rides into neighborhoods in Lacombe and Red Deer to mix up a thick and tasty brew for people. As they sip his coffee, Abma gets to know them. He shares the transformation that has reshaped him and his view of the world and life. At the same time, using more traditional methods, he occasionally holds Bible studies and corporate times of prayer, in his home and elsewhere, often mixing these times with cups of coffee and food. "Hospitality is important . . . Jesus taught us of the importance of being hospitable to our neighbors."

## A Visit to the Brew House

The crisp morning sun was climbing into the sky and the rolling, snow-covered Alberta plains stretched in all directions outside Abma's rural home as he showed us his espresso machine and bike, and then led us into the building where he stores the sacks of coffee from Central America. The large room was filled with the smell of coffee beans. Every week, he will spend time breaking open the sacks, roasting and grinding beans, and placing the finished product in bags. He sells coffee to area grocery stores as a way to cover expenses, but the coffee also provides him a way to connect with people. Many individuals in Lacombe and Red Deer are his customers. The coffee is about more than just money. "The coffee is as much about a gift that I have to offer. It is something I can bring to the table," writes Abma in *Neighbouring for Life* (2017), a book in which he reflects on his ministry. "I share my coffee with my neighbors often, and I encourage them to share the coffee with their neighbors as well."

## Meeting with Friends

One evening, Abma and his wife, Joyce, sat at a table in the Good Neighbour Coffee Shop with three friends, Thelma Ten Hode and Denis and Doreen Hainsworth. The friends spoke of why they decided to link with Abma and his Neighbourhood Life ministry. They talked of how he has helped them see that God is more than the church; it is a group of many people in many places, alive and reckoning their worth with the help of each other wherever they happen to be.

After Abma left Woody Nook, Denis and Doreen wanted to know what caused the change in his life. They were curious as to why he entered a new life of such risk. When he told them about his focus on bringing Christ to people in the neighborhood, they responded with enthusiasm. This made sense. What he was doing appealed to them. They also appreciated that here was a minister who didn't act like the pastors they had known: distant, serious, and often judgmental. They had stopped attending traditional church, not because they had drifted away from their Christian faith, but because the congregations they had been part of kept breaking apart over personal struggles and pastoral leadership. They began to believe that it wasn't worth the effort to be part of a church. Too many rules and a bent toward legalism, driven by the egos of people who thought they were in the know, drove them away. They were not bitter, not even angry; rather, they were sad that the churches they had loved became too infested by little things that grew into major obstacles. They learned they could pray and stay close to God without attending Sunday worship. They could do it in their everyday lives. Following Christ didn't require Sunday praying and listening to a sermon. "We liked what Rick was talking about—that what is expected of us in the New Testament is to be vitally connected to people," said Doreen, a Christian school teacher. "As soon as you have a structure in place, it can be the undoing. I find it liberating to meet new people and not feel it is necessary to invite them to church." At times, they have gathered with Abma for prayer, reflection, and discussion. Other times they find ways to link with people in their lakefront neighborhood—such as helping to support an annual Christmas party at a local community center. Denis added, "Being part of Neighbourhood Life helps us be aware of being more intentional and finding ways to connect with people . . . It's not that all institutions are bad, but we do live in an age in which people have become more suspicious of institutions."

Thelma Ten Hode, also sitting in the coffee shop that evening, met Abma after returning from doing overseas missionary work with her husband. When they came back, they weren't sure where they fit in. She felt the need for something else, a different focus than the traditional church. Meeting Abma and connecting to Neighbourhood Life gave her this; he taught her to keep her eyes open to the little things. Ten Hode mentioned, for example, that she would not normally go up and introduce herself to strangers. The year before, however, the three cherry trees in her backyard had a bumper crop. Once she made jam, she took some over and knocked on her neighbor's door. The elderly neighbor—a stranger—invited her in and they have since gotten to know one another. Sure, this was a little thing, but it was a gesture that felt meaningful to her; a gesture that felt genuine. "I grew up in the Pentecostal church and mostly met with people who were already in the kingdom," she said. "I still don't think I do Neighbourhood Life very well, but Rick teaches us to relax and let God do the work and make the connections."

## Working on a Roof

In his book, Abma describes his neighborhood ministry—how he was asked by a single mother who wasn't much of a believer in God to conduct the funeral of her father; how he had the chance to see neighbors gather regularly to support a family whose home was destroyed by fire. He also describes going for a walk one day and approaching a muscular guy whose body was etched with tattoos and who works in the adult entertainment business. Even though he didn't know the guy and was a little scared by the man's appearance and the glowering expression on his face, Abma asked him if he wanted to attend an upcoming block party. The man, one of Abma's neighbors, was more than willing to come and was eager to help out when he arrived at the party. That experience again emphasized for Abma our common humanity and how being willing to go beyond appearances is what God calls us to do.

One key story comes to mind. In his book, Abma recollects how he and twenty or so neighbors had asked their neighbor, Joe, if they could fix his roof, which had fallen into disrepair after his wife had deserted him and left him with their four children. Joe was in a bad and lonely place; he seemed to want to live in his grief alone. He was trapped. But he was their neighbor and it seemed he needed help. Even though they were wary of asking Joe if they could work on his house, they made the effort and to their surprise, he said sure, to go ahead. It was a good lesson in being a neighbor: ask and the door may be opened. And once the work began, Joe was on the roof hammering away and laying down new shingles. They laughed and talked and poured sweat together. Slowly the roof was covered with a new covering. And while working on that roof, a car pulled up in the driveway and Abma watched as an older couple got out. They looked curious, gazing up at the crowd on the roof. Climbing down, Abma went over to greet them and learned they were Joe's parents. They had made the nine-hour drive from Regina, Saskatchewan, to be there. Tears filled the mother's eyes as she told him that they made the trip to see for themselves how the neighbors had come together to help their struggling son in his time of need. When Joe had told them what the neighbors wanted to do, the parents weren't sure what to think. Later, when the roof was finished, they all sat around a campfire and Joe's parents spoke "about Joe's hard story and how grateful they were that this community was rallying to support him," said Abma. "They said they had been telling Joe to move to a different area, to get away from this place, but now they were glad he stayed where he was."

As for Joe, he has remained a loner, and yet he is fairly friendly. At the same time, the fruit of the roofing project keeps emerging. For instance, two neighbors, Tom and Henry, had been enemies for years, sometimes threatening one another because of one dispute or another, but both showed up to work on Joe's roof. As they joined in the effort to help Joe, they seemed to get along, chatting and joking. Later, neighbors reported seeing Tom and Henry waving to one another on the road. Perhaps they had set aside their resentments and had mended the fences that had driven them apart. Theirs is a story reflecting what Christ came to accomplish: breaking down the barriers of sin and bringing on reconciliation, the unfailing love a father has for his wandering people.

This is a story that encapsulates why Abma left Woody Nook, venturing out into a world in which he already lived. "Joe's story, and the Tom and Henry story humble me," said Abma. "It reminds me there is always so much more going on than I could control or plan for. I have simply tried to be obedient, but God does the real work of transformation."

With neighbors on all sides of him, Rick Abma has no problem figuring out who his neighbor is. His neighbor is whomever he comes across in his ministry and in his life. His neighbors are in his coffee shop; they come to barbeques; they buy coffee from him when he rides around on his bike; they sit with him in Bible studies; they stroll along the streets of his neighborhood—and they gather to reroof the home of a man struggling as a single parent to raise four children.

# Part Two

## Community of Peacemaking, Hospitality, and Compassion

"Say 'peace to this house!' . . . Eat what is set before you . . .
Heal the sick who are there." —Luke 10:5, 8, 9

# 4

## "Peace to This House"

### [or]

### Homes of Peace in Visalia, Detroit, and Olathe

"When you enter a house, first say, 'Peace to this house.' If someone who promotes peace is there, your peace will rest on them; if not, it will return to you." —Luke 10:5–6

*Randall and Beth Grimmius have created a peaceful home in the Central Valley of California for needy children, many of them sons and daughters of migrant workers, in their city of Visalia. One of them was Erica Martinez, who showed up on their doorstep one night, at the end of a very hard journey and ready to get off drugs. Beth Grimmius—in true Luke 10 fashion, reflecting the call to "remain and stay" and to welcome the guest/stranger with hospitality—stepped aside and let her into their home to start a new life. Meanwhile, in one of the poorest and most violent neighborhoods of Detroit, Hesed Community Church—Hesed means "abounding in love"—works from a small home in the midst of a neighborhood filled with gangs, single-parents families, and abandoned homes. We visit Hesed on a day when Momma T, a local woman, seeks a Bible study out of Galatians to help her cope with fierce family challenges. And we feature two stories from Pathway Community Church in Olathe, Kansas—one about a former missionary couple seeking to bring peace to an inner-city neighborhood of immigrant families, several of them undocumented, and another about how women from the church gathered one day to thoroughly clean a home and bring a sense of well-being to a woman struggling with depression. Spending time in each of these places helps us get a sense of what shalom—biblical peace—looks and feels like when it is lived out in light of the Luke 10 narrative.*

65

## Taking in Strangers in Visalia, California

R andall Grimmius was deeply shaken when one of his employees, Juan Cisneros, was accidentally run over by a tractor and killed on a Sunday morning in May 2006. As the owner of Grimmius Cattle Company in Hanford, California, Grimmius worked hard to run a safe operation, seeking always to care for the welfare of the people who worked for him. The accident shook him to the core; he knew and liked Juan, who began working for him in 1999. But, as painful as this tragedy was, it ended up evoking a crucial change in the life of Grimmius and his wife, Beth, and their children: Katherine, Jessica, Nicole, and Rebecca. Although Randall and Beth, who are members of Visalia CRC, had been connecting with at-risk children and their families before the accident, it was after Juan Cisneros died that they got even more involved in this effort. Their home isn't a formal church; but it certainly acts as one, as a refuge for God's hurting children. Neither Randall nor Beth had a strategic plan of how to proceed with what has turned into an under-the-radar kind of ministry; they simply did what they considered the next right thing. In the process, this family expanded the borders of their life together. God's grace expanded in every corner of their house in an upscale suburban neighborhood. Their home has become as much a haven for troubled kids as it is a place of prayer, praise, and peace. Many midnights kids from all over Visalia have stood in the kitchen with Randall and Beth and talked about their troubles and their faith, often in light of hardships faced that day. Randall and Beth Grimmius have listened to the unspoken words of God's Spirit and responded to the call of Christ to welcome the strangers and the aliens, to make room for the least of these. Doing this, they have fostered an intricate network of relationships that seem always to be in flux and yet are grounded in and nourished by the always dependable Spirit of God.

## God Spoke

Beth Grimmius says she knew, following Juan's death in the tractor accident, that the Lord wanted them to do all that they could to smooth the way forward for Cisneros's wife and three children. The suffering she saw in the family and the deprivation they faced broke her heart. The mother, Antonia, was grief-stricken and struggling, and it became clear she was not able to provide very well at that time for her children. Antonia allowed

Beth and Randall to step in and be there for the children, taking an active role in their lives, as well as for her. They worked to fill the grief-filled gap left by Juan's death.

Over the past twelve years, many children, including the Cisneros children, have come into the lives of Randall and Beth and have lived for periods of time with them. In some cases, with the permission of the parents, they have taken on guardianship for the children. The couple has essentially created a large family of people living under one roof, regularly facing life's challenges together. The home is always busy as the children, many now grown, stop in to talk and share what is going on. This is an unusual house church where faith formation often comes on the fly, between visits to the doctor, times before and after school, over meals, and during experiences such as shopping or heading out to the soccer field. "When you look at these children who have so many needs, you can't [just stand by and] do nothing," said Beth Grimmius. "You do what you can. You need to reach out and fight for those who can't fight for themselves." Beth Grimmius knows this because she experienced abuse as a child and has found that caring for their biological children and their guardian children has helped her deal with her past and matured her relationship with God. Opening her home to so many children has helped her see more clearly stories of struggling children and how God can step in and help in her home and beyond. "Our story is bigger than what is happening here. God is inspiring many others to take an active role in coming alongside at-risk children," she said.

## Roman Tries to Find His Way

Roman Cisneros was only nine years old when his father died. He and his siblings had been raised Catholic but he wanted no part of the church as he grew older and angrier over the loss of his dad and difficulties at school. As his two sisters—Lizette and Maria—connected with the Grimmius household, Roman stayed with his mom, started hanging out on the streets of Visalia, and joined a Hispanic gang. Being tough, hiding behind rough language and acting like he didn't care, kept him going. But a few years ago, while he was in juvenile detention after being arrested for committing a crime, Roman got really scared. It seemed Satan had a hold on his life and he was going to hell. Imaginary fires coming from the devil seared his soul. Unsure how to escape this feeling of being boiled alive, he picked up a Bible to find out about hell. Reading the book cover to cover in detention, something amazing happened. "I found out who Jesus really was, and I wanted to give my life to him," Roman recalled. "I wanted to change, but I didn't know who to talk to."

When he got out of juvenile detention, he talked to Randall and Beth about his experience behind bars. They were troubled by what he had to go through, but were delighted to hear about his openness to the Lord. "That same day," said Beth, "he got so excited and committed himself to Christ and quit the drug and the gang life."

Randall offered Roman a safe environment to live in and invited him to church, and he started going. Randall also bought him a computer and talked to him about Scripture. But the transition into this new home setting was tough; there were rules to follow, so many people to deal with, important values that he needed to learn and work to accept. "Like others who lived here before, he experienced a major culture shock," said Beth. Still, this house was full of goodwill. God was alive in this home, and Roman felt this take hold. "I grew a lot. I got close to Jesus, and in the end, I could be myself there. I could get my feelings out," said Roman.

Still, there was the lure of gang life, the supposed freedom of the streets, so one day Roman left—"which was so hard," he said, "because it made Randall cry. . . . I was out there for two weeks before I threw in the towel and came back." He was back for a time. But he drifted off again—and his falling away has hurt Randall and Beth. Still, they haven't given up on him and leave the door open. And they pray for his return.

## Roman's Family

Meanwhile, Roman's sister, Maria, said the Grimmius family gave her the strength and courage to move to Mexico to attend college a few years ago with the intention to return to this country and obtain legal status. The day that we visited the Grimmius home Maria was home for a few days from Mexico. "Randall and Beth have been like real parents to me. They are what healthy parents look like," said Maria. "And they taught me so much about God, who loves us so much that when we are struggling, he is hurting too." Lizette, her young sister, lived there as well but, like Roman, has struggled. "There were times when we were very worried about her," said Beth. "But we worked with her, and God worked with her, and she settled down. At this time, she is going to college near Los Angeles at Biola University with my daughter, Jessica."

## Makings of a Ministry

Even as a child, Randall Grimmius had a strong sense of God working in his life and letting him know what he needed to do. For a time, he considered entering the ordained ministry. But as he grew into an adult, it was clear that he was to be a loving husband and father, to work as a rancher in the cattle business, and serve as a mentor and role model for the children whose lives he has been able to enter. You could say this good-natured, hard-working rancher with a friendly smile has been ordained by experiences, not a seminary education. "We've invested a lot in all the children," said Randall. "We're fortunate to have what we have. We've been able to send them to Christian schools and even college. But, in the end, we realize everything we have is God's."

## From Fighting to Faith

Erica Martinez, in her thirties, came from a broken home. Both of her parents battled a drug addiction. When she was twelve, she started to smoke weed. By the time she was fourteen, she was using meth. She dropped out of school and was in and out of juvenile detention. Authorities put her in a group home, and she ran away. On the streets, she got into fights and had a series of boyfriends, many of them violent, and got pregnant. She had a daughter, Sarah, and a son, Daniel. More than six years ago, she met Beth Grimmius at a local ministry home that is supported by area churches, including Visalia CRC. Beth invited her for coffee, and they went for a drive all around the area, up and down hills and past cattle ranches and almond orchards, talking for hours. Both women knew something significant was at work. "When we talked, I cried—and I had never let anyone into that place in my heart where I hurt so bad and didn't have any hope," said Erica.

Still, Erica wasn't ready to change; she kept to the streets. But the encounter with Beth stuck and kept coming back to her, a nagging sense of missed opportunities. One night, after a tough bout of things on the streets of Visalia, Erica came to the Grimmius home and knocked on the door. She was strung out and desperate. They weren't sure what to do at first, but they let Erica in, and she started her rehabilitation right there in their home. Slowly, a sense of God's love and acceptance—mirrored by the Grimmiuses themselves—cut through her hurt and anger. Things started to turn around in her life. She got her driver's license back, finished high school, and started a job at Grimmius Cattle Company. Best of all, her children were returned to her. Amid all the turmoil, she made the Lord the center of her life. She knows now, even in times of wandering and struggling, that she can come home and trust others because God, through Randall and Beth and others, has brought her out of complete chaos she was living in. "Erica is one of those rare stories of transformation," said Beth. "When she came to us, she was weary to the marrow of her bones. But God got hold of her and turned her around . . ."

## "A Lot of Redemption"

Katherine Grimmius, now in her mid-twenties, remembers when Erica moved in and was coming off the drugs. But even in her discomfort, Erica could joke, and they talked. They slept in the same room. At night, before falling asleep, they told stories, shared dreams, and they laughed. "We talked about any and everything," said Katherine. It was great. Even so, having had her parents open their home these past years to so many young people such as Erica has been hard because it took away from the time she and her sisters got to spend with their parents. Yet it has also held a profound blessing. They have seen God's grace at work in their home in so many ways and on so many occasions. It is a grace that is real and true, said Katherine, and would otherwise be missing if her parents hadn't opened themselves—and their children—to it. "I love what my family has done," said Katherine. "This is who God called us to be. I feel like I have my foot in two worlds"—the safe, predictable world provided by her parents and the harsher, more turbulent world in which her guardian brothers and sisters have lived. "I certainly now have much more empathy when it comes to how other people live and what they have to cope with. It's been really rewarding to be here. We see a lot of redemption happening in our home." Theirs has been a home of peace, she said.

## Inspiring Others

Nearly every Sunday, the Grimmius family arrives at Visalia CRC a few minutes late for the late-morning service. After all, getting everyone ready can be pretty chaotic and takes time. Since the rest of the church is mostly full, they slide into the first couple of rows, front and center. "This instantly changes the atmosphere," said Pastor Joel Renkema. "It becomes a little more rambunctious and 'alive.' We reflect the body of Christ more completely once they join us, and that is kind of 'subversive'—playing out in worship in ways that I'm not sure most of those attending are aware of."

Over the years, as Randall and Beth have built relationships with at-risk families, he and Randall have chatted. In the course of one of their conversations, "Randall once mentioned to me that money itself cannot solve the problems," said the pastor. "We have also talked about the complexities of disciplining children that are not your own. . . . Randall and Beth will tell you this journey has not been made without mistakes." Throughout, though, the pastor said, "their goal has never been to remove children from their parents or to make the children into images of Dutch CRC kids." In fact, despite the fact that often the kids stay with them at their own home, what has impressed him is how Randall and Beth have poured themselves into and brought peace into the lives of the parents of these at-risk children. "They have learned throughout the years that ministry 'to' and 'for' cannot compete with ministry 'with,'" said Renkema. "In this they are paragon models of incarnational ministry for the church. On average, perhaps twenty people a Sunday are in church just because of their relationship with the Grimmius family."

Because of what Beth and Randall have done, there are now several families in the church who are getting involved with the adoption agency Bethany Christian Services and its Safe Families Program that temporarily places children in Christian homes as their parents attempt to stabilize life. "I'm not sure that would happen if the Grimmiuses weren't members of our church," said the pastor.

## Hesed: God's Covenantal Love in Detroit

Momma T asked if they could read from the book of Galatians for the weekly Bible study at Hesed Community Church, located in a small house in Brightmoor, one of Detroit, Michigan's poorest neighborhoods.

A frequent visitor here, even though it's tough making the two-block trip on her legs that hurt, Momma T was angry. She said a man, who used to be a boxer, had been storming into her brother's house and abusing him, his daughter, and the daughter's new baby. The man had been the daughter's boyfriend. The police apparently weren't part of this situation. "It's terrible what's happening, and I can't do anything to stop it," she said. "I need to hear Galatians today."

Momma T didn't say exactly why she chose Galatians, in which Paul rebukes his readers for abandoning the gospel he preached. But she paid close attention as Nate Bull, one of the Hesed pastors, cued a recorded version of it on his phone. As they began, Mark Van Andel, the other pastor, prayed: "This is the day the Lord has made, and let us be grateful for his Word and its nourishment to us. Stir up the Holy Spirit in us today." Then the recording of Galatians began, and eventually, they heard this from Galatians 6:7–8: "Whatever a man sows, that he will also reap. For he who sows to his own flesh will reap corruption, but he who sows to the Spirit will from the Spirit reap eternal life."

"That's it—the flesh!" said Momma T, apparently indicating that the boxer was reaping corruption. Then she said, with assurance, "God has filled me with the Holy Spirit. I'm a vessel!"

Meaning the peace of God in some Hebrew translations, Hesed is a joint church-planting, urban ministry effort by the CRC and the Reformed Church in America. It arose out of an initiative in which the denominations worked together across the US to start churches. In some cases, these are stand-alone CRC or RCA congregations, while in other instances, as with Hesed, the church plants are joint projects.

## Planting a Church in Brightmoor

Bull and Van Andel, who came together in 2017 to plant a church, decided to focus on Brightmoor to start the ministry because of the many challenges facing this four-square-mile area on the far west edge of Detroit. More than 35 percent of the houses and businesses in this neighborhood, once home to a thriving community of autoworkers, are abandoned. Unemployment is high, and nearly 80 percent of the residents live below the poverty line. Drugs, gangs, and prostitutes have been active in the area, and the crime rate is substantially higher than the national average, according to police statistics.

Opening a ministry in the middle of a blighted neighborhood is certainly not a financially wise choice. Nonetheless, it is a reflection of the church stepping out from its more comfortable places and taking a chance to spread the word of Christ in an area rife with burglaries, assaults, and carjackings. "We are not your normal church with its programs, Sunday services, and a big building," said Bull. "Our main aim is to find out how we can care for people."

For a long time, Hesed had no Sunday services at all; now they hold one once a month in a rented building, filling the time with stories and testimonies, prayers and praise and music. Bringing together other house churches, they seek to offer a traditional message in ways that seem to work best for those living in the midst of a city that is crawling out from hard times, including the near-collapse of the auto industry, the Great Recession, and the 2013 Detroit bankruptcy. "We feel it is our call to be working here and to wrestle in faith for the people in Brightmoor until they are brought out of their addictions," said Bull. "We fight for them until they are free to make decisions on their own on how they want to live."

Hesed is open seven days a week, and someone is there most of the time, at all hours, to minister to the needs of people coming in the door. Besides Bible study, visitors stop by for a weekly discipleship program, meals, and free toiletries. The house church also provides a shower for those who need it, and the use of a washer and dryer. Young people also regularly drop in to use the free Wi-Fi. "Many of the people around here have no electricity or water," said Van Andel. "This is an area with so many needs in a city that is still grieving from undergoing so many losses."

## The Neighborhood

At one point, Hesed did a survey of the immediate neighborhood and found that about 20 percent of the people owned their own homes, another 20 percent rented, and the rest were squatters—and these include families—living in abandoned homes.

Take a drive down the streets of Brightmoor, and you see homes boarded up and decorated by graffiti, some of it pleasant images painted by church groups that come in to clean up the area; some of it stark and ugly. A few homes are sturdy-looking, but some bear the scars of arson and others looked bombed-out. It's hard to imagine people staying in houses—whether they are owners, renters, or squatters—with crumbling roofs, sagging foundations, and collapsed porches. But that is how things are—and Hesed is there to provide attributes of a home for those who need them. Hesed wants to bring stability and a sense of peace back into this area in which many of the businesses are closed. Only bars, a party store or two, and other churches show signs of life. "Our goal is to start a neighborhood-focused ministry, beginning here and branching out in partnership with other mission-minded people who want to make disciples of native Detroiters," said Van Andel. "We want to be in this small home because it doesn't carry the baggage of a church facility. When they come here, that kind of catches some people off guard."

The home has a large front window with a couple of bullet holes; it also has a new floor they put in; two bedrooms, a bathroom, a meeting area and kitchen, and a breezeway where the washer and dryer are located. Paintings by Bull hang on the walls—one shows a man in a baseball hat, wearing sunglasses and speaking into a microphone. It's titled "Preacher Man."

## Finding a Mentor

Outside, in the backyard, are a couple of plastic chairs. People from the neighborhood often drift by to sit down, relax, smoke a cigarette, check their phone, and talk. Out here on this afternoon was Josh Cook, who is now the house supervisor. He explained that he met and became friends with Van Andel several years ago. At the time, Josh was in his mid-teens and homeless. He wasn't in school.

"Mark has been my mentor. He's helped me out of a lot of situations," Josh said.

God has been there for him as well, Josh said. He recalled a time when someone was shooting at him and the bullets kept missing. "I realized God was real after that, and my faith really started to grow." Through the ups and downs of his life, he and Van Andel have stayed connected: "Mark helped change my life over from what it was. Really, he's had a massive impact on me. No one from my past, from the 'hood where I grew up, ever expected me to be where I am today." On Tuesdays, about fifteen people from the area come to Hesed, and Cook talks to them "about God and how it should be. I give it to them in ways they can understand. I want to show the genuine power of the love of God for people who are hurt and broken." As for himself, Cook is still adapting into this new life and his role of house supervisor and teacher. "God has brought me this far—and that is pretty good."

## Seeing Christ in a House of Peace

Van Andel and Bull are hoping to raise up leaders such as Cook from the local area to run house churches. Typical seminary training isn't necessarily on the agenda for them. "We want to work with them where they are and bring them along at their own pace," said Van Andel. "We see ourselves meeting tangible needs as a way to raise up disciples." The church planters see Christ in everyone and see their role as tapping into that, bringing it forth so that people can be transformed and show others the same love for God that they have come to experience.

As the afternoon wore on, Momma T got busy sweeping the kitchen and front room, where they had held the Bible study.

She met Mark and Nate a couple of years before while they were prayer-walking the streets as a way to meet people. As they walked, they would drag a wagon full of cold soda pop along behind them and hand it out to thirsty folks, some of whom were open to prayer. Such was the case with Momma T, a lifelong Detroit resident whose past is filled with abuse and violence, poverty and suffering, and yet an ongoing closeness to God. "I come here almost every day," she said, taking a break from sweeping. "They really show genuine love to you, regardless of who you are. I'm a believer and a saint, and I love this type of ministry."

Truly, this is a house of peace, something Momma T needs since so much else in her life—like the situation with the abusive guy—is a roller coaster of bad things. This is a home she can visit when she needs prayer, when her life is going crazy. This is a home where she finds God. "I love it here," she said—and then she went back to sweeping the floor.

## Pathway Church: Finding Mortgages for Immigrant Families

We stood one drizzly morning on the front porch of Kurt Rietema's house in the poor, Latino neighborhood called Argentine in inner-city Kansas City, Missouri. Inside his house, his wife, Emily, and children were finishing breakfast. Gesturing with his hand up and down the street, Kurt explained that since he and his wife arrived here a few years before they have worked slowly, diligently, and steadfastly to get to know people and then, over time, learned that their biggest worry and need was to obtain permanent housing. With owning your home, they told the Rietemas, comes stability and peace of mind. In several cases, even though many of the people had been able to obtain documentation and had jobs, they had come from unstable places and feared being evicted. Many of those who live in this neighborhood are immigrants from Mexico or Central America. "When we moved in, almost every one of these houses was a rental," explained Rietema.

The Rietemas are members of Pathway Community Church located a few miles away in the well-to-do suburb of Olathe. Founded in the mid-2000s by church planter Kevin Schutte and his wife, Kelli, the original plan was to start and build a megachurch that would offer a multifaceted, high-octane service on Sundays out of a sprawling building surrounded by a large parking lot. But that plan changed in 2008 when Schutte was doing a sermon series on the Gospel of Matthew and became convinced that Jesus would not want a big church; Jesus would want a place of worship that lifted up its community, however large or small, and that began ministries to serve the community. The church has worked since then with ex-offenders, young people leaving foster care, and they worship not in a spacious church but in a small, comfortable place that sits on the property once designed for the megachurch. Its sanctuary is paneled in wood and has windows looking out on a rolling landscape. Every Sunday, people step forward to receive the bread and wine; the Eucharist is a strong bond, a way to feed the members before they are sent out to do their work and live their lives until the following Sunday.

## Missionaries in the City

Kurt Rietema and his wife, Emily, two of those who are sustained by the Eucharist and have been sent, served for several years as missionaries in Mexico for an organization based in Kansas City. When they returned, they started attending Pathway and then, inspired by Pathway's renewed vision of serving the community, they moved into Argentine. Located near 35th Street, a road that once thrived with businesses that are now closed and shuttered, the neighborhood can be dangerous. Kurt pointed across the street to a spot where someone had recently been shot. Still, it is a good place to live, especially for those who now have mortgages. "We ended up finding out that many of the people couldn't get a mortgage because of the language barrier," said Kurt, who is fluent in Spanish, as is his wife. As a result, they could help bridge the language barrier and were able to make connections with banks and then help their neighbors navigate the complex process of filling out the paperwork for a mortgage. It was a meticulous, time-consuming process that required lots of paperwork and documentation. But they kept at it.

## An Immigrant Family Expresses Gratitude

After Kurt took us on a tour of the area, showing us houses and businesses that are being spruced up because a sense of hope is slowly returning to this area of Kansas City, we had a great Mexican lunch in a party store in the area. After that, we visited one of the families whom he and Emily helped to buy their home. Because of the weather, the men who lived there had left their construction jobs early and sat around with three women and spoke—with Kurt translating—of how the Rietemas helped them. Because some of those who lived in—or were visiting—the home are not US citizens, or have no legal documents to be in the country, they asked we not use their names. But we had the chance to hear how a couple of them had walked many miles across the sweltering Arizona desert after leaving Mexico to find a home in the US. We also learned how the first members of this family to arrive in the US settled initially in another town, but moved to Kansas City so their daughter, who was very sick, could be treated at a local children's hospital. Unfortunately, she eventually passed away and her smiling photo sits on top of a shelf in the living room. Even though grief-stricken, they stayed here, met the Rietemas, and the husband and wife were eventually able to buy the home. The wife cried with gratitude as she talked about this. The husband said they were the first to buy a home in the neighborhood and since then many others have followed suit. Leaving the home, Kurt said: "We are here being good news and good neighbors—and not just to help save others but to help change ourselves. We are here to see God at work. We are here to see a kingdom vision for our neighborhood on 35th Street."

## The Snack Shack

Kurt has also met and got to know young people in the area. He didn't bring a formal youth ministry to them; instead he took the time to learn what was important to them and what they wanted—as he did with families in his neighborhood. They told him they were troubled by the number of empty storefronts in the area; they also said they wanted a place to hang out. Out of this came two years of work and planning, which led to obtaining a lease from the local school district for an empty site in which young people helped to create the Snack Shack. Kids drop in here to eat and play foosball, air hockey, video games, and board games.

"We hope that Snack Shack KC just becomes a cool place for kids to hang out. My little sister has already been asking how old she has to be before she can start working here because she just loves to hang out," said Zaira, eighteen, one of the young people who founded the drop-in center. "We've already seen a lot of excitement in the community just by fixing up an old storefront. Maybe this will inspire other people to fix up other places too."

Bringing peace has come in many ways in the ministry of the Rietemas. Generally, it is a quiet peace, finding out what people need and exploring ways to help them get it. Although the Argentine neighborhood is improving, work yet needs to be done. With the help of members of Pathway, they have already helped to rehab houses and plan to do more, said Kurt. "We believe God is out here, providing for us even in the face of some pretty hard issues."

## Helping Revive a Woman's Home

Being "sent out"—just like Jesus sent out people in Luke 10—comes in many forms; at Pathway Community Church that sometimes means staying put to be there when a new person, such as Dana Cooley, shows up. Years of struggle and disappointment—from her own life and the life of others she had come to know—are etched in Dana's face. Deep wrinkles crisscross her skin. After working for several years with rape victims in Chicago, she moved back home to the Olathe area. A survivor of bad experiences at different churches, she one day saw the Pathway sign out front and eventually slipped into the church one Sunday. She sat in the back, feeling a shame she didn't understand and couldn't quite shake. Church had never worked for her because of the rules, the complex doctrines she could never grasp, and relationships that seemed to be based on family and ethnic ties. She never seemed to be part of the "in" crowd and couldn't connect with God. Sitting there at Pathway, she said, "I was scared that they wouldn't accept me." Although she liked Pathway, she remained wary of church and the people. But, feeling something hard to name but pleasant, she kept coming back. And one Sunday Kelli Schutte, wife of the pastor, Kevin Schutte, sat down next to her; after church, they began to talk and eventually became friends. Kelli got to know her and her life and felt led one Saturday to gather a few other members of Pathway. They drove over and knocked on the door of Dana's mobile home. Knowing she was battling depression, cancer, and other challenges and that she had a hard time organizing things and items had been piling up all over the place, they asked if they could come in and help clean her home. She put up a fuss. But when she relented, they asked her to visit with a neighbor while they cleaned and sorted and arranged things. It turned out taking several hours to clean the home. When Dana returned, she was stunned to see everything in order. It helped her feel like something that had been shaky inside of her had been fixed. From there, going to church no longer made her feel shame. "They didn't look down on me. I felt they were really into this Christian stuff, and I started feeling more comfortable in church," said Dana. "I began to have faith in God. I went from being tortured and alone to having what seems like what they call a peace that passes understanding."

After our trips to these places, we reflected on how all of these communities, like others we visited, are made up of ordinary people being God's people of peace and offering that shalom to the broken, hurting, suffering in their midst. Randall and Beth, Kelli, Kurt and his wife, the pastors at Hesed are all normal people just like any of us, but they are living extraordinary lives because of the presence of God's Spirit in their lives and in their homes and in their acts of obedience of saying Yes! to God.

# 5

# "Eat What Is Offered to You"

[or]

## Sharing Meals and Hospitality in Tucson, St. Thomas, and Denver

*"Stay there, eating and drinking whatever they give you, for the worker deserves his wages. Do not move around from house to house. When you enter a town and are welcomed, eat what is offered to you." —Luke 10:7–8*

*Setting aside the need to control and be in charge, reflecting a fresh vision for a world of necessary commonality, Luke 10 people learn to live as a guest—even as a stranger. The shift is from always being the host and bringing in people to your church to, in humility, accepting the hospitality of others. Again, Luke 10 people seek to give up control and follow what the Spirit is already doing in a particular place. This chapter is about the value of eating together, of sharing food and conversation and fellowship, of partnering in a place, about being clear on what God is doing among a particular group of people. These values are evident in the ministry of The Village Church in Tucson and The Table in Denver. Both shape their work around the ministry of food. In St. Thomas, Ontario, we stop at Destination Church to join in a weekly "Stone Soup Supper"— this is soup made from a potluck of ingredients brought in from people in the community. The soup simmers all day in the kitchen as the cooks place new ingredients in the pot. In the late afternoon, the people at Destination grab their soup and sit at tables, in easy chairs, and on couches in the sanctuary that doubles as a meeting space for services and things such as the Stone Soup Supper.*

# The Village

A large, lumbering man with a deep voice, Rod Hugen had hopes years ago of planting a big church in his home state of Iowa. In order to do this, he attended a church planter boot camp at the CRC headquarters in Grand Rapids. But he found out that the process you had to follow to begin a church didn't seem to fit with his personality. It was so formal and had so many boxes to check. He eventually had a hard time seeing himself coming into a town, meeting people, and launching a church that had to be built under certain, measurable guidelines. Nonetheless, he longed to start a church. He loved the gospel and firmly believed it was for everybody. After struggling through the boot camp, he did try to start churches to varying degrees of success. It was a tough journey that led to many disappointments and to sleepless nights in which he tossed and turned and asked God what exactly he ought to be doing. Eventually, he opened more and more to new ways of starting a church, ignoring much of what he learned in boot camp.

About fifteen years ago, he was living in Tucson, Arizona, when he met Eric Cepin, now a CRC pastor, who wanted to start a church in the community. They both had a vision for the church they hoped to start. A vision based on a blockbuster, 1999 science fiction movie. Hugen and Cepin used *The Matrix* as their template for The Village, a church now worshipping in a nondescript neighborhood near downtown Tucson. With its cutting-edge special effects and computer-driven, futuristic action, the movie struck a chord with millions of viewers around the world. But for Hugen and Cepin it was the main message, in an era of falling church attendance and brash skepticism, that hit home. "We wanted to tap into something about the culture itself, especially about how younger people were feeling—and the movie helped us to do that," said Cepin.

The message the founding pastors took from the Oscar-winning movie, starring Keanu Reeves as Neo and Carrie-Anne Moss as Trinity, was that most human beings are trapped and subdued by artificially intelligent machines. With the help of a character named Trinity, Neo defeats the machines. Afterward, before flying off into space, Neo—who some consider a Christ figure—promises to return and show people a new world "where anything is possible."

## Neo-Monasticism

In the movie, the two pastors saw reflections of our contemporary culture in which it is easier to live in darkness, without any real faith in God, than to undergo change and be able to live in the light. They wanted to reach people who need to find a space—a place, a church—where they can be transformed, even if that means things can get pretty raw in the process. Hugen and Cepin wanted to help people, through the gospel, to understand sin as turning away from God—as basically deciding to stay in and be controlled by the matrix. Begun with the help of funding from Christian Reformed Home Missions, the church's approach resonated with people, especially those born between 1980 and the mid-1990s, who are considered millennials. Although the ideas in *The Matrix* played a role in forming the vision for The Village, the slick cyberworld of the sci-fi film is not particularly evident in the church building itself. A former grade school, the church is located on a side street lined with trees and includes a scattering of homes and small, industrial businesses. In the sanctuary, you see well-worn couches and easy chairs spread out in front of the pulpit and the table where the Lord's Supper is served every week. On the wall above the table is a striking desert scene showing three cacti sprouting wings—an image of the Trinity painted by a church member. To the right is a stage area where musicians play during worship, using songs composed mainly by church members straight from the Bible. When they play, the music is often in a minor key, which creates sounds of lament and sadness and somber praise as befits a world in which struggle and suffering are too real and common. At the same time, the music has an underlying beauty and reassurance to it. To the left is the large, open kitchen and dining area. As the regular Sunday worship goes on, smells from the kitchen drift into the sanctuary from the meal that everyone will eat at long tables or outside after the service. Sharing meals is an important aspect of being part of The Village.

A key element of every Sunday service is reciting the Apostles' Creed. The children lead the congregation in reciting the Apostles' Creed one week and in saying the Lord's Prayer the next. The sermon at this congregation is always biblically rooted, often full of stories and advice for living and touching others, and at the end, the preacher, either Cepin or Hugen or one of the other pastors, will include time for comments and discussion. Sometimes the discussion gets heated, but that is fine. "People are free to move around during the service," said Hugen. "This is a value-oriented

82

church built around accessibility and authenticity. Our vision is to help all people—and many who show up here are hurting deeply—come to God." This happens through discipleship, which is more than just telling people the good news; it involves each member seeking to live out the gospel and share it with others. "We believe that along the way, we have to help each other walk this experience of life together," said Cepin.

The church is committed to something known as neo-monasticism, a movement including churches of many denominations. It takes on different forms. But normally it is characterized by a communal life expressed in various ways; a focus on hospitality; and intentional, practical engagement with the poor. "In our case it means that we eat together, worship together, share places to live, and work together in the church, taking turns as janitors, cooks, teachers, nursery attendants, in much the way a monastery operates," said Hugen. "It is not just worship and Bible study but being deeply involved in each other's lives."

## Eating Together

We were there on a Tuesday evening as a group of church members gathered around the table in the home of Eric and Sue Cepin for a dinner of hot dogs, salad, fruit, and soup. There was a sacred, festive quality to the meal. It was a time of sharing, of receiving the hospitality of the stranger and taking a risk; it was about eating what was set before you. It was also a time to share testimonies. As people ate, they took time to talk about their church and how it expresses itself as a neo-monastic community. Layne Crawford, a former teacher now working part-time at the University of Arizona, has been connected to The Village for many years—ever since a college roommate suggested she attend. Right off, she was attracted by the questions the church prompted her to ask: "What do I believe? What do I think? What does Jesus say?" she said. "I've learned that the gospel incorporates story and that you ask, 'How does Jesus' story apply to your story?'"

She has also learned "to listen with grace as people tell their stories. This is the most powerful thing we can do—to listen with a heart of grace," she said. Crawford sees neo-monasticism as a way of being in order for the whole group to be fruitful. Imagine the church and home as always working together for the same purpose: a welcome unity that grows as people share stories and their faith, moving together into the uncertain world. At The Village, said Layne Crawford "people want to know you and what your burdens are." And then, turning to Jesus, they help to make one another's burdens lighter.

## More Stories

Ashley Cousineau met her husband, Michael, when she was in law school in Boulder, Colorado. He has been attending The Village for several years. After they got married, even though she hadn't landed a job, they came to Tucson and she has loved The Village. "We, all of us, vow to be together and stay together," she said, looking around the table. "This is about God and commitment and love." But someone else at the table said that being in community can be hard: "Community is like sandpaper against flesh. Sometimes things hurt, and you realize I'm not always going to come through for you. This is hard; but this is real when you are building relationships."

Mark Crawford, Layne's husband, grew up in Tucson but wanted badly to leave. When he received a job offer, he was ready to pack his bags. But he believes God told him in no uncertain way—although it is hard for him to describe—to stay and be part of The Village, where he has now been a pastor for several years. He especially appreciates the church's annual belonging service in which members renew their covenant with the church. "I'm part of a community that at first pursued me because they loved me," he said.

Rod Hugen knows about that love; he has felt it and he shows it in his ministry. At The Village, they teach how you are burdened by sin, your own sin, sin around you, and sin in the world. They know things are broken and wrong and harsh; that society is filled with injustice and sorrow that comes in many forms. "Here we confess our sins and talk about what we are doing and where we need to go," said Hugen. A picture, painted by a church member, hangs in a room off the sanctuary of the church. It shows Hugen having broken free of and leaving behind chains, the pain and hardship of the past, and carrying a cross—the symbol of Jesus—up a hill.

As the dinner ended and people set aside their silverware and plates and bowls, Sue Cepin, a University of Arizona admissions evaluator and musician at The Village, picked up her guitar. Everyone got quiet as Sue, sitting on a stool, played a song, based on Isaiah 55:1–3, in a minor key, her fingers picking notes that were sad and yet full of life. In many ways, this song exemplifies the missional aspects of the church; it also is the kind of lament they sing on Sundays. "Bring your emptiness . . . I will have, I will have, I will have compassion," she sang. "Come, all you who are thirsty, come to the waters. . . . Give ear and come to me; listen, that you may live. . . . Come, all you who are thirsty, come to the waters. . . . Come to the waters and drink; all you who have no money, come, buy, and eat!"

## Destination Church: The Stone Soup Supper

Devon Davis was shooting darts in a local bar when someone told him about the weekly Stone Soup Dinner at the nearby Destination Church in downtown St. Thomas, Ontario. It sounded interesting. Maybe he'd check it out. Not long after, he ran into Beth Fellinger, the pastor of the church, which is located on the main street of town in a building with a checkered history, including time as a bar and strip club. Devon asked about the dinner and learned he could come and eat, even if he didn't have much to bring. He decided to give it a shot and his first trip to Destination for the meal ended up filling much more than his stomach. "A lot more happened: my life changed," said Devon Davis.

Having his life changed sort of hit him weird. He didn't even know he needed what the church offered. But like many people who call this church home, he found some of the hope his life was lacking. In his case, he was grieving the recent death of his parents, who had died separately several months apart. When they died, it hurt and he didn't know what to do about it. Nor did he know how—or wasn't able to acknowledge—how much it hurt. So he drifted into the bars and played darts. Then he heard about the Stone Soup Supper at Destination—and the church became exactly that—the place to which he was headed, even if he didn't know it. Destination offers him so much. "I love coming here now and listening to Pastor Beth's messages on Sunday. They really hit you and get under your skin. You get good feelings and ideas from them," said Devon, a slender young man wearing a stocking cap.

## A Church Planter with a Broad Vision

Beth Fellinger worked in other denominations before becoming a church planter for the CRC, where she caught a new vision for how to start, maintain, and grow a church. A few years ago, she was attracted by the CRC conviction that the world was changing and the church needed to change with it.

Supported by CRC Home Missions, Beth founded Destination in 2011. From the start, this ministry in downtown St. Thomas, Ontario, focused on welcoming and embracing people such as Devon Davis who live in the immediate community. Hit by poverty and unemployment, St. Thomas has some industry, but several businesses have closed or moved on. At the same time, the city is working at redevelopment, especially in rebuilding its historic train depot, and the central city area was coming alive again. "We knew that planting a new church in the traditional style of a church building on the outskirts of downtown wouldn't do us any favors here where we are in St. Thomas," said Fellinger as she took a break on the day of one of the Stone Soup suppers. "We wanted to create a DNA that would honor Reformed theology and at the same time honor the times we are living in and the community in which we find ourselves. We wanted to add value to people's lives, to be a spoke in the wheel and bring Jesus to the center of the city."

The former bar has been refurbished with a bamboo floor, new windows, glossy wood walls, a small platform for worship, and artwork from church members. During the week, tables line the walls, and on Sundays they are pulled out and placed in front of the platform for the service that includes lively music. "In coming here, we were joining God in what he was already doing," said Fellinger. "We are also doing whatever we can to be part of this community and to help the people in this place." Destination holds a farmer's market every Saturday, provides space for Alcoholics Anonymous meetings, invites Indigenous people to hold gatherings here, teaches people life skills such as how to dress and prepare for a job interview, offers debt counseling, and provides a group for single moms. "We are a ministry that builds relationships with people where they are. God is working in everyone who walks through our doors," said Beth.

## Visiting Destination

Eva, who struggles with depression, was sitting at a table that afternoon with her son, a young man with long hair and wearing a black trench coat. They come in here often, just to be together and to talk with others. Before becoming a part of Destination, Eva had tried different churches, including a Catholic and a Baptist church. "When I went there, I just felt a void," she said. "But from the first day I came in here, I fell in love and thought this is where I have needed to be all of my life." Fellinger's smile and upbeat personality were "like a ray of sunshine." It felt like a loving blanket of acceptance was wrapped around her. "Something clicked, and so I kept coming here," said Eva. "To help out, I hand out bulletins on Sunday morning. I help in the kitchen and clean up."

Roy Heikamp grew up in a distant city in a "stodgy old Christian Reformed Church, and . . . didn't like it." A couple years ago, after losing his job in a furniture store when he was sick with cancer, he got connected with Destination Church. He does odd jobs around the church and likes playing euchre at a table with friends during the day at Destination. Taking time to pray alone and with others and to worship are also important. "We are an outreach church. People come in grieving and drunk and in pain, and we try to give them God," he said.

George Cutney, who helps with the Stone Soup Supper and does other jobs, recalled going to another church where people were nice enough on Sundays. But outside of church, when they saw him on the street, they often looked away, as if they didn't know him. "I guess I wasn't good enough for them," he said, taking a break from helping prepare the weekly dinner. "But here at Destination they are open to people of all walks of life who can come in and have a cup of coffee and get warmed up and talk about God if they want to."

## Coming Close to Dinner

As the afternoon moved toward evening, Devon stood at the door and greeted people coming in for the supper. Stocked with various ingredients that people donate for the meal, the dinner draws its name from folk tales about people who don't have enough food for a meal but can bring a bit of food that they do have to help make a meal for everyone. Also, said Devon, he's been told that the practice has a connection to a Bible passage, Ezra 1:6, which says, "All their neighbors assisted them with articles of silver and gold, with goods and livestock, and with valuable gifts, in addition to all the freewill offerings."

## The Sunday Gathering

Outreach ministry during the week gives way to lively worship on Sunday mornings at Destination. On one of those Sundays, Fellinger gave a sermon on Matthew 12:46–50, in which Jesus is teaching people inside a house when a man told him his mother and brothers were outside and wanted to see him. Gesturing to his disciples, Jesus said, "Here are my mother and my brothers. For whoever does the will of my Father in heaven is my brother and sister and mother."

In her sermon, Fellinger said that the people worshipping at Destination were members of a new family whose significance goes beyond blood relationships. And as a family, she preached, we all have the job of doing the will of the Father. "We are to take stock of whatever gifts we have and ask if we are using them to build the body together. We are to pray with one another, to lift one another up."

Finishing her sermon, Fellinger asked everyone to stand and hold hands. As they did, she asked people to look at their neighbor, really look at them, and imagine the Spirit of God at work in that person. While the Spirit is ever-moving, at the same time it takes root and rests in the hearts of God's people. In many ways, Destination Church has opened itself to the fullness of the Spirit. It weaves people together as a family; it does this in mysterious and yet oddly predictable ways. In looking at their neighbors, Fellinger reminded them that they were all part of a family, of God's family, and all of them were called to use their gifts and love to build their family. This is a family of mutual hospitality; it is a family rooted in one place; it doesn't move around; it grows together in the passage of time come what may. Waving a hand at the worshippers, Fellinger said, "Say to your neighbor, 'I love you and I need you and we are members of the same family.'"

She waited a moment, but then the people did as they were asked, sharing glances and letting others know that they were in this together. Come hard times or times of plenty, they committed themselves to the journey—to walk the path to the destination for which Jesus died and to which Christ wants all of the people to arrive. This is a rugged path, harder for some than for others, but it is a path made easier and much smoother by the feet of many trodding together in one direction.

## The Community

St. Thomas, a city of about 38,000 people, was hit hard during the 2008 recession when two automobile plants closed. It is also a city with a significant number of people who are connected in one way or another to the provincial mental health system. For many years, a large psychiatric hospital was located here. As a result, generations of people came from all over Ontario to the hospital. After being released, their doctors and various programs were here, and so they stayed. But then when the government shut down the hospital a few years ago, some of the patients ended up homeless and others were put in group homes in town. Several of those who come to Destination live in group homes or often have no home at all.

## Members of the Family

Although not everyone who attends Destination is dealing with intellectual challenges or disabilities, everyone is helped in their walk of faith—and this is because everyone comes before God with his or her own set of shortcomings, fears, and feelings of shame.

Rebecca Anderson got connected to Destination several years ago, not long after the church was begun. She learned of Destination through a friend and showed up. "I instantly felt comfortable," she recalled. One memory especially sticks with her. When she first attended, her children were young and were not always willing to sit quietly. They squirmed and talked during the service. This embarrassed her. But one of the people sitting near her smiled at her and the children and told her to take a breath—they are children. Rebecca immediately relaxed and was able to take in the service. Destination, she said, has helped her flourish as a Christian. "One of the most important things that Destination has helped me with is actually being more comfortable praying with others." She often worried that when she prayed, especially in public, she would not say the right thing or not sound as reverent and articulate as others. But by allowing herself to be vulnerable she has learned that others feel the same way. Now she knows she is not the only one who has fear and she is happy to pray freely from her heart.

After spending only a few months at Destination, David and Cindy Feddema began to see its resemblance to the early Christian churches described in the book of Acts: churches that shared their lives and worldly goods; churches that followed the leading of the Spirit. At the heart of Destination, said David, who has been attending the church since 2013, is the keen desire to be part of a community that sees the face of Christ in everyone—a church that is about seeing others and being seen. They are a family with room for anyone who is seeking faith and the love of others. "As a church, we actively share the good news of the gospel with those willing to listen," he said. "We welcome everyone to come as they are and try to add value to each person's life. We are connecting with others and helping them connect to God."

## Stone Soup for Dinner

On the night of the Stone Soup Supper, many people filed in and, as they did, Devon greeted them, inviting them to sit at tables spread across the sanctuary. People chose their seats and chatted, a friendly buzz filling the large room that was once a raunchy nightclub. After a time, people filed up to get a bowl of soup and some bread. As they did, Devon smiled broadly. When he was shooting darts in the bars and wandering the streets, Devon had no idea he would one day be here, in a church like this, a Luke 10 person offering hospitality in this special space and helping to gather people for dinner. "See how we eat together here. Everyone is invited for the soup," he said. "We don't always know what is in it. But it is always good."

## The Table in Denver

From the start, The Table has been a nontraditional ministry community. It calls itself an urban farm, and its focus has been to gather people from the Platte Park neighborhood—and nearby areas in southwestern Denver—who want to help plant and harvest food, mostly in front and side yard garden plots donated for that purpose by local residents. Members of The Table have distributed their produce free of charge to schools, in parks, and in other settings for the last several years. In addition, they meet to share meals and have conversations on a range of topics.

People who have been drawn to The Table are generally not regular churchgoers or even believers. Rather, they have been attracted by the chance to help plant and harvest vegetables and fruit for the local community and then to spend time together. Hospitality is a kind of hand-holding holiness that they share around food. The abundance from the earth is what sustains them and leads them in unexpected directions.

"The Table is not just about food, but about life," said Rev. Craig Broek, who served a church in New Jersey before he and his wife, Jeanine Kopaska Broek, moved west in 2011 to start work in Denver. "We do church in non-churchy ways. We bring in the divine in ordinary ways."

## Realizing a Dream

In 2020, the ministry was realizing the dream to renovate a former Veterans of Foreign Wars hall beside the South Platte River and along a popular bike path in Denver, into a meeting space for The Table. But the space in the onetime VFW hall—as it is being built—won't include a platform for preaching, a place for the choir, or rows of chairs for people to sit during a service. Instead, there will be a coffee bar, a tap room, and a commercial kitchen for educational classes on cooking and healthy eating. That area will also be used to prepare food for gatherings. "This will be a new beginning for the way we function. It is unexpected, but God is bringing us to this place in ministry," said Jeanine.

The new coffee shop/tap house/food education initiative will enable them to have a public and permanent presence as well as extend hospitality and educational opportunities to their neighbors in a brand new way. "It will provide us access to the community on a daily basis throughout the year, something we have never had before," said Craig. It will be a big change. For several years, people have had to meet in various locations on Sunday evenings for a meal and to discuss a topic. During the week, they have also met, often in the Broeks' home and in the homes of others, for soup or another kind of meal. Increasingly, and yet without compulsion, during the Sunday evening gatherings people began to take part in communion.

## The Table's Patient Approach

Early on, Ryan Hammons was interested primarily in helping to grow food in the garden plots donated by local residents. But, over time, he saw something in the Broeks—a sense of giving, a kindness, a keen willingness to share—that made him wonder if they had a deeper motivation behind what they did. "This was a new thing, and it really appealed to me," said Hammons. "They weren't trying so hard to say, 'Come and join us,' or to put pressure on us." While they do speak about matters of faith, mostly when they come up, the Broeks don't evangelize in any traditional way. They keep their beliefs, which are strong, low profile because the people they have been trying to reach are those who live in their mostly upper-middle class neighborhood and who tend to go to the mountains on weekends, visit the local farmers' market, or simply stay at home and rest after a busy workweek. Church isn't important to them.

Visiting The Table gave Hammons, a former Catholic, a chance to get comfortable before moving into speaking about his faith, a difficult area because his experiences in formal church settings had been unsatisfying. "I have come to The Table for a few years, and very gently and subtly I have had the chance to ask questions about faith," said Hammons, an environmental permit ecologist. "Coming to The Table has given me good friends, and Craig gives us the space where you can freely talk about spirituality. It is a good place to be, to come and hang out. I know I have friends who have my back, and I have their back." Hammons lives in the area and played a role in gathering support for the project to rehabilitate and furnish the VFW hall. There was a time when he wouldn't have thought that having a permanent space was wise for a group whose focus was on being loose and open-ended. But the Spirit seems to be moving The Table into a new home, a fixed place where people can come and take part in the various activities. It's still not a church building, but the people making up The Table have become a church-like community. In their new place, they could get a business going—the coffee shop and tap room—and provide a kind of educational ministry in the back area for the community, while at the same time making money to help support The Table. But, especially, it would be a permanent home for people connected to The Table to meet for meals, for Bible studies, for larger events, times of worship, neighborhood gatherings, to have one-on-one discussions, and different kinds of classes. "The Holy Spirit is definitely in this—the way conversations flow. We share forgiveness, sorrow, and grace," said Hammons.

## Planning for the Future

The new space is located by the river near Grant Frontier Park, the site of a former gold mining town, Montana City, the first settlement in what is now the Denver area. Besides renovating the building, The Table will use outdoor space for a demonstration garden and a small greenhouse. The property will also provide space to help store the produce they grow in neighborhood plots, and that will help to free up space in the Broeks' home. "We have been able to donate 30,000 pounds of food to people and groups in the area over the years—and most of that was kept temporarily in our kitchen," said Jeanine Broek. "We'll now have a place for it all to go before it gets distributed."

## Sharing Larger Life Questions

Even though The Table will now have a permanent location, much of the gospel teaching and reflection will still take place in front yards and side yards, in those readily accessible and visible spaces where the food grows and Jeanine and Craig use the reality of creation to share messages about God. Jeanine recalls getting into a conversation with a group of young people who visited one of the gardens. "The process of growing food gives you time to open up and talk about larger life questions," she said. "I was pruning the tomatoes and explained how pruning is hard work. But if you don't prune them, you end up with a mess of branches and very little fruit."

They try to draw on biblical lessons in tangible ways. For instance, Jeanine speaks of how growing and giving and taking and receiving food are acts of grace. "I talk about how in our work around food we exemplify honoring and preserving life."

They talk about planting and tending and having patience for the plants to bear fruit. They talk about the gifts of water and land; they talk about using compost, things we might otherwise throw away, to enrich the soil and help things grow.

Jeanine looks forward to having a new place along the river and the bike path near the park. But she will still find joy that comes when she is out working in a garden and someone drives by, tapping their car horn in encouragement, or even pulls up to learn more about what she is doing and why.

"Certainly, there are a lot of brick-and-mortar churches in our area" that people can find and visit, she said. "But when they see a garden, they want to stop and talk to you. Out of a simple thing like a garden can come some major things," she said, such as conversations about food that can help people grow closer to God. Like being part of a conversation and context in which the sharing of God's plenty can shape and lift up people.

# 6

# "He Felt Compassion for Him"

## [or]

## Meeting Good Samaritans in Hudsonville and Grand Rapids

Then a despised Samaritan came along, and when he saw the man, he felt compassion for him. Going over to him, the Samaritan soothed his wounds with olive oil and wine and bandaged them. Then he put the man on his own donkey and took him to an inn, where he took care of him. —Luke 10:33–34, NLT

*Jesus told the story of the Good Samaritan after an expert in the law asked who was his neighbor. Clearly, our neighbor is the one who looks out for us and is willing to care for us when we are sick or injured in body or spirit. In this chapter, we look at how addiction to drugs and/or alcohol can lead many of us to dark places; addiction can trample over us and leave us by the side of the road. But we need not lie there, bludgeoned by the bad choices we have made; lured there by our own hungry minds, seeking the solace of drugs or alcohol. We can end up in place—such as the pig sty in which the Prodigal Son found himself. Or, just as the Jewish man going down from Jerusalem to Jericho, we can be beaten and robbed and left for dead by our addiction. Caked in mud and wounded in many places, even as we are helpless on that road, we know we need help. And there are those, such as Tom Kragt, whose story we tell here, or Jerome Burton, whose story similarly is told in this chapter, who can come to our aid. Driven by their faith and their own experiences, they pass on the assistance they themselves have received in their lives. In writing about Jerome, the story takes on a personal aspect since he helped me (Chris Meehan) at a time a decade or so ago when I found myself*

94

*lying half-dead on the side of a road, when I, as so many others, was lost and wondering just what God wanted for me.*

## Evergreen Ministry: Focus on Recovery

R ev. Tom Kragt opened the Sunday evening Faith and Spirituality service at Evergreen Ministries in Hudsonville, Michigan, by leaning into the microphone and describing in a few words who he is. "Hey, everyone, I'm Tom, and I'm an alcoholic." Many of the people seated in chairs in the room serving as a sanctuary replied, "Hi, Tom!" A number of those attending are also alcoholics, drug addicts, or persons addicted to other things such as gambling or overeating. "Let's get this thing going tonight with the Serenity Prayer," said Kragt, at that time pastor of congregational life and recovery at Evergreen, a large church that was built several years ago amid cornfields in West Michigan.

Standing by their seats, people followed the pastor's lead and said the prayer written many years ago by theologian Reinhold Niebuhr: "God, grant me the serenity to accept the things I cannot change, the courage to change the things I can, and the wisdom to know the difference."

## A Church for Misfits

In a powerful way, this recovery service exemplifies the spirit at Evergreen Ministry, founded in the early 1990s. At Evergreen, the focus has always been rooted in Scripture but constantly finding ways to express the truths of the gospel in programs that help people—and in the case of the recovery service helps save them from addictions that threaten to kill them. The Faith and Spirituality recovery worship service at Evergreen was inspired by the Twelve Steps of Alcoholics Anonymous, but bases all of its prayers, music, and sermons on the Bible. "We have always been a church that opened itself to the broken and the lost, to those people on the edges who were familiar with church, who knew the language but could no longer find a place for themselves in a church," said Rev. Larry Doornbos, who planted the church and helped to guide it as a ministry for people who feel forgotten and for those seeking a more contemporary style of worship and messages with everyday applications. Especially in its recovery ministry, the idea is for Evergreen members to have open hearts and open arms to welcome people who have wandered and stumbled and hit bottom in the world. Many of these are those who have been beaten and robbed of their dignity and left by the side of the road. Depleted of hope, they often want to find their way back to a better way of living. Yet, they wonder where can they find that? Doornbos had this group in mind when he began Evergreen, which sits in an area full of thriving CRC congregations and yet, especially in the early 1990s, offered little more than the tried-and-true weekly Sunday services. Back then, go to one on a Sunday and you'd get what you'd get a few miles away.

## A Father's Open Arms

Whether someone is recovering from an addiction, trying to find their way out of a divorce, or hurting from a bad experience at another church, what is evident here at Evergreen is being able to see imperfect people trying to find a better way and in the process receiving God's grace. And this is the kind of openhearted grace shown by the father in the familiar story of the Prodigal Son (Luke 15:11–32), said Tom Kragt in his sermon on that evening. "The power of God's love is clearly shown in this story that Jesus told," he said. The father's love for his lost son is incredible, given the tribal Middle Eastern culture in which it was set. Populated by close-knit families run by patriarchs, it would have been unthinkable for a son to come right out, as did the prodigal son, to ask for his inheritance. "Those who listened to this story must have been shocked to hear how shamefully he was dishonoring his father," said Kragt. They would have expected the father to explode in anger, but instead the father let his son go, giving him his share of the inheritance to do with as he wished. And so the son went off to a "distant country and there squandered his wealth in wild living," only to end up working, as severe famine covered the land, for "a citizen of that country, who sent him to his fields to feed pigs" (Luke 15:13–15). And it turns out the pigs ate better than he did. He was bereft; a lost, forgotten soul. The son was sprawled in a sty, at the end of himself.

Realizing just how far he had fallen, the son decided to get up and return home to plead with his father to take him back and make him one of his servants so he could have something to eat. But when his father sees him from far off, he runs out to welcome his son home. This is the spirit of the recovery program, a welcoming spirit that makes no judgments and opens its arms to the lost. "This is Jesus' posture to us—acceptance and love," said Kragt. "We are all deeply loved by God; you can't make God love you more than he already does. God is there waiting for you to grab his hand and to begin this beautiful journey through the Twelve Steps."

## Breaking Bad in Chicago

Several of the people listening to Kragt know what it is like to end up covered with filth, desperate, badly in need of a drink or a drug and yet wanting to quit. Many, like Don, know what it is like to end up in the far country of drunkenness with seemingly no place to turn. Their drinking led them down dark alleys they couldn't escape. They have fallen far and are in need of someone to help them and bandage up their wounds. After years of drinking, Don landed in a recovery program in Chicago. The program asked people to believe in a higher power but didn't define that power. That was OK; he could buy into that as far as it went. He appreciated the care he received in that program—yet the God part eluded him.

Then, on a family visit a few years ago to Hudsonville, Don attended Evergreen. At first, he didn't like how the church connected recovery with Jesus Christ. It seemed too churchy—a quick and simple answer to his complex problems and challenges. How could this Jesus lift him up from where he lay? But, with time, he got over that, seeing the power in having a higher power, a power he began to believe worked through others who, like him, had been cast aside and driven down by addiction. He started to see Jesus as a loving presence alive in others. When his family moved to Hudsonville, he joined the church and has become part of the recovery ministry. "Being here now, helping out with the service, and being part of the community helps me have a bigger purpose and a direct impact on people who come here for healing," Don said after the service. "I know people want to correct their mistakes. This ministry is a perfect gateway for them to do that."

Donna Sills and her husband, Don, have been attending Evergreen for many years. Reared in the traditional CRC, they appreciated Evergreen's willingness to color outside the lines, to share the message of Christ to ragged people who longed for a faith in which they felt they belonged. Often, she and Don attend the evening recovery service to show support for the ministry. "It is awesome to see those people who are hurt and ignored and to see them accepted and become outstanding members of our church," she said. What they say is straightforward: God lives and God forgives us all, and especially his children—his sheep—who have left the fold and have gotten lost in the bleary cloud of addiction, a force that has a demonic power—a spirit that makes its users susceptible to evil in its many forms. They see how they, solid in their faith, can open their arms to the addicts seeking that new road to recovery.

## Sharing the Meal

Tom Kragt sat down in the Evergreen cafeteria for the meal that follows the service. In a few minutes, he and others would attend a meeting dealing with the overall topic of addiction. And this was open to everyone, since it was designed by the church and not by AA. Evergreen wants to remain open to all who have questions and yet not to direct them on a spiritual path, unless they want to explore faith in Christ. "We want to be a church for God's world, for all people of all places, and our recovery ministry reflects us," said Kragt.

More than twenty years ago, Kragt lost his job at a Reformed Church in America congregation because of his drinking and landed at a recovery center in Grand Rapids, Michigan. Before that, he said, he "had danced around the edges of recovery." It was a very difficult time; like the man in the story of the Good Samaritan, he had been robbed of just about everything—his livelihood, his dignity, his health, his relationships—by alcohol. But something inside of him began to shift; he knew he needed help and reached out his hand and checked into the recovery center, where he learned something he already knew but had a hard time accepting—addiction was a powerful foe and he needed to take recovery seriously. In the center, he found support; he found friends; he found people willing and able to help him heal. Kragt came to see that even though he'd been a pastor, supposedly a man of God, he had not taken the first three of the Twelve Steps. He had not admitted, as the first step states, that he was "powerless over alcohol" and that his life was unmanageable. Nor, as the second step says, had he come to believe that "a power greater" than himself could restore him to sanity. He also hadn't, as the third step directs, turned his "will and life over to the care of a higher power"—in his case Jesus. After taking those steps in the recovery center, in fits and starts, he delved into the rest, which all demand humility and a deep willingness to change, often brought on by the desperation of alcohol addiction. In fact, some call it the gift of desperation, without which it is next to impossible to allow God and others to help you return to a sane and solid life. Kragt considers the steps as a to-do list that he has to keep going over and working at, but not a theology. His belief is in God as defined by the Reformed creeds and confessions, and that fits comfortably in how he works with Evergreen's recovery program. "I see the steps as helping me in the process of sanctification," he said.

Once he got sober, Kragt worked for a time as a counselor at the Grand Rapids treatment center where he had been a patient. He found that helping other alcoholics powerfully blessed him. Reaching out and embracing others who had fallen by the side of the road helped to lift him up and deepened his connection to God. Meanwhile, he started attending Evergreen and was happy being an unconcerned church member trying to figure out "this recovery thing" when he began meeting with Doornbos and was eventually offered a job.

After a time, he began his work in this recovery ministry, and he started the recovery service. Over the years, many people have come to the recovery service, hurting and alone, with no belief in God whatsoever, and Kragt has seen them turn around. He has seen them come to faith, not as an event, but as a process, "as a series of things that bring our faith to fruition."

As he spoke, people around the cafeteria were sharing a meal. So many had come from out of addictions that had trapped and made their lives unbearable. Like Kragt, they were here on this night to keep working on their recovery—a slow, lifelong process. But watching people eat and laugh and talk, it was easy to think of that Good Samaritan who, unlike the rabbi and Levite leader, paused to stop and sought to help the man who had been beaten and left for dead. Many of the people there had been on the side of that road and had then been brought to a place where they could recover from their wounds. And then, as they recovered, like Tom Kragt, they began to reach out and assist others—not because they thought it was a good idea, but because their very life depends on it.

## The Crucible of God's Love: A Personal Story

Jerome Burton, pastor of Coit Community Church, got a call one day from someone who told him a family member was near death at a local hospital. The caller wasn't a member of the small, Grand Rapids church, but told the pastor that he had heard about Jerome and that the pastor was someone willing to help people regardless of if they had any connection to the church. Later, Jerome told me (Chris) he went and prayed for the man and others in the room. He also baptized the man before he died. And this was not an isolated instance. Over his more than twenty-five years at Coit,

Jerome had been called or found someone knocking on his door many times, asking for help, and he has given it.

There is so much here to tell: how Jerome grew up at the height of the civil rights movement in Selma, Alabama, or how he came to faith in the haze of his own drug and alcohol addiction after his mother died. Or there is how, once he went through rehabilitation, he moved to the area in which Coit is now located and spent hours on the streets telling people about Jesus and holding Bible studies in homes and then one day showed up for a Sunday service at Coit. He is a Black man and most of the people, if not all of them in church that day, were white. But he stayed there, through thick and thin, and was eventually ordained by the CRC as a Minister of the Word for the church. And there is so much more.

He talks of how his church is an emergency room for those with bleeding souls, broken lives, and shattered dreams; many of whom have been in prison for a range of crimes and after they get out have ended up here. Although I've (Chris) never been to prison, I am now at Coit and serving, because of Jerome's inspiration and support, as an associate pastor. And that is the story I want to share—how he found me on the side of my own road, offered his hand and helped me step into a role in ministry that all my life I had thought about but never embraced. As he has for so many others, Jerome has been a Good Samaritan to me.

## An Offer to Help

Although we had met before, we really didn't get to know one another until we were sitting together in a class on Reformed doctrines at Calvin Theological Seminary in 2009. After being a newspaper reporter for many years, I was then working as a writer for the CRC and decided, why not take a seminary class or two? In fact, I'd been in a Catholic seminary for a couple of years in high school, but left when I was a junior as it became clear I didn't belong there. Anyway, Jerome and I got to know each other at Calvin, especially during breaks and in conversations after class. It was after our final class that we were talking about Coit and he invited me to attend, telling me he could use some help at the church. For many years I had been a practicing Catholic, and still very much appreciated the church, but had drifted away for different reasons and tried various congregations in the CRC. Without a church home at the time, I told him I'd give it a try. My wife, Mary, was attending another church and was happy to stay there.

# Joining Up

Some forty people, maybe 60 percent Black and the rest white, were in the sanctuary on the first Sunday I attended Coit. After the service, I talked with a couple of people, including Jerome, and told them I'd be back. On my part, I felt something tugging at me to come to Coit and, as Jerome had said, to help out. My reasoning, even then, however, seemed a bit foggy. Looking back, I think it was probably the Holy Spirit telling this former Catholic boy from Detroit that this was where I needed to be. I'd like to say it was a clear-cut process, but it wasn't. At times I dragged my feet; at others I was inspired to be there; while at others I wondered why God wanted me to be at Coit, which worships in a former Methodist church building in a slowly gentrifying neighborhood on the edge of downtown Grand Rapids. Conflicted as I felt, that began to change as I got to know church members and heard their stories and shared mine. Bonds began to form. Same thing with Jerome; we never had deep, intimate conversations and yet I sensed something growing solid between us. Maybe a year or so in, he asked if I might want to become a Commissioned Pastor, a position in the CRC that is generally focused on one church for which you are ordained to preach, teach, marry, bury, and baptize. At that time, I had finished a few classes at Calvin and decided it might not be a bad idea to keep going and to consider Jerome's invitation seriously—to realize a dream to be ordained I'd held for many years, since grade school actually.

# Water in the Basement

Here is where the twists and turns in the road really begin. As an alcoholic, I landed in lots of trouble, lost one marriage, and caused more damage than I want to admit. But I got sober in 1984 and haven't had a drink since. However, around 2011 I found myself in a bad way. I had had a heart procedure and then neck surgery to repair some bad discs and was given narcotic pain medicine, which being an addict I should have shunned but I found very much worth taking. It was in the midst of this that my train ran off the tracks. A neurologist who I visited to check pain in my legs told me there wasn't much he could do other than prescribe a high dose of a painkiller. I filled the prescription and began popping the pills. I liked the warm feelings that came over me; I enjoyed the fuzzy buzz, even though my mind got muddled and my behavior turned south fast. Instead of reaching out to others for help, I settled for a time into that narcotic cloud.

Maybe it was the drugs; maybe not. But I began to feel lost and unsure and especially questioned God and wondered if I was in any way qualified to become a pastor of a church. The doubts had been there, but now the painkillers opened the door wide, filling me with a fear I hardly knew was there. Doubts slammed into me until one day, as providence would have it, the washing machine in our basement began bouncing, knocking off a paint can, and then started overflowing. Suds and water and paint spread throughout our basement. Still recovering from surgery and still taking the pills, I had to spend the day going from room to room shop-vaccing the sludgy mess. I had to clean up the water and paint alone because my wife was at work. And as I worked, pressure inside of me built; I began thinking about Coit and about becoming a pastor. My friend Moses Chung, my co-author, came to mind and I gave him a call in my desperation. I told him I wondered if I ought to become a pastor. If I really had a vocation. He told me we should talk more, which we subsequently have done quite a bit. But what I didn't tell him is that those pills were killing me and, probably because of them, I had so many questions about the future. Emotions that are hard to describe suddenly overwhelmed me. When we got off the phone, I knelt down in the water and spilled paint and began to cry. Deep, hard sobs spilled from me and I called out—in loud words to God. I'd never really done this before; but I ached and hurt and wanted to know what God had in store for me. Maybe this sounds melodramatic; but I wanted to know if I was worthy enough to be a pastor, to be a preacher. Here I was not drinking but I'd become a pill popper. Still crying, I asked, "God, what do you want from me? Please, tell me." I got no answer from on high; but I called another friend and we met and I told him the fix I was in. He didn't know what to say, but he listened. That helped.

## Getting Better

A couple of weeks later, at the urging of my wife and doctor, I entered a short detox program. My emotions were raw and in turmoil. My mind was a mess. I realized I was sicker than I'd thought because I'd been taking other medications besides the pain pills. After three days, I went home from detox. But it was only the start. Coming off all of the drugs, dogged by fears I couldn't name and inklings of suicide, I went back to the hospital for ten days and then to a treatment center near Detroit for another ten days. In the treatment center, I went to meetings and started to feel a little better. At some point, I met with a chaplain and told her how, in the midst of it all, I was so unsure about wanting to go into the ministry. I mentioned how I hadn't really even talked this over with my wife. The chaplain wasn't much help. More helpful were the men in the hospital and treatment center; they knew where I'd been and where I was. They helped me up and carried me along, telling me to let God be God and God would get in touch with me when the time came. Also of great help was my wife who, even though I'd kept the big picture of what I was going through a secret, had seen me go down and wanted me to be back up, standing on my own two feet.

When I returned home, now ashamed at what I'd done and where I'd been, I decided I needed to talk to Jerome to tell him I couldn't move ahead to be a pastor. Even though I was finishing my program at the seminary, a deep place in me felt I couldn't do it; I couldn't stand in front of people to preach. As for God, I'd called out and only received silence. Or so I thought. Regardless, late one Saturday morning I drove over to the city park where Coit members were holding what they called a Gospel Fest, a time of music, games, food, and fun for people in the neighborhood. Trudging from my car to the park, suddenly something lifted, a burden of some sort I'd been carrying. I'm not quite sure why. I felt feathery; as if the storm might be passing. I felt a puff of a sifting wind. Nearing where everyone was, I stopped next to Larry, a wise Black guy who is my age—a church elder who had been around many blocks many times. I was about to tell him I wasn't coming back to Coit when he put an arm around me and said: "Welcome back, my brother." Hardly anything more. Relief began to flood me. Maybe I was getting an answer to my basement prayers.

## Formed for Ministry

Soon, Jerome came up and asked me to go with him to get ice to keep the food and soda pop cool. I wondered what I ought to say, but, again, it went pretty simple. Jerome turned to me and said: "I'm glad you took care of that." Later, he would say my experience with the pills and being in the hospital and my struggle with ministry made sense. If you are going to work for God, he said, expect opposition from good old Satan. The devil had his teeth in me and wanted—because I had strayed too far in the wrong direction—to take me down. Being in the ministry was not on the devil's agenda. He wanted me in the wilderness. And, to an extent, that is what happened. I floundered and got beat up, mostly by myself and my poor choices. And was left in a heap on the road, closer to death I realize now but certainly didn't really realize then.

I graduated from the seminary with a diploma in missions and not long after was accompanied by my wife, Mary, in many ways one of my most important Good Samaritans, to my ordination. My best friend from high school came up from Detroit to talk, a friend in the congregation gave the sermon, another friend from CRC headquarters offered a prayer, and Jerome did the ordination—in some ways fulfilling the dream that went back many years but had seemed unattainable. Several friends and family members were there to watch and afterwards we had lunch. No loud music played; no huge fanfare took place. I was now a pastor and, having gotten the answer from God that I'd been calling out for in my watery basement, could move forward serving God in whatever ways seemed fit.

I've had a chance to enter into the lives of men and women at Coit; I've been able, I hope, to be a channel of God's grace for them. It is especially in these times, and when I preach, that being a pastor seems right; it is a calling I am grateful for answering, even if the road to my ordination was filled with some pretty big potholes.

Looking back on this experience, I see the movement of the Spirit in it, the movement of God speaking and filling me with experiences that have formed my ministry. I see the backing and support of many people, and especially I see how Jerome helped in making room for me in ministry. Like someone who is a first responder to the calls of so many people, he has been a Good Samaritan to so many, lifting the broken from the side of the road, including me.

# Part Three

## Sent to Every Town and Place

"Jesus appointed seventy others and sent them
two by two ahead of him to every town and place
where he was about to go." —Luke 10:1

# 7

# "Blessed Are the Eyes that See What You See"'

[or]

## A Mass Killing in Calgary, a 9/11 Service in Toronto, and Card Tricks in Chicago

"Then Jesus turned to his disciples and said privately, 'Blessed are the eyes that see what you see.'" —Luke 10:23

*We feature ministries that have helped people see God at work in people and in the places in which they happen to find themselves. We stopped at the University of Calgary, where a multifaith ministry, opening the eyes of students to other types of belief and showing love to your neighbors is important. It was here that campus ministers had to muster their resources to respond to a mass killing. In Toronto, Gideon Strauss makes sure every Tuesday morning during the academic year to attend Wine Before Breakfast, a service created by the CRC campus ministry at the University of Toronto that helps make him more acutely aware of a sovereign God who allows him to share in the rich mix of Reformed theology and a kind of progressive Christianity that focuses on a Luke 10 approach of proclaiming the kingdom in the here and now. Living in this kingdom, he believes, helps us learn and engage with the tough issues. We also visited a campus ministry on a Catholic campus outside of Chicago, where the chaplain holds a Bible study on the tale of Abraham and Isaac that offers young people new insight into this Bible story.*

## University of Calgary: Doing the
## Hard Work in a Time of Crisis

I t was a tragedy that no one could have predicted—a mass murder that
took place in April 2014 near the campus of the University of Calgary.
When he came to the school many years before to serve as campus chaplain, Paul Verhoef never dreamed he would be called in to try to bring some
hope and healing at a time such as this. Nevertheless, he was no stranger
to being the voice of the loving presence of God at times of crisis. He had
helped to hold services for students who died from suicide and been there
to speak with and listen to students and family members grieving a death.
But there he was in 2014, helping Debbie Bruckner, director of the university's wellness center, provide assistance to students and staff after the
stabbing death of five young adults attending an end-of-year, off-campus
house party. Matthew de Grood, the son of a Calgary police inspector, was
charged with the crime but found not responsible due to his mental condition. Students across the campus were shocked and devastated by the mass
murder. Friends had been killed; many had been there when the killings
took place. Emotions ran high; questions about why this happened seemed
unanswerable. Verhoef knew it was necessary to reach out to students and
staff and others and gather with them in many places—in classrooms and
dorms, in areas outdoors both on and off campus, in dining halls, and in
the chapel. Helping Verhoef in his outreach was the other CRC campus
chaplain at Calgary, Pearl Nieuwenhuis. "Paul and Pearl were there and
able to help young people navigate through the painful process," said
Bruckner. In meeting after meeting, they sought to give a sense of God's
grace, but early on grace was not what people wanted: They wanted to cry
out and the chaplains let that happen.

Nieuwenhuis joined the campus ministry more than ten years ago.
She is a trained spiritual director and meets with students in all kinds of
situations, from trying to deal with a tragedy or just the everyday challenges of college life. "I'm here to accompany you wherever you are," she
said. And, along with Verhoef, she did this during that time of devasta-
tion. It was a time, in the wake of those five deaths, that Paul and Pearl
still recall with a shudder. Yet they also remember the resiliency of the
students and staff, the way they stood with one another—whether they
had a faith family on which to rely or not—to help one another through a
time of sorrow and grief.

The response of Verhoef and Nieuwenhuis during that mass killing reflects the work that the CRC is doing at some thirty mostly secular universities and colleges across North America. Certainly, the ministries aren't called very frequently to serve among a student body experiencing grief and lament following an incident such as the one that occurred in Calgary, but they have the heart and desire and "eyes that see" the needs that the students and faculty experience. Ministering in secular settings, in schools in which God is not necessarily on the agenda, they bring the sacred and holy into the lives of those they meet. They show love for their neighbor, said Verhoef.

Over the years, Verhoef has seen how God is always at work—that the Spirit of God is always moving, breathing, creating life, reconciling God's world back to God, and doing this on the campus in Alberta—and he is grateful to have had the chance to be part of if. Looking back over his time at Calgary, Verhoef is confident that in many ways—such as when he and Pearl Nieuwenhuis connected with the students, families, and staff in the aftermath of the mass stabbings—he has become a good neighbor. With God's help, he has sought to touch hearts and minds with Christlike love, and he has tried to be a voice speaking into a secular world that tends to look away from things that are divine. Because of these things, Verhoef hopes and prays the university would miss the CRC's presence—a palpable example of God's kingdom—if it were no longer there.

## University of Toronto: Wine Before Breakfast

For twenty years, the campus ministry at the University of Toronto has held its Wine Before Breakfast service starting at 7:22 AM every Tuesday during the academic year, in the Anglican chapel at Wycliffe College, an Anglican seminary, at the University of Toronto. This worship community began just after September 11, 2001, when Brian Walsh, director of the ministry, and others decided to hold this gathering as a way to offer lament and acknowledge pain while "the smoke was still smoldering . . . and the world was in a state of deep shock" after the attacks that took place in New York City, Washington, DC, and involved a terrorist-driven plane crashing into a farm field in Pennsylvania. We attended the service on Tuesday, September 10, 2019, not long after the start of the academic year and one day before the September 11 anniversary. As always, the service offered a special blend of Anglican liturgy and Reformed prayer and preaching.

It was a powerful service mixing prayer and song, liturgy and a sermon, all leading to the sharing of the Eucharist. It was a time of pause; a time to look inside and see how God was working in us.

The focus here is on ministry to graduate students, older students whose faith has started to mature, often with the help of this campus ministry. A ministry with a keen sense of its place at the university, it also provides a type of Christian worship and reflection that calls into question the behavior and beliefs of the wider culture.

This was obvious in the way in which Brian Walsh interpreted and preached a sermon on Luke 1:39–56, as well as how the service itself was shaped on the morning we were there. In the Gospel text, the focus was on the Magnificat, the prayer that the teenage Mary spoke in praise after learning she was to bear the child Jesus. In this prayer, Mary goes from praising the child in her womb to offering a prophecy of what this child will grow up to do. Using this Scripture as inspiration, as always, music was key in underscoring the message being shared. From week to week, the music ranges from popular and traditional hymns and songs to rock, jazz, and other forms of music. Deb Whalen-Blaize, the music director, chose as the prelude today, a moving and startlingly apt piece titled "Mothers of the Disappeared." A song by the band U2, it is about mothers in Argentina who gathered before the presidential palace in 1978 to protest the kidnapping and killing of their children. In part, the lyrics were: "Midnight, our sons and daughters cut down, taken from us. Hear their heartbeat. We hear their heartbeat." The next song was "Canticle of the Turning," by Rory Cooney. A song based on the Magnificat, it begins: "My soul cries out with a joyful shout that the God of my heart is great." The final piece was "Dancing Barefoot," by Patti Smith. Tying in with the theme of the day, one verse reads: "She is the essence of thee. She is concentrating on He who is chosen by thee."

## Lamenting September 11

Also included in the service was a litany of lament, based on the Magnificat and written in free verse, poetic style. In part, this read: "We are waiting, waiting for those who are called by name, waiting for the poor to receive your Kingdom, waiting on the streets of Toronto, waiting in the refugee camps. . . ." In this service, we were called to open our eyes, to see ourselves and the world, from a slant, a different perspective.

In his sermon, offered before the altar in the Wycliffe College chapel, Walsh linked Mary's words to September 11, 2001. "Where do we find ourselves in the abrasive prayer that Mary prays as we look to the anniversary of 9/11?" asked Walsh. In the Magnificat, he pointed out, Mary prays words that challenge the powerful: "He [God] has scattered the proud in the conceit of their heart. He has put down the mighty from their thrones, and has exalted the lowly. He has filled the hungry with good things, and the rich he has sent away empty." Mary was a young woman, said Walsh, who reminds us that God is on the side of those who struggle and have little—such as this teen who did not come from an important family. God stands with those who have been pushed to the margins of society. Listening to Walsh, it was easy to picture Mary, this young woman, startled by the announcement by the angel Gabriel and yet having the spunk to speak this brave prayer that—in a surprising and satisfying way—calls the powers that be to task. She is obviously aware of who this child in her womb is and that he will challenge and seek to turn the world on its head. Mary mirrors a deeply faithful person willing and able to see beyond the normal and the narrow to a wider world in which God was active and promised incredible opportunities for transformation. She can glimpse beyond the traditional, the tried and true, to a new place that God, who would soon be born, would assume in the world. Walsh helped those in the chapel to see this—to see the role Christians need to play in upending the ways that offer only comfort and to embrace practices and approaches leading to a depth of experience and personal commitment to one's faith and to justice. "Mary knows that praise and protest always go together, knows the holiness of God is always about justice," he said. "So can we sing the Magnificat on September 10, 2019? Dare we sing the Magnificat at 7:22 in the morning, while the powerful remain in their boardrooms?"

## The Eucharist

Everything in the liturgy leads to the Eucharist. This is the "wine" in Wine Before Breakfast and functions as the heart of the liturgy. In breaking the bread this morning, Anglican priest Rev. Susan Spicer said "In the face of hunger, you are bread. In the face of deep thirst, you are wine." After blessing and praying over the elements, she passed them to the people. We shared them as we stood. We took the bread, the body, and the wine, the blood, allowing it to suffuse us, to provide a sustaining power, to give us—in a tangible way—a strong sense of God being among us and of what Christ did for all of us on the cross. We took in the communion Jesus instituted on the night before he went to that cross. We did it because we sought to do what Jesus wanted—to share the meal in which we remember that terrible day on the hill called Golgotha, and the hope Jesus provided by staring death in the face and rising from the tomb.

## The Lasting Value of the Ministry

When the service ended, people gathered downstairs for coffee, tea, bread, and jam in Walsh's spacious, book-filled office. Besides serving as chaplain, he has taught for decades at the University of Toronto School of Theology. He and his wife, Sylvia Keesmaat, also a theology professor at the school, live on a farm a few hours outside Toronto, and when he is in town he sleeps on the couch in his office. Gathered in Walsh's office that morning was Carmen Schultz, who is working on a master's degree in pastoral studies. This had been her first time at Wine Before Breakfast. She had heard about it, met with Walsh, and decided to give it a try. She had been looking for a different way to worship, seeking perhaps a new approach to expressing her faith. Between sips of coffee, she said she was glad she came; this might prove to be what she was seeking. She especially liked the social justice thrust of the sermon. "I respond with the idea of having an active faith. What does it mean to have faith in a world that is ignoring the environment and is all about making money?" she asked. "If my faith is not engaging the world, what does it mean to be saved?"

James Sholl, a pastor at Wellspring Worship Center in Toronto, stood nearby. He comes to Wine Before Breakfast when he has the time to find refreshment from a busy ministry that includes working with youth at his church in a Toronto suburb and prisoners in jail. What he heard in the sermon that morning reinforced how he views Scripture. "I read the Bible as a subversive document," he said. "Coming to Wine Before Breakfast, you see they aren't offering a cookie-cutter approach. Often, if someone feels they don't fit in in other churches, they fit in here." Peter Greidanus is one such person. He takes time out of his work at an electronics calibration laboratory to attend Wine Before Breakfast. He grew up in the CRC, but drifted away years ago, unhappy with the messages and overall tenor of the services. They just didn't grab him; he was looking around for another church when he heard Brian Walsh speak at Redeemer University College in Ancaster, Ontario. After that, he stopped by Wine Before Breakfast and almost immediately felt at home. "This is not the standard campus ministry set up," he said. "It's not just about standing alone in your faith. . . . And I liked how they do music. It's not usual church music."

Attracting Gideon Strauss to Wine Before Breakfast is that it offers a mix of rich Reformed theology and a progressive approach to Christianity—for some people, he said, a contradiction in terms, given there is a notion that being Reformed requires you to hold to conservative views of the Bible and society. "My theology is Christian Reformed. I am a Kuyperian [following the thought of Dutch theologian Abraham Kuyper]," said Strauss, academic dean of the Institute for Christian Studies, which is on the University of Toronto campus. "I appreciate Wine Before Breakfast's rock-solid preaching and I'm startled time and again by how well the songs are deeply integrated in the liturgy." Attending the weekly service is emotionally, intellectually, and spiritually moving for him. A spirit moves through the service, creatively opening him to a wider vista of God at work and alive in the world. Everything works together, from the prelude, through the Scripture reading and the litany, to the Eucharist. When he eats the bread and drinks the wine, he is reminded—in a way that is hard to describe—of the example of the self-giving love that Jesus showed by facing the violence of the Romans and going willingly to his death. Taking the Eucharist, recalling this sacrificial act, he joins in a community that tries every day to live out a full-fledged gospel that speaks to all things. Wine Before Breakfast creates a texture and offers a meaningful experience at a time of cultural turmoil for him. It is a shelter and gives shape to his life. He sees it as a "pioneering ministry."

## Ministry Helps to Reorder Faith

The University of Toronto Campus Ministry is a place for graduate students to ask questions, to face their doubts and come closer to a substantial faith. This is what happened to Aileen Verdun. While studying for pastoral ministry at the University of Toronto School of Theology, it began to slowly dawn in her there was a lot missing (and misguided) in what she had learned growing up in a nondenominational evangelical church. That church formed and taught her about God's love, yet gave her a laundry list of what she was supposed to believe and do if she wanted to be a Christian in good standing. In school in Toronto, it came to her—and not pleasantly because these thoughts were so disruptive—that "the things I believed about the world, my neighbors, and justice didn't fit, so I wondered if I was really a Christian." It was a very hard place to be.

Now an emerging leader of the Christian Reformed Church campus ministry at the University of Toronto, Verdun shared these reflections while meeting in the Campus Ministry office with Walsh and the rest of the ministry's staff team. It was a chance for all of them to discuss their roles and what brought each of them to this progressive campus ministry. Collectively, they talked about how this ministry offered them a path to deeper faith in the midst of a world troubled by terrorism, poverty, racism, and violence. They spoke of being equipped, in this university setting, to ask hard questions and find answers that have helped them to move forward, taking up the mantle of leadership to assist others on what they see as a difficult journey in an era when religion and commitment to Christianity have been relegated to the sidelines.

Continuing her story, Verdun spoke of how she came to Toronto in 2016 hoping the seminary could help answer her questions and shore up her beliefs. But many of her theology courses dished up more of the same easy answers, a rote reading of what to do, and left her questioning and nearly turning her back on the faith she had known for many years. Still, she didn't give up. "I kept looking for people who were intellectually honest, loving, hospitable, and focused on justice and Christ." She wasn't finding those things until she took a course taught by Sylvia Keesmaat, who is married to Brian Walsh. Keesmaat is an adjunct professor of biblical studies at Wycliffe College and the co-author (with Walsh) of a pair of books on biblical interpretation through a justice lens: *Colossians Remixed* (2004) and *Romans Disarmed* (2019). She is also the editor of *The Advent of Justice: A Book of Meditations* (2014), authored by Walsh and others. "Sylvia was doing theology that hooked me," said Verdun. "She really brought the Bible to life for me."

Keesmaat also invited Verdun to Wine Before Breakfast—and that grabbed her right away, both the service and the people she met. "Here I could have deep, respectful, and thoughtful conversations. It became home for me." Verdun found an even deeper sense of home and community when she joined the campus ministry's Graduate Christian Fellowship, which meets on Thursday evenings for a meal and a time of discussion and conversation. There she had the opportunity to tell her faith story to the group. Speaking with others, she began to see a wider, more ecumenical view of Christianity that she could embrace. Going into your story and expressing all your doubts can be scary stuff, but Verdon found it to be important and worthwhile.

## An Expanding Worldview

Co-leader of the Graduate Christian Fellowship, Geoff Wichert first met Brian Walsh during the last year of his undergraduate studies, when Walsh was leading a workshop on *The Transforming Vision: Shaping a New Christian Worldview* (1984), a book he had co-authored. Wichert was deeply impressed by Walsh and his vision of expanding the Christian worldview to include areas of society that had seen little emphasis by much of mainstream Christianity. Walsh gave him a vocabulary for a Reformed vision of how faith relates to the whole world, including what he was studying. Until then, he didn't have the biblical language to articulate what he already believed and had been trying to practice. He had many years to mull this over and incorporate a new Reformed vocabulary into his life; he didn't encounter Walsh again until about twenty years ago when Wichert began attending the University of Toronto. They talked and became friends and, after a time, Wichert joined the campus ministry staff. Meanwhile, he has helped to shape the Graduate Christian Fellowship into a community where graduate students and other young adults can explore the Bible and examine their faith. A community that helps members to see and articulate how faith can play a role in the future, the graduate fellowship also offers an opportunity to better understand the many cultural and intellectual complexities confronting the world today. "The fellowship is a place to ask, explore, and wrestle with hard questions about faith and the Bible, where the wrestling is taken seriously, and the answers, such as they are, are neither glib nor simple," said Wichert.

In the fellowship, leaders don't try to sway people into believing something but instead seek to honor the Holy Spirit, who is already at work. This is key: evangelism is meeting people where they happen to be, given that God is already at work in different ways with different people. It is a matter of seeing the kingdom alive in others, about kindling the fire already burning in a person's heart. As those sacred flames come alive, leaders of the fellowship invite people to tell the story of how the Spirit has been active in their lives. Members of the fellowship pray for one another, socialize, and support each other to form a strong bond of faith that will be integral to who they are and what they do after earning their graduate degrees and leaving the university. Besides providing a community for graduate students, the campus ministry also has a monthly gathering for faculty members. "This is an unflinching ministry. If it gets uncomfortable, we are on the right track," said Marcia Boniferro, one of the campus chaplains. "We help graduate students dive in all the way. When you face the hard questions, you find that your faith can survive."

## Sharing the Story of God

In the graduate fellowship, the participants often speak about a God who sits with people in their pain and accompanies them in their joy. This is not a God you petition for things you want, a cash-register God who delivers requests on demand, said Carol Scovil, another chaplain who helps oversee the fellowship. "We don't believe you flip a switch and God will make everything better," said Scovil, who joined the Graduate Christian Fellowship in 2005 while doing a postdoctoral fellowship in biomedical engineering. Scovil divides her time between the weekly fellowship, rehabilitation research, and working in a clinic that helps people paralyzed from spinal cord injuries to access and find assistance from computer and smartphone technologies. Living and working in the two worlds gives her a unique perspective and has helped her to reflect on God's role in helping people. "You can't skip over the painful things," said Scovil. "But we know that [no one] understands pain and suffering and injustice better than a loving God who will be with us so that we can sit and lament together—which is a holy and beautiful thing."

## An Overall Perspective

Brian Walsh prays and hopes that the campus ministry can be a place where, maybe for the first time, a student, a faculty member, a staff member can feel love, can meet the abiding love of God who comes to us with open arms. But there is more to it than that—the need to build self-awareness and recognition of the forces at work that shape and misshape the world. While love is key, Walsh says the reality of who we are as broken people, as people afflicted by our own sin and that of others, undergirds the campus ministry. Key is realizing that suffering, often coming from awareness of our own brokenness and fallenness, is an important part of developing a solid faith. Laments plays into this as well—lament over a world that often seems to be spinning too fast on its axis. But what Walsh seems to be referring to is not about simply feeling pain, which we all do, but about something much deeper—a sense of being split open at our core. And only when this happens, when we are cracked and shattered, when we've examined and aired our beliefs, when we've recalled and touched those places bleeding inside of us, can we come face-to-face with the nature of suffering. And growth in faith only comes out of this struggle. Facing one's shortcomings, in a sense one's demons, and asking God to purge them is necessary for us to move closer in a very real sense to God. We must clear the way in our lives for God's grace to flow in and take hold. By becoming aware of our own suffering our eyes are opened to the suffering of others. It is a matter of seeing what is inside and outside of us—and that is God's unfolding kingdom. In *Colossians Remixed: Subverting the Empire*, Walsh and Keesmaat write about this, making it clear that reconciliation, peace, shalom, can only come by confronting and living with the suffering in ourselves and the world. In fact, only in suffering and in acknowledging and sharing that suffering can people—such as those in a campus ministry—become a community. The suffering that is shared builds relationships. Reflecting on the early church, Walsh and Keesmaat write in *Colossians Remixed*: "Is it any wonder that a community shaped by a narrative of a suffering God would itself become a cruciform suffering community?" A community formed by and following the way of the cross. This is the kind of community that they have sought to form at the university—a community that shares its pain and out of that its joy. A community that sees itself living counter to the ways of the dominant culture. A community that is forged by sharing in the true gospel—the gospel of peace, the gospel of the cross—brought by Christ. The kind of peace that the seventy of Luke 10 sought to bring to every town and place.

In a reflection Walsh wrote in summer of 2020 shortly before his retirement, he said: "Our campus ministry office has become a sacred space, baptized in tears, ringing in laughter, echoing in prayer, resonating with song, fragrant with coffee and good food, filled with wonderful, and often hard, conversation.

"In that office, in our worship together, and for some, in a weekly email, many of us have found our way on the path of discipleship, often after being lost, or at a dead end. Many of us have discerned our place, our calling, our life direction. And many, many of us have come home, in community with each other, to God, made flesh in Jesus of Nazareth."

## Offering a CRC Campus Ministry on a Catholic Campus

Wagme Ravindran was eating lunch in the Damen Dining Hall at Loyola University in Chicago when he saw Alec Kenny doing card tricks at another table for a number of the students. Flipping one card, another seemed to disappear while another showed up in his hand. They sure looked like they were having fun over there; and those card tricks fascinated Ravindran, a healthcare administration major. Wagme wondered: Who was this card-trick magician? He looked like a nice guy. Not long afterward, he found out that Kenny was indeed a good guy. Wagme was playing basketball in the university gym when he came across Kenny again. The two talked; one thing led to another and eventually they became friends. At some point, Kenny let him know about the campus ministry of which he was a part and invited Wagme to join in an event or worship celebration. Kenny did it in an open way; no pressure. Why not give it a try? Wagme thought and began coming to Ecclesia, the campus ministry's Sunday worship service. Wagme also began sitting with Kenny at the table in the dining hall on Thursdays—where the card tricks took place—when the campus ministry meets for lunch. That lunch is always an enjoyable time as students come in and out as time permits. With a break between classes on Thursday, Wagme—a young man with a slender face and quick gestures—likes to hang around and talk to people. Sitting at the busy table, Wagme said: "I'm not super religious or even a Christian." Wagme grew up as a Hindu, and his parents still practice Hindu traditions—and Wagme will join them half-heartedly when he returns home. But at Loyola, it is a different story. For someone not very religious at all, he enjoys being part of a community that doesn't demand much from him. This freedom has felt like an escape valve. "Most places push their religion on you, but they don't do that here," he said.

Welcoming all students, regardless of their faith or lack of it, is an important aspect of the campus ministry, the only Christian Reformed Church campus ministry located at a Catholic university in the United States. A focus of the work at Loyola is to offer the gospel message in often subtle and yet scripturally solid ways to students who tend not to be interested in or to embrace formal religion, even though they are at a Catholic school. Regardless of who the student is or their religious background, says Alec Kenny, all people need to know they are loved, especially because many students who come here have had negative experiences—often meaning they couldn't follow the rules or embrace the rules and doctrines—in the church in which they grew up. In campus ministry, Kenny sees his role as connecting with and befriending students by playing sports with them or perhaps showing them magic or card tricks, or sitting with someone and playing a video game. "I try to plug in and hang out with them," said Kenny. "I think it is important to listen to them and ask questions. I don't know what to do or ask unless I listen."

## History of the Ministry

Before lunch, we met with Tyler Ward, director of the campus ministry, and Mike Moore, who founded the ministry more than a decade ago. Ward and Moore spoke about themselves and the history and purpose of the campus ministry.

During his studies at Northern Seminary in Lisle, Illinois, in the late 2000s, Moore was inspired and had his eyes opened by teachers who spoke of North America being a rich mission field. One of the teachers and leaders who influenced him was Alan Hirsch, an author who has taught at Northern Seminary. In his work—and this is what resonated with Moore—Hirsch criticizes the church's common approach in doing evangelism; it is not enough to basically ask someone to accept Jesus as their Savior and let it stop there. Sharing the good news is crucial; but that is only the start—in fact, coming to understand and accept Christ is not usually a onetime experience. Hirsch has said, "Here's the deal . . . evangelism gets done along the way as you do discipleship." It is done in the context of relationships and community. In seminary, this idea made total sense to Moore, especially as he became aware that mainstream churches were experiencing a decline in membership. In the wake of this decline, Moore believed, there was a crying need for fresh ideas and practices to be used in ministry—to encourage people to grab a living faith, a faith made fresh by a newer view of Jesus—a faith that went far beyond the "make a decision for Jesus" approach to evangelism.

When he graduated, Moore wanted to serve in some way in this expanding mission field—and decided to do so as a campus chaplain. He particularly wanted to work with young people, to be with them in the tension of the questions they ask about issues of faith and to let them know that, even if they had no desire to attend a church, God is still there for them. Moore sent out resumes to a number of colleges—and Loyola was the first to respond. He was intrigued by the idea of establishing a campus ministry in that setting. But he wasn't drawn there to give a counterpoint to Catholicism. Instead, he wanted to offer students, especially non-Catholics, the chance to examine and ultimately expand their faith. In fact, Loyola seemed to be a fitting place to launch a Protestant ministry. Loyola was a school where Christianity was not alien. Offering a Jesuit education that challenges the faith of students and even of the Catholic Church, Loyola requires all students to take core classes in theology and philosophy, which can help students to re-evaluate matters of faith. When Moore arrived, he knew, echoing the teaching of Hirsch, that coming at students with a hard-sell approach would not work at all. He had to get to know and build a relationship with students. A Wednesday evening Protestant Bible study was already going on when he showed up, and this offered him a way in. Having been started by Protestant students, the Bible study was losing attendees after the study leaders had graduated. Moore started to attend but didn't barge in and try to take over. Seeking to become part of the place in which he was sent to spread the gospel, Moore knew that creating a ministry of attraction, and not through high-gear promotion, meant he needed to spend time listening and looking at the possibilities of working together with students who attended the Bible study. Over time, as he built relationships with students, Moore became a leader of the weekly gathering, and he called it Agape.

Once the Wednesday night worship gathering and Bible study took hold and started drawing a committed core of students—an average of sixty to seventy a week—Moore began to see that there were additional ways to offer campus ministry where "things were fluid and there were all kinds of ways to engage people." He helped to begin Sunday worship as an alternative church called Ecclesia. It was for people who had been going off campus to attend services. "Things really started to grow from there," said Moore. Reflecting on his time in campus ministry, Moore said, "Students have seen significant cultural shifts on issues such as race and sexuality." This frequently means needing to address the concerns of LGBTQ students who ask what their place is in churches that shun them. Mental health and other issues, from anxiety and depression to eating disorders and suicide prevention, have also become increasingly important for the campus ministry to address. "At the end of the day, students are dealing with a lot—and campus ministry needs to be a part of reaching out to them," said Moore. "We need to be flexible, always keeping God in mind."

## Changing of the Guard

After Moore left the ministry in 2017 to start a new church, Tyler Ward was named leader. Also a student at Northern Seminary, he needed to earn credits as a ministerial intern and moved to Chicago in 2013 to join a couple who were planting a nondenominational church in the area. During that time, he also started serving as an intern with Mike Moore at Loyola. Moore was a good mentor, showing him how to connect with and especially learn to listen to what was on the minds of students. Slowly the work at the church diminished and his work at Loyola grew. Like Moore, he wanted to work with and help to form the faith and worldview of young people during their college years—a time in which students often made decisions about how they wanted to live their life in the future as well as study for a career. Being in his early twenties, Ward found it easy to relate to the issues students have to address. Ward has sought to help these young people—caught between their adolescence and the reality of finding their place as adults in the early decades of the twenty-first century—to navigate their way and to help them see how God can help them. "I have enjoyed it here," he said. "I've found that with the students, if you aren't their parent, they will listen to you." In working with students, Ward sees amazing leaps of faith as they go deeper into their relationship with God—and that often touches and helps him in his own journey of faith. Overall, the ministry offers students a place where, through worship, various events, and building friendships, they can find ways to deal with the challenges of college life.

## Back to the Thursday Lunch

Taking a break from eating, Hannah Hinerman, a sophomore studying dance and psychology, told us she appreciates being part of what the ministry offers. "I heard about this at a faith fair before I started college, and I found and met friends who are pursuing a life with Jesus. People welcomed me with open arms, and it felt right away like a family."

Hinerman grew up in the Lutheran church, which taught her many things about Christian living. But as she grew up, it sometimes seemed that people didn't always practice what they preached, which is not the case at the Loyola campus ministry. The campus ministry has offered her hospitality, forgiveness without judgment, and encouraged her to use her spiritual gifts. It has taught her what a Christian community is like. She is among people who receive encouragement when she has to deal with hard things. "Whatever happens, there is a swarm of people who are around me and teaching me to love."

Another student, Alex Schorr, grew up in a Christian home and came to Loyola in 2012. She met Mike Moore at the Faith Fest and started to attend Agape. Right away, she was attracted by the honesty of students who offered testimonies of their lives and asked for prayer at the beginning of Agape every week. "There is something special about the way people share about the highest of highs and the lowest of lows. . . . I was so nervous when I started, but then I found my footing."

Schorr especially recalls a time when she was spiritually dry and met one-on-one with Moore: "He helped me to hear the voice of God in my life. He gave me the space to ask questions." Listening to the small voice of God speaking to her, Schorr began to hear a calling to work in ministry, and she enrolled at Northern Seminary after graduating from Loyola in 2016. Today, she works part-time for the aid agency World Vision in Chicago and also serves on the staff of the campus ministry. "A decent number of students I work with have faith, but many others don't know what to believe," she said. "As a CRC ministry on a Catholic campus, we are in a unique position to minister to students."

As a ministry worker on a Catholic campus, Schorr has become a young Luke 10 person who is blessed because she has come to have the eyes that see God's Spirit alive in so many ways in this particular place. She has been able to glimpse the places the church—and its young people—need to go in the future.

## Agape Gathers

Besides being part of the lunch, we had the chance to join about seventy Loyola students as they gathered in the Information Commons building for the weekly Wednesday-night Agape worship service and Bible study. It was a lively event, an outgrowth of the Bible study Mike Moore encountered when he arrived on campus. Ward now helps oversee this ministry. Standing at their seats, students began with a song of praise. "Holy, there is no one like you. There is none beside you. Open up my eyes in wonder. Show me who you are and fill me. . . ." Some students raised and waved their hands, and a few put an arm around the person next to them. Clearly they were in the mood to sing and worship.

Some students at Agape come from a CRC background, but many don't. What they share, above anything else, is the desire to connect with God in an environment in which they could feel comfortable and be friends. The goal here, said Tyler Ward, is to help students of whatever religious persuasion gain a sense of how the Holy Spirit is at work in their lives and why that can matter. "We talk of how one of the fruits of the Spirit is faithfulness and how the Spirit helps you to slowly and carefully see something in you that you didn't think was there," he said.

## Offering Stories

After singing a few songs that night, students had a chance to go forward to the front of the room to offer brief testimonies about things they are dealing with and to ask for prayer. In this way the campus ministry hears about many matters, big and small, that it can seek to address and help students with. One of the first students to speak was a young woman who said: "Pray for me because lots of crazy stuff is going on between my stepdad and stepbrother." Another young woman gave praise for landing a job, but also mentioned, "When I am under stress, my immune system tanks and I get migraines." One student said: "I was so nervous coming here to college. Now I see this as my new home. Everyone has been so good to me." A fourth spoke of the need for her ninety-seven-year-old grandmother to move into a nursing home. "Please pray that it goes well," she said.

## Abraham and Isaac

After students shared their testimonies, the young people formed into small groups to read and discuss Genesis 22:8–13, in which Abraham is asked by God to sacrifice his son Isaac. Most of the groups left the large room to gather elsewhere; we decided to stay with Tyler Ward, who asked a few students to gather around him in a circle of chairs. It was an opportunity to read and review the Bible story and for students to share thoughts on what it meant to them. It was clear that the story touched a chord when Ward asked everyone to imagine being asked by God to sacrifice your son. Even though the story has a happy ending because God commands Abraham to put down the knife before using it on his son, some students wondered what kind of God would ask a father to do something like that. It sounded outrageous. Could they follow such a God? "If a dad took you off to sacrifice you, I wonder what the conversation would be like with the mom afterwards when he told her all that had happened," said a young woman. Another student said it was stunning to think of what Abraham might have done. "A son can symbolize so much," she said. "He can symbolize your wealth, and Abraham was putting all of that on the line."

Ward told the students that it was important to realize that child sacrifice was fairly common at the time. This story shows how God went against that practice and how Abraham came to realize that Isaac was truly God's child, not just the son of him and his wife, Sarah. "God was challenging Abraham to once again have faith, and he came to realize that God would provide in all situations and wouldn't leave him stranded," said Ward. "At the end, we find God saying, 'I'm not going to ask this thing of you that has been asked somewhere else,'" he said.

One student said it was difficult to imagine people these days having the kind of faith that Abraham showed. In today's world, another said, many people have trouble with this story, seeing it as showing a brutal God instead of being a story about strong faith. Clearly, the students had some ambiguities about God, especially as he is portrayed in the Old Testament. At the same time, there were lessons here if you looked for them. One student said the story inspired her to think of how God shows us what is important. It made her consider the different paths you could take to success. Do you follow your heart and the urging coming from God that may seem to go against everything that others, including your parents, are telling you? Or do you follow a path of faith that seems to open inside of you—and is it God who is opening this path? "What is success to parents and others these days . . . to strive toward material wealth and to get a good internship opportunity that would lead to success?" She spoke of a practical decision regarding her future that this story hinted at it. "Or do you have the faith to go ahead and find meaning in work you want to do instead of getting a job that would give you material things? I think this is something you have to give to God."

Ward wrapped the Bible study up by asking students if they wanted to share any prayer requests. One student asked for prayer, speaking of how her mother at home had started drinking heavily and her father was having a hard time coping. A few others offered things that were on their minds, just as students had done during the time for testimonies. Then Ward bowed his head and, serving among a group of young people who often teach him as much as he tries to teach them, began to pray. "Lord, show us your love. Be with us all as we live and grow together and come to know you better . . . as we come to see the Spirit alive and at work in our lives."

# 8

# "Lord of the Harvest"

## [or]

## The Lord of Harvest at Work
## in LA and Vancouver

"The harvest is plentiful, but the workers are few. Ask the Lord of
the harvest, therefore, to send out workers into his harvest field."
—Luke 10:2

*The tall towers of apartment buildings, home to thousands of new
Chinese immigrants to Canada, are everywhere in Vancouver,
British Columbia. Pastor Albert Chu saw the harvest and gathered
around him a group of people who sought to share in the harvest
and the need to grow a Luke 10 community seeking to share their
faith with the community around them. Four new churches have
grown out of the vision of the ordinary people of this congregation—many immigrants from China who saw and, responding to
the movement of God, took action.*

*In this chapter, we focus on the story of Tapestry in Vancouver. But
before looking at the Tapestry, we're going to take a sidetrack and
offer a little history on the ways in which the Christian Reformed
Church has grown and begun to respond to the various needs of
ethnic groups—the harvest—outside of itself over the last nearly
165 years.*

## A Little Background on the CRC

Having roots in the Dutch Reformed Church of the Netherlands, the
Christian Reformed Church was founded in Holland, Michigan in

1857 by Dutch immigrants. For the first century, the church hewed close to its Dutch Calvinist roots; it didn't decide to use English in its services until well into the twentieth century. Keeping to itself, the church remained primarily Dutch and white for decades—until touched by the changes sweeping society in the 1960s. A history on the CRC's website says: "The flood of changes in values, lifestyles, and social interactions precipitated in the 1960s profoundly affected the CRC. Tidier patterns of church life gave way to a rising disenchantment and disagreement over how believers should respond to the social chaos around them. While the CRC never overtly held racist teachings, members debated long and hard over the ways the church should combat racism—if at all."

In Grand Rapids, Michigan, in the 1970s and eighties, the church began to open up to the wider world as congregations welcomed refugees from Vietnam. President Gerald R. Ford, the US chief executive in the mid-seventies, was from Grand Rapids and his administration helped smooth the way for thousands of these refugees to settle in West Michigan. Many joined churches that helped to sponsor their journey from Southeast Asia to West Michigan.

Responding to the demands of an increasingly complex and diverse world, the CRC began in the late 1970s to send a small army of church planters across North America to begin congregations in a range of ethnic groups. By the turn of the twenty-first century, progress had been made in forming churches among African American groups in cities such as Chicago. In Texas, a group of churches was founded that focused on Spanish-speaking people as well as on groups of people from Africa. Other efforts in the CRC include a congregation of Rwandan refugees in Grand Rapids and, most recently, a Farsi-speaking congregation in Willowdale, Ontario.

Notably, also expanding as a group in the church have been people from Korea, especially flowing into California, where two of the CRC's largest and more prosperous congregations took hold. We'll pause here a moment to look at them.

## Ttokamsa Mission Church

One of those congregations, with a healthy Luke 10 focus of having a strong missionary identity of "sentness," is Ttokamsa Mission Church near downtown Los Angeles. This is a congregation that often devotes more than 90 percent of its annual multimillion-dollar budget to doing missions work around the world. Ken Choe, longtime pastor of Ttokamsa, says they have worked, for instance, shipping thousands of tons of food to North Korea, a country known by some as "the hidden kingdom" and for which Choe's church constantly prays. They also work closely with and send assistance to Christians in such countries as Pakistan, where Pakistan minister Shahbaz Bhatt, who was a close friend of Choe's, was assassinated in 2011. While shipping goods overseas is important, that is only one aspect of the mission work at Ttokamsa. "We don't just send money," said Choe. "We get involved with mission. Seeing a global harvest, many of our people go overseas every year to work with people and bring them the gospel."

For instance, several groups have gone to the Philippines to build schools. Others have traveled to India to present traditional Korean dance, featuring dancers in colorful, authentic costumes, to people in schools, churches, and other settings. After the dance performances, they take time to share their faith. And behind their widespread mission work, which also involves the inner-city LA area around their church, are prayers—intense prayers, often spoken in the traditional Korean style in early morning every day of the year in the church sanctuary. This style of prayer involves speaking out loud, often with words that flow unchecked from the heart. "Prayer is sensing where God is leading," said Choe, who served for several years as a missionary in the Philippines before becoming a pastor at Ttokamsa. "In prayer we are not only offering our requests; we are hearing from the Lord, who works many mysteries in our lives."

One Sunday afternoon in 2018, we had a chance to have lunch with Brian Park, who went on a mission trip to the Philippines with Ttokamsa. His story reflects what going on an international mission trip can do. When he left, he still held on, if lightly, to the Buddhist faith with which he grew up. But on that trip to a village that was mostly Muslim, something important happened. Trying to sleep one night in the elementary school they had come to help build, he felt something shift in him: God sifted into his soul. He wasn't sure exactly what was going on, but over time he realized that, having gone overseas to work, God had been working on him. And since then he has gone on many overseas trips. "It's not easy. It can be scary. But as missionaries for our church, we choose to go to places where no one else goes," said Park, who runs his own small manufacturing facility in Los Angeles. "When we are on a field, we touch people's hearts with the gospel, and we see them change, even though we always strictly follow the local rules when we do our work and don't openly evangelize."

# All Nations Church

Another large Korean congregation with an all-out focus on reaping the harvest for God is All Nations Church, located in the foothills north of LA. Not long after forming as a congregation more than twenty years ago, and even before having a permanent building, the pastor and members of the church in Lake View Terrace began driving every weekend on a four-hour round trip to Tijuana, Mexico, to meet with people. As part of this effort, the church, which explicitly sees spreading the gospel as a key element of its mission, purchased space in a prison, where every week they held regular worship and baptism services. As this longtime initiative in Tijuana illustrates, All Nations has been a church that lives up to its name, said Tae Kim, lead pastor of the church. "Our congregation is 99 percent Korean, but our heart is where God is—for the nations," said Kim. "By the grace of God, even from the start of our church, we have given more than half of our resources for missions. We see ourselves as doers, but we want to do healthy mission. We don't want to do it with paternalism."

Jinso Yoo, All Nations' founding pastor, first organized the weekly visits to Tijuana. In addition, the members bought seven acres of land in Juarez, Mexico, to build All Nations Seminary. More than 600 miles east of Tijuana, Juarez is on the Mexican border near El Paso, Texas, and has been known for drug-related violence. Even so, All Nations and those with whom it has partnered have stayed there and maintained a setting where people can train for ministry. "We have graduated more than 500 [Mexican] students, and they have gone on to start many churches [in Mexico]," said Tae Kim.

# The Tapestry: A Full Story

Benjamin and Nerini Shen stood in their familiar spot at the end of a row of seats in the sanctuary of The Tapestry Church in Vancouver, British Columbia. The Shens had big smiles on their faces, looking happy as they clapped their hands in time with the praise band that was opening the service at the main location for this multisite congregation. Today's service would include the lively music, intense prayer, and a sermon by Tapestry's founding pastor Albert Chu. As always, the sanctuary in the former First Christian Reformed Church was packed. And the Shens, who are from China, are here most weeks, often taking the same spot near the back of the church. They are among hundreds of Tapestry members who have been drawn here by a mixture of engaging worship, solid preaching, accommodations to their ethnic background, and the chance to build strong friendships.

Before the service on this Sunday early in 2019, the Shens sat in an office near the front lobby. As people started showing up for worship, they spoke of their lives before coming here and what has happened since they joined The Tapestry.

Life for Benjamin Shen was all about making money when he lived in mainland China. Having a good job—in his case, selling garments to companies in North America—and being able to provide for his family came before everything else. His god, if he even thought about having a god, was working hard and accumulating the things that could make life more comfortable. The more he had the better he felt. His goals were simple: get ahead and build his bank account. Hoping to become even more prosperous, Benjamin moved with Nerini to Vancouver several years ago. They joined thousands of Chinese and other Asian families who have settled in Vancouver—a city built along the Puget Sound that has opened itself to immigrants, especially those seeking to invest in the Canadian economy. When Benjamin Shen and his family moved, joining the flood of Asian people uprooting from one culture to another, it seemed like they had made the right choice. They enjoyed the city. They experienced a honeymoon period when everything seemed to click. They began to build a new life for themselves. But then, suddenly, Benjamin lost his job. At the same time, his wife got pregnant. Soon, the predictable became unpredictable. The old ways weren't working and he needed to make changes.

Those changes eventually led him and his wife to seek solace in religious faith and brought them to Tapestry Church in Richmond, a suburb of Vancouver. Friends told them about it and they decided to check it out. It was a Christian Reformed Church congregation that welcomed a wide range of people. They liked it right away. The upbeat music and open friendship of others were very appealing. And the more Benjamin attended and paid attention to the sermons by Albert Chu, the more he learned about a personal God, a divine entity who became man. Slowly what he experienced and learned at Tapestry shifted his perspective—as well as that of his wife. Especially, he began to consider that his priorities had been off: he had been living without any lasting purpose. "Over time as we attended Tapestry, the Holy Spirit moved our hearts and started me thinking about what I had experienced in the past. I've learned that there is a God—and it isn't money," said Benjamin.

## Weaving the Tapestry

Over the last fifteen years under the leadership of Chu, Tapestry has sought
to bring together people from many cultures and walks of life by offering a
gospel message that is both about eternal things and yet also accessible and
understandable, meaning it is practical, to people such as the Shens. Begun at the one site in Richmond, Tapestry now has four places of worship.
It has expanded and touched people across Vancouver. The Tapestry also
has an active outreach ministry, supporting churches overseas and, for instance, working with residents of a senior care facility across the parking
lot from the church. The church offers classes on the Christian faith, food
for those in need, and space for a variety of gatherings in many settings. At
a time when many other churches are struggling, Tapestry has grown and
held fast to a vision of Spirit-led ministry and provision, drawing support
and resources from the expanding Asian population in Vancouver. This
is a Reformed church that finds God's grace in all places: they see harvest
fields everywhere that are rich for the gathering. "God has been so good to
us here at the Tap," said Nerini Shen. "We've learned that being a Christian
is not [mainly] about God's blessings. It is about providing community
and facing challenges together."

## Meeting in Marpole Among the Tall Buildings

After giving the sermon that morning in Richmond, Chu hopped in his car
and headed for the nearly three-year-old Tapestry church plant meeting
in a movie theater in nearby Marpole. Once a month he does the "shuffle,"
leading worship at one of Tapestry's church plants in addition to the service at the main congregation. Located near the Vancouver International
Airport, Marpole is one of the oldest communities in Vancouver. Historic
neighborhoods here mix with towering high-rise apartment buildings
and businesses. Abject poverty also sits side by side with affluence. And it
is here that Tapestry has been spreading its influence in a city, spread out
along a vista of snowcapped mountains and shimmering water, that is ripe
for the work of a church sharing Christ's message in culturally valuable
and relevant ways.

On this day, the new *Avengers: Endgame* was premiering at one of the
theaters in Marpole, so Chu had to circumvent a long line of action movie
lovers to make it into the theater where the worship service was already

underway. More than 200 people—many young families with children—filled the seats that rose from the front to a series of rows in the rear. The praise band had played a few songs to open worship, and many people stood, raising their arms and swaying their bodies to the upbeat music. They sang in loud voices full of vigor and praise.

## A Baptism in the Theater

Soon after Chu arrived, Linwood Siu, a member of the praise band, and his wife, Winnie, brought their child, Kassia, forward to be baptized. They gathered with Chu around a small table on which a container of water and folded white towel sat. Using a microphone, Winnie spoke of how her pregnancy had been touch and go and how grateful they were to have a healthy baby. People from the church had stuck close by them through many months of trial and tension. "God was always watching over us," she said. When she had finished, Chu opened his arms, asking the parents: "Do you confess Jesus Christ as Lord and Savior and profess the Christian faith as proclaimed in the Bible?" They nodded, saying that they did. "And do you promise to do all in your power with the help of the Holy Spirit to help Kassia be Christ's disciple?" As they nodded, Chu poured water on Kassia and explained: "Water is cleansing. . . . God's Spirit is reaching down and blessing Kassia."

Repeating the sermon he gave earlier in Richmond, based on 1 Corinthians 15, Chu touched on some of his own life. He recounted how his father lay on his deathbed in 2014. Instead of focusing on his own condition, his dad kept thanking the doctors for all they had done for him and asking the nurses and others about their families. "You can tell a lot about a person's life by the way they die," said Chu. "My father died well; that's because he had a steadfast faith. The resurrection gave him—and it gives us—comfort and peace, the hope of heaven and future eternity with God." People in the theater listened closely. Later, someone said the sermon was vintage Chu—solid theology peppered with personal reflection.

## "Time to Find My Feet Again"

After the service in Marpole, Shelaine Chu, no relation to Albert, sat at a table by the refreshment counter of the cineplex and spoke of growing up in a Pentecostal church. Now an elder at Marpole, her story reflects the stories of many who attend Tapestry: how disruptions and changes, culturally, demographically, and spiritually, led them to seek another place to worship. All of Shelaine's family, including sixteen cousins, attended the Pentecostal church. Her father was on the church board. For several years, she immersed herself in the life of that spirited church and in working with youth. She was so busy that she hardly had time to consider what she was doing—and if she was doing it for God, for herself, or to please her family. Her reward simply seemed to be being busy for a good cause. But a few years ago, she got burned out and decided to take a break from the church. And soon she decided to try going somewhere else. It didn't take long before she landed at Tapestry in Richmond. Like so many when she first arrived, she was drawn in by the dynamic music. It spoke to and enlivened her. Still, something felt off. She came to church on Sundays, sat toward the back, and tried attending small groups, but nothing stuck. The faith she thought she had held so close for so long seemed to be ebbing. She felt torn: stay or go. Lethargy, weighed down by inaction, defined her times of worship. But the Spirit, behind the scenes, was at work. Gently letting her know she had to make a decision, the Spirit nudged Chu into asking herself how much longer she could be a "benchwarmer." And that's when she learned that Tapestry wanted to plant a church in Marpole. They needed sixty or seventy people to get it started. It was all hands on deck, deciding to join up was good; she decided to become a Luke 10 person—someone willing to go out and join others on a new effort. "I got involved in the hospitality team, and now I'm an elder," said Chu, a marketing specialist. She also found friends and has built strong relationships. Looking back, she appreciates how Tapestry let her sit in the back of the church, not demanding of her more than she was ready to give. "Tapestry gave me time to find my feet again and to say 'yes' to everything God wants of me," she said.

## Reaching the Neighborhood

Over lunch at a Thai restaurant, Jesse Pals, a pastor at Marpole, looked out the large window and pointed out all of the extensive real estate development in this area. Cranes stood on many street corners. Expensive cars were parked on the streets; windows from the apartment structures glittered in the Sunday sun. Given how crowded it was, trying to find space for the church to meet had been tough. But when they finally came across the theater, it was a blessing, an answered prayer and a welcome opportunity. Renting space in the theater allows them, Pals said, "to meet in this neighborhood and break bread together" with people who live here. Although they are located in a place of growing affluence, there are also homeless people tucked away in alleys and doorways trying to scrape by. Many live in the shadows, but a handful live temporarily in a nearby facility built to meet their needs in small efficiency apartments. Marpole members visit there and share meals with people. "We have the chance to get to know and love them," said the pastor.

Marpole members have developed a vision for the church through prayer meetings and by visiting people in the nearby homes and apartments to ask what they like and don't like about this changing community. Many of those with whom they spoke feel lonely and cut off from the world around them, a world that seems to be moving too fast, that is growing higher and more distant as those cranes reach farther and farther into the sky. The community they once knew is vanishing and with it their place in it. Marpole is home to many seniors while at the same time young families are moving in. "We want to get to know and be a part of this neighborhood. We don't want to assume anything about what we can bring," said Charlotte Au, a church member who works in real estate, which gives her a good chance to see what is selling and what will be going in. "God has started us on a journey. There is excitement and fear. We hope to find a way to breathe new life into this community."

## 9/11 Opened Her Eyes

The Tapestry's roots go back to the early 2000s when First CRC of Richmond was faltering and uncertain about its future. As she thinks back to that time, Hennie Beeksma, a long-time First CRC member, recalls the day terrorists attacked the World Trade Center Towers on September 11, 2001 and the impact that had on her and her view of her church. That afternoon, she got a call at the bakery she owned with her husband, Gerben, asking if they could provide food for people who had been grounded at the Vancouver airport. Planes across North America were prohibited from flying until it was clear no other attacks were imminent. The Beeksmas willingly provided bread and other items for travelers, but what troubled Hennie was to learn that a local Baptist church, not her own, had stepped forward to help people in need in a variety of ways. To an extent, she wasn't exactly surprised: First CRC of Richmond was in decline. Energy for ministry was low as the membership was growing older; people were tired and not inclined to turn their attention to new things. The church members had helped to build and knew for decades was evaporating, but they still held on, if for no other reason than they weren't quite sure what to do or where to look for answers. But Hennie saw it differently. "I thought, 'If they [the Baptist church] could do it, why weren't we?'" That triggered the thought that First CRC didn't have the ideas and vision for what a church could do. The church was in a downward cycle that needed to be broken. Inertia had left them clinging to a way of worship and doing ministry that no longer worked. It was hard to see and even harder to realize and accept this reality. But the Beeksmas and others did. And that began a process that led, after much discussion, to closing First CRC and eventually launching the Tapestry out of the same building, with Albert Chu as the pastor.

But, even though the Beeksmas wholeheartedly supported the transition, it took some getting used to. During an early worship service, Chu asked people to turn and pray aloud for the person next to them. Gerben felt uncomfortable, never having prayed like that before. Even so, he did it; and almost against his will he loosened up. It felt good. "God used that to make me grow" and, he said, it helped him to realize that "when all you have is your tradition, you think your spiritual life is your own." Getting to know the others who were attending Tapestry opened his eyes. "I had been very judgmental. But being part of this new group of people of all ages, I found new friends. I was blown away by their struggles and the depth of their faith."

## Standing in the Fraser River

David Louie works as a pharmacist on Sunday mornings and often slips into Tapestry in Richmond a few minutes late. But he is always greeted warmly at the door. It might seem like a small thing to place greeters there after the service starts, but it has mattered to him—a smile, a handshake, a connection inviting him in. Outside of Sundays, he and his wife are involved in a program mentoring young married couples. Before attending here, he had gone to churches in Toronto and elsewhere, but he has never felt as comfortable as he does at Tapestry. "There is a sense of belonging that we have here." More than that: there is the sense that in some important ways they are linked by their human brokenness and lifted up by the God who gave the life of his Son to open new life for others. Knowing and feeling this tight tie, cemented by grace, helps people to realize they are all fallen, and all brought forth into new life, and, said Louie, "no one will judge us." There is a bond that goes beyond words, a glue that comes with the Spirit as they journey into the fields full for the harvest.

One memory in particular sticks in his mind. A few years ago, he stood in the nearby Fraser River with other church members. Cool water flowed around him as he held his son, Nathan, in his arms and Albert Chu conducted a baptism. It was a deeply moving experience, holding Nathan while standing in the water and seeing members of the church gathered along the riverbank. He felt that he was part of a large family of people who were at the river for the same reason. They came down to the river, as the old hymn goes, to pray, just like the good old days—and yet at the same time these were the new days of harvest and grace they all came to experience and share. "The theme of Tapestry is that we come from all walks of life and try to weave that all together and live it out," said Louie.

## Making the Change in Mundy Park

Neil Roos was a longtime member of what is now The Tapestry Mundy Park. For many years, he was perfectly satisfied and fulfilled by all that was so familiar in his church in Mundy Park. From the 1960s on, church membership grew to about 250. Well into the 1980s, the children's ministry flourished; they had a vibrant women's Bible study outreach; the Sunday choir filled the sanctuary with sacred hymns and holy sounds. But then in recent years, Roos watched as young families drifted away, membership aged, and ministries began to dry up for lack of resources. While many others scratched their heads and began to fall into despair or lived in denial in hopes things would turn around, he knew something had to be done if the church, founded in the 1950s, was to survive. He wasn't sure what that would be. Someone suggested connecting with Tapestry for help. At first, he wasn't sure. He worried the big church in Richmond would simply want to come in and gobble them up. Yet, he reluctantly supported the move to have Tapestry come in to consult with them about the future. Sitting around the table with Tapestry representatives as they discussed the future, Roos felt at home in that role. He worked for many years sitting around tables hammering out agreements for the Christian Labour Association of Canada. Around that table, listening to and getting to know the Tapestry representatives, he had lots of questions but began to sense there might be a way forward. Perhaps God wasn't done with them yet. Roos realized the faith life they had been living need not be discarded but could be poured into a new wineskin. He listened as Sam Lee, one of the people from Tapestry, laid it all out. It wasn't always easy to hear: Lee and others said that without major shifts in worship style and outreach, things at the longtime CRC church looked bleak. At the core of this message, Roos began to realize, was the need to shift power—the realization that unless they let go of the old, the new could not be poured in, filling them with a new life. They need not set aside being Reformed or being part of this larger denomination, which they loved, but they needed to consider the idea of following directions and the suggestions of others. "We'd always been able to run the show by ourselves, and now we had brought in these new people who seemed to be telling us what to do," said Roos, who, it turns out, is now a leader of Tapestry Mundy Park.

Over a series of meetings, the two groups began talking about the feasibility and desirability of a possible merger and what that might look like. Roos began to see the Spirit at work, leading the church into a new day in which it opened itself to a wider range of people and possibilities. "We increasingly realized this wasn't a church grab," said Roos. "Tapestry wanted to help us. It was about disciples making disciples." It was a new harvest opportunity. After one year of discussions, they decided to merge and called Sam Lee as the pastor.

## A New Pastor

Lee served as a chaplain for several years at a juvenile corrections facility and then took a position working for Tapestry as a chaplain at Kwantlen Polytechnic University. Throughout that time, he didn't see himself becoming a pastor of a church—not to mention one emerging from a largely Dutch heritage and seeking to find a way in the diverse world that is increasingly characterizing Vancouver and its suburbs. But being a chaplain and having worked with people of many faiths prepared him to be a pastor in ways he could never have imagined. Encouraged by Albert Chu, Lee underwent the assessment process to become a church planter and was called to serve as the pastor at Tapestry Mundy Park. It was a leap of faith, but he soon realized all of his experiences, including a time of drifting and discouragement in college, led to this. "I've come to realize that I love starting new things," he said. "I like the whole process of bridge building." He uses the analogy of viewing a family portrait—such as the one that once defined the Mundy Park congregation—and helping to expand that portrait with new shades and a harvest of new colors.

After deciding to merge, members of the former, well-established church in Mundy Park agreed that it was a good idea to take a few weeks off and hold no Sunday services. "There was a feeling of sabbath rest and then a time to replant, a time of ending and a time of looking forward," said Lee. About forty Tapestry members joined the remaining members of the former church to make up Mundy Park. They held a grand opening in 2017. When they began to worship again, they did so in a freshly painted and spacious sanctuary that had a feel of openness and freedom. Roos, who is a woodworker, crafted a large cross that hangs on the front wall. It is a welcoming work of art, one that seems to draw people and help them feel comfortable. Now a praise band, instead of a choir, performs on Sundays and Lee doesn't stand behind a pulpit to preach. He speaks and moves around in the front of the sanctuary. A new sense of purpose and joy is palpable on Sunday—and it is drawing seekers. Lee recalls how a retired college professor who said he was an atheist started coming. "He was having a crisis of faith that sent him in search of churches. He came here and now loves this place and may get baptized," said Lee. While the number of children who had come to the former CRC had dwindled to four or five, Mundy Park now has twenty-five. "We have come to realize," said Roos, "how important it is to somehow share God in a way that is working and speaks to the situation."

Through this process, Neil Roos came to see that it is important for churches to look beyond themselves, asking how everyone can be the church together in this time as God's people. The CRC reminds people that they have a local and a global calling—and at Mundy Park they, said Roos, seek to answer that calling.

## Building a Future

Church planting is starting to make its way into the overall fabric of Tapestry. Besides the church plants in Marpole and Mundy Park, Tapestry has begun a Saturday evening service at its main campus "that has a different vibe" for "soccer moms and dads and others who have a hard time making it on Sunday mornings," said Albert Chu. The leaders of Tapestry are also beginning to work with other churches facing declining membership, he said, "to help them dream what they can do to better serve God in their context." Tapestry offers no magic solutions; rather it stays attentive to the Spirit, watching and listening and praying for the wisdom to follow it as it moves into new places, into new fields. No books can clearly define this, no set strategy can provide a spreadsheet to follow. What seems to work is trying new things while staying close to the message and ways found in Scripture and using them to make it clear that the gospel of yesterday is still critical for today. But you have to have the imagination to live it in a world that constantly points you in other directions. Ironically, what worked centuries ago in the early church works today: people gathering, supporting one another, breaking bread, and going forth from place to place to share their stories. With this in mind, Chu said his hope is that the churches in Marpole and Mundy Park can plant other churches over the next ten or so years. "Let them plant other churches, and let's make sure their children plant churches. We don't want this to be a one-generation thing." The harvest, in other words, is a lifelong, ongoing process.

## And More: Starting a Church at Home

Mae-Ling Yen, a longtime member of Tapestry, and her husband, Russell, are there nearly every Sunday to greet people coming in for the worship service in Richmond. Hospitality is their gift; welcoming others is a ministry to them. But Mae-ling has thoughts of extending that hospitality and perhaps even starting a small church in the apartment building where they live. A couple of years ago, she attended Inhabit, a conference about new missional neighborhood church movements in Seattle, Washington, that encouraged people to embrace new ideas for extending the walls of a church into the community. Being there fired her imagination. It wasn't long until Mae-Ling and Russell sold their home and moved into an apartment building. Since then, she has tried to share her faith, more through actions than words, with her neighbors. She invites them over to eat, she engages them in conversation, and she keeps the door to her apartment open for children to stop in if they wish—and they often do with the permission of their parents. The future for her has arrived. "I'm done talking about where will we go on our next vacation," she said. "I have said to God, 'Here I am, send me.' We need to be sent out and be able to love our neighbor right next door. You don't have to preach Christianity but to allow relationships to build."

Her neighbors include people from Iraq, India, and Haiti. A global crowd lives right next door and she tries to make them all feel welcome.

Albert Chu is watching what Mae-Ling and Russell are doing and wonders if planting a church right where they are makes sense.

Church is not a building; church is where people gather to worship God. Church is as much about meals as it is about following a set liturgy; it is a place and space of honoring and accepting the divine grace Christ so freely offers. "Physical presence is an important thing," said Chu. "We have to be always asking what we can do with the spaces we inhabit to be a blessing to our community."

# 9

# "The Kingdom of God Has Come Near"

[or]

## Navajos Shake the Dust off Their Feet in New Mexico and Arizona

"But when you enter a town and are not welcomed, go into its streets and say, 'Even the dust of your town we wipe from our feet as a warning to you. Yet be sure of this: The kingdom of God has come near.'" —Luke 10:10–11

*Churches across the Navajo reservation in New Mexico and parts of Arizona were formed by and worshipped for decades under the auspices of the Christian Reformed Church missionaries who were part of the Doctrine of Discovery, a doctrine linked to what is called white privilege. While many people on the reservation were helped by the missionaries, there remained a sense that the primarily Dutch missionaries were essentially channeling the Lord's will and Word to and for them, instead of allowing them to grasp the Bible message for themselves. In recent years, the Navajo churches began to shake the dust off their feet and, with help of an indigenous leadership program, have taken responsibility for themselves and their congregations. They see the critical need to adapt their particular history to their current approaches to faith. We visited people and congregations across the reservation and feature stories of a minister who never thought he would ever stand in a pulpit as the preacher; a couple who, spurred and supported by their church, have created jewelry sold around the world; the janitor at the Rehoboth Christian School who talks of attending the school as a native youth and what it meant to him when he lived in its*

*dormitories during the academic years he was there; and then we
feature a veteran pastor who feels, after many years in the ministry,
like he is finally working in the place where God has placed him to
be a source of hope for the people.*

# A Hard Gospel

A soft wind was coming in from the desert, ruffling the curtains, as
Caleb Dickson began preaching in the sanctuary of Red Valley CRC.
His sermon was on "Suffering for God"—a topic familiar to many in the
sanctuary that morning in late July. Located in Apache County in Arizona
on the border with New Mexico, this is a rugged country of mesas, twisted,
stretching cacti, long stretches of emptiness, and mountains. The rich red
rocks filling the countryside are what give the valley its name. Work has
always been scarce; the harsh, pounding sun, lack of rain and dry, dusty
heat define the days. In this climate, the Navajo people have lived and
survived, often struggling against forces that have been hard to understand. For hundreds of years, they have to deal with the legacy of white,
European oppression and domination. Only in recent years have they
begun to move beyond that powerful influence and start to experience
their own chance to forge a future for themselves. There have been many
ironies and mysteries and struggles in their history, both for Navajos
who have been part of the CRC and those who have not been part of the
church. And Dickson, a slender man in a brown shirt and bolo tie, was
talking about some of this. A Luke 10 follower, he is a pastor who walks
the dusty desert path to share the gospel with a tender but aching heart
with his people. This morning, he was preaching about the hardships of
life on the reservation, of being a Native American in a predominantly
white denomination. And of the elements that surround them. "There are
things God does and allows to happen in our lives that make us wonder,"
said Dickson. "We don't live on easy street. . . . The Christian life involves
things we don't understand—and yet, when we pray and seek God's coun-
sel, some of these things become more apparent."

Dickson grew up as the son of a Nez Perce evangelist and the family
traveled from place to place as his father preached the gospel across the
southwest. Married to a Navajo woman, Dickson worked for many years as
a mechanic at the San Juan Generating Station in Waterflow, New Mexico.
It was hard work, but paid the bills. Attending to God and the ways of faith

weren't always firmly set in his life—and yet he thought of his father often and of the strong words he preached, and Caleb couldn't ignore a calling that he suspected lay in his own heart. As he came close to retirement in the early 2000s, a sense of that calling got stronger and he learned he could fulfill the dream of being ordained as a minister.

In 2011, he was among the first students to enroll in the initial class of students in the Red Mesa Leadership Development Network—a program designed specifically to train and raise up native leaders on the Navajo reservation. Arising from the Reformed faith that CRC missionaries taught for many years, it is a program engendered by native people for native people. Right away, Dickson appreciated the program and what he learned, traveling twice a month from his rural home to Rehoboth and Shiprock for weekend classes. It was grueling since he was still working at the power plant when he began, but he kept at it, frequently inspired by the memory of his dad preaching in tents and churches, in fields and in other places, to native people. After graduating from that program, Caleb received a license to preach and served the CRC congregation in the tiny town of Naschitti. Meanwhile, he went on to study to become a commissioned pastor. Hours of work and one-on-one mentorship with an area CRC pastor prepared him to be ordained in March of 2017 and to become one of the first Native American commissioned pastors in the area. Now able to preach and perform the sacraments of baptism and the Lord's Supper, he took over the Red Valley Church. He soon found in answering the call that he felt a depth of purpose that surprised and has filled him with joy.

## Doctrine of Discovery

Dickson and many other Navajos in recent years have become familiar with what is called the Doctrine of Discovery, through what is called in the CRC the Blanket Exercise. In this exercise, which takes place in churches, gymnasiums, community centers, and elsewhere, people lay out and stand on blankets and move from blanket to blanket as a group of people read from a script that recounts the history of the Doctrine of Discovery. In this exercise, the leaders explain that the doctrine dates all the way back to 1492, when the Catholic pope issued it to give white explorers the right to claim the land in North America and elsewhere because it was home to pagan savages. White superiority was the driving force behind the doctrine used as a blueprint for conquest and the various forms of oppression that followed. Many churches, including the CRC, came to fall into it in one way or another. As was the case with so many churches and institutions, this doctrine helped shape the CRC and especially how it conducted its ministry among the Navajos and Zunis—another tribe—in the southwest starting from the late 1880s. Missionaries going to those places did not make the journey to destroy, but, they sincerely believed, to build up and save native people living in spiritual darkness. But as the wheels of history have turned, as the Spirit has helped uncover the fatal flaws in the doctrine, as a deeper awareness of just how much the doctrine kept native people on the sidelines of their own Christian faith, the CRC and its agencies began to come to grips with it—and in places such as New Mexico a new indigenous culture of praise and worship and ministry has arisen. A cultural shift, away from outside dominance to local leadership, is occurring. And with it comes the advent of native identity and deeper participation in churches. Native people have shaken the dust off their feet in the desert spaces spanning their reservation.

## A Poison in the People

Dickson's sermon on that Sunday in July—as the soft desert wind kept sifting through the curtains—touched on the book of Esther and how God uses people, often mysteriously, for his purposes. Esther is the Jewish woman who became queen of Persia and, despite her fear, successfully implored the king to hold off killing the Jewish people. "Suffering will prove and improve our faith," said Dickson. "In suffering and in fear, such as Esther felt, we learn to persevere so that we can be preserved by God. And as we suffer, we can learn to help others in their suffering." Besides touching on Esther's role in saving the Jewish people, Dickson's sermon connected with and spoke to the history that a number of members of this church have experienced and observed. Adversity out in this remote area of red-rock mesas and mountains has come in many, often unsuspected ways. Looking around, except for a couple of men holding cowboy hats in their hands, few men were there that day. And there was a reason for that. Men remain scarce here. In the late 1940s, at the dawn of the nuclear age, the US government came to the reservation and opened uranium mines and offered lots of jobs to extract the material needed to make atomic bombs. People here were poor, many of them subsisting as shepherds or farmers, so getting a job in the mines, with higher pay, was attractive. Many Navajo men signed

144

on. But the government didn't make clear—and perhaps it wasn't really sure in those early days—just how dangerous it was to work with uranium, and the miners received few protections. But, as the decades passed, the effects on the miners from Red Valley and elsewhere on the Navajo reservation became clear. Although uranium is radioactive, the chemical compounds in it are what cause sickness, especially kidney failure. Having had close contact with uranium, dozens and dozens of people got sick and began dying. Slowly they began to realize, too often on their deathbed, what had happened. Government officials, facing mounting evidence of what this type of mining meant, began closing the mines and cleaning up toxic waste. Funds were made available to those who got sick. But for many, it came too late. The legacy of that time endures. People here know what it means for the promise of good work to turn to disaster. They know—in their bones and blood—a history that includes being misled and exploited, and this reflects many aspects of the Doctrine of Discovery. As their pastor, Dickson gears his ministry to a people whose hopes have been broken, sometimes by outside groups, sometimes by the pure indifference of history. Yet faith endures; they keep turning to their Creator for help in such things as building their church community. "We pray that Red Valley will pick up new growth. We have to help those who are sick and getting older," Dickson preached. "We can't let the Word of God leave this area. We need to keep the children of the next generation in our prayers."

## A Cooling in the Mountains

During one of the prayer times on this Sunday, Alice Dickson, Caleb's wife, said the Red Valley area is not just about suffering: it is also about hope. And it was good to pray about that, to have hope and praise God for it. She had recently driven up into the mountains. As always, she was refreshed, being able to leave for a time this world of many tribulations, a place in which rain comes far too infrequently. Going up there brought her to a special place, where things still ran wild, where creation can seem new, pouring right out of God's hands. It brought her thoughts around to Jesus. "What did Jesus feel as he went into the wilderness? It was a vast place," she said. "Did he fear the wild animals, the demons? I don't think so. But he needed to go there, just to find the Spirit, the voice, the whispering of God in the wind. He must have felt it vast and uncertain, wondering how long he would be there." Alice would say later it is crucial to go to the wild places, to those places lacking the normal things of comfort, because the Spirit is a restless Spirit that seeks to break us of comfort and take us into the desert with Jesus. It is there that, through hardship and discipline, the church can better know itself; it is there that flowers can poke up through the rocks; it is there that clouds can part and light shine on us and, if we listen, a whispering voice tells us where to go next.

After the service, people gathered in the church basement of Red Valley Church for a potluck. Food was set out on a long table and everyone had a chance to fill their plates and to find a table. Among them was Annabelle Barber, who has lived in the Red Valley area for many years. During the service, she had thanked God for the rain they had gotten over the last few days and asked prayer for people who were getting older. During lunch, she recalled how you had to walk everywhere when she was growing up. Going to church was a daylong process. Even today, people and communities scattered across the red mesa buttes and desert find it takes time getting anywhere. Barber appreciates coming to church because she gets to know people better. A stronger community can grow. "But," she said, "we need more little ones to come so we can start new members classes." Although the church is aging and needs to be fixed up and numbers are down, Annabelle Barber is grateful they have a new pastor. They have been without a full-time pastor for many years. And she especially appreciates that he is a Native American, someone who knows their hardships, their joys and hopes, and who can speak to them words coming straight from the Creator. Caleb has come at the right time and, she hopes, will help them to grow into a deeper community, defined by their local place and significant age-old customs. "We keep praying and the Spirit of God is showing us to reach out to the family of God that is ever growing," she said.

## Shaking the Dust Off Their Feet

Traveling from Native American churches across the Four Corners area—the area where New Mexico, Arizona, Colorado, and Utah touch—about twenty Indigenous people came to Bethel CRC in Shiprock, New Mexico on a Sunday afternoon in July to talk about their leadership roles in their congregations. Gathered around a long conference room table, they spoke of how, guided by the Holy Spirit, pastors, elders, deacons, and others have assumed greater ownership of their churches. Instead of taking direction from outside the Navajo reservation, they are beginning to guide the ways in which they express and live out a Reformed faith they have come to understand and appreciate. They especially spoke of becoming aware of the need to step into a new way of expressing their love for God, the Creator who they have known and yet are only now beginning to worship and praise in a context that works best for them. "We realized we needed to step out of our comfort zones and be servants of the Lord and build up the churches in this area," said Alice Dickson, Caleb Dickson's wife and a leader at Red Valley Church. "That is what is behind the leadership network."

The others agreed: People who had been on the fringes in their churches had begun to see that they needed to join in the Holy Spirit's work to stabilize and grow the churches in the Red Mesa Classis, the regional body of the CRC. Clearly, they said, the Spirit was moving, uncovering the ideas in the Doctrine of Discovery and making it more obvious how the domination they and their ancestors experienced was part of a much bigger historical pattern. It is also likely, given its constantly shifting nature, the Spirit had been at work and helping change the priorities of the CRC, making it possible through the leadership program that people in Red Mesa were more able to embrace and become leaders of the faith in which most of them were raised. Times have begun to change; people on the reservation see the need—*feel* the need—for them to step into the pulpits and take on leadership roles in their churches. "The church is at a crossroads today, and we can be a part of helping to develop a strategic way of proclaiming the good news of Christ in a time when young people aren't coming," said Janelia Smiley, an Leadership Development Network student and member of Bethel CRC.

## Following the Path of the Spirit

On a warm day Monday morning in July of 2018, Stanley Jim was holding an empty balloon in his hand as he spoke to children attending Vacation Bible School at his church, Window Rock CRC on the Navajo reservation in southern Arizona. The VBS theme was "When you walk through the waters, remember God is with you," based on Isaiah 43:2. Sparkling on the sanctuary stage behind Jim was a "waterfall" made of silver streamers and a tent that welcomed the VBS campers. In another room, a Navajo teacher was moving a plastic fish around in a small tank to teach a lesson about swimming in turbulent waters. She was acting out a message similar to Jim's—the need in all things, especially when the going gets tough, to lean into God.

The balloon Jim held represented a life raft. "Sometimes in your lifetime you will feel like this—an empty balloon." Then he blew air into the balloon and showed how it took shape. "See what happens—this is how the Holy Spirit will fill you and your raft so you can float and live." This is how, he seemed to be saying, the kingdom of God comes near.

A low-key man with a taciturn dignity, Jim's energy for ministry was evident that day as he dashed between craft and teaching stations, blowing a whistle to let everyone know a new session had begun. For years this well-respected Navajo leader worked as an ethnic ministry leader for Christian Reformed Home Missions. One of his abiding projects was the creation of the Leadership Development Network, of which Caleb Dickson and others are graduates. Satisfied that the program to form native leaders was up and running, Jim left his role as an ethnic ministry leader in 2016. He is now settling gratefully into parish ministry. "I love what I'm doing now. I have the chance to be working down here with other native people who have the chance to be native leaders. I'm able to keep offering them things I know and have experienced," he said.

## A Gun to His Head

Jim grew up in Teec Nos Pos, a solid two-hour drive north from Window Rock. Life growing up, as is the case for so many on the reservation, was hard. He was in junior high school when his mother left the family and things, already on the edge, went downhill. His father tried to provide love and stability, but he was often gone, working in the uranium mines or for the railroad. So Stanley spent a lot of time alone, walking in the mountains and began in his teens to drink heavily to wipe away his hurt, loneliness, and depression. In the depths of his struggles, far out in the mountains one day, he put a gun to his head. But then he recalled Rev. Corwin Brummel, a CRC missionary who first introduced him to Christ by stopping by his house with a hand-cranked phonograph on which he played Navajo hymns. Even as a youth, Jim had listened with fascination; for the first time back then he got the notion of a God who spoke to him in his own language. He taught himself to read by pondering hymns in the Navajo Hymnbook, compiled in Navajo by L. P. Brink, another CRC missionary. On the mountain that day, as thoughts of Brummel and those hymns filled his mind, he slowly put the gun down. Those hymns and their words offered hope and a different way. Touched, he knows now by the Holy Spirit, things began to turn around. He walked slowly back down the mountain into a new life. Looking back, he realizes that was when he began taking his first steps into the world of ministry. He eventually went to Grand Rapids to learn more about Christianity, a world of rules and practices that was mostly foreign to him and yet whose theology taught him God sanctified the whole world and made everything in it holy. He started to see how those mountains and the desert he loved were part of this abundant holiness. He graduated from Calvin Seminary in 1995, already wanting to link what he learned at the seminary with his culture. As a man who experienced being in both worlds, the Anglo and the native, he believed the Spirit had given him the mission to be an apostle to his people. He saw that it was time for Christianity to transform the culture in the Red Mesa area and to make it new in Christ. He knew leadership had to change. In the book, *Flourishing in the Land* (1996), a history of Home Missions, Jim said: "The music has to change to become true to who we Navajo are as people. Churches down here have been seen as being 'missioned.' . . . Instead of being on the receiving end, we need to be on the giving end."

## Talking About Native Leaders

Jim's presentation using the balloon was the last one of the morning. As the children left and teachers cleaned up, Jim invited us out to lunch at a restaurant near the church to talk about his ministry work and especially about training new leaders. Taking a seat in the restaurant, Jim said that on Monday mornings tribal leaders of the Navajo Nation, based in Window Rock, usually meet here, and sometimes Jim is invited to pray for them and their work on the reservation. He appreciated this chance. After ordering lunch, Jim spoke of how the Holy Spirit who can fill everyone's life began especially to fill Classis Red Mesa after the formation of the Leadership Development Network. "The best thing that ever happened to us here is leadership development," said Jim. "It is helping people rely on themselves instead of someone else coming here to help us."

As far back as 2003, Classis Red Mesa approved the Red Mesa Indigenous Leadership Development Network program. But it took time to put together a program that met the needs of Indigenous people. In September of 2007, the program began. Of the nine students to enroll in the first year of the LDN program, several were people that Stanley Jim identified as potential leaders. Like a shepherd, he devoted many hours to care and being with them, teaching them about the Reformed faith. In the restaurant, Jim spoke of those early times and reflected on some of the keys to good leadership. At the top of the list is working in partnership with others. "I'm not here to work for someone but to partner with you. That was my upbringing. Being a pastor means being a partner," he said. Jim often tells young leaders to keep their minds, hearts, and ears attuned to what is going on around them and to what others are saying, especially in a church setting. "We need to be open and shaped by the church so we can become messengers for Christ," Jim said. Having been in ministry for many years, and having played a role in helping to build the ministry of others, Jim is a leader who turns to God regularly for guidance. "God chooses different people for different jobs," he said. "Whenever you want to say 'yes,' the Spirit will get hold of you. . . . Much of ministry is being willing to take a risk, and God will take us as far as we're willing to go." The sermons he preaches on Sundays at Window Rock are based on Reformed theology that has close connections to Native American experience. "We understand the covenant of grace. In our culture, the child is part of your family for the rest of your life," said Jim. In the past, missionaries taught Navajos there is a difference between the sacred and the secular. But elements of that are changing as Indigenous leaders take their place in the Red Mesa churches. Still, there is a strong Reformed element to the faith. Referring to a quote by Reformed theologian Abraham Kuyper, Stanley Jim said: "If you start by going back to recognizing that 'every square inch' of the world is full of the activity of God, I embrace that as a Navajo person."

## Dealing with the Past

Donovan Carlile worked for thirty-five years building and designing roads for the Navajo tribe and retired a few years ago to become maintenance supervisor on the campus of Rehoboth Christian School. He had been thinking of continuing for a few more years in road work, but then he learned of the position at the school while he was serving on the Rehoboth school board. When they offered him the job, he thought it over and accepted, excited by the prospect of a new high school being planned and because the school means so much to him. He attended and graduated from Rehoboth, founded as a mission school in 1903 by the CRC. Many former students are critical of their education at the school, which required them to speak English and not their native language, forced them to have their hair cut, and sought to have them adapt to ways that would make them more successful in the white world. Carlile has a more nuanced view—perhaps even a surprisingly contrary view. "This school has been the building block of my faith. The people at the school have put a lot of blood, sweat, and tears into me and many others," he said.

After graduating from the school, Carlile attended the University of New Mexico, where he studied civil engineering. The years of constant travel and the hard work of civil engineering, building bridges, abutments, and roads, along with some personal challenges, have at times set him back. But the friends he met at Rehoboth and at CRC congregations he's attended have been there to help. "I've been through a lot of mud, but these guys from the school and churches have stood by me. It can be hard to find people like that who can articulate their faith and then live it out."

## Charting a Path for the School

One of his friends is Bob Ippel, choir director, former middle school teacher, and now executive director of Rehoboth Christian School. Ippel came to Rehoboth in 1993 and has known Carlile and members of his family for many years. The Carliles have been strong supporters of Rehoboth—and they know from their own lives and experiences what a school like this means to people facing hardships. "Rehoboth is a very important place. It can be a refuge for people when they are hurting," said Ippel.

Over the years, he has seen people living on or near the Navajo reservation struggling with poverty, addiction issues, family strife, and other things. "We do see brokenness and hurt and people just wandering in this area," said Ippel. "But we believe God has a plan for each of us, and the school has played an important role in Donovan's life and the lives of so many others."

The school is a community center, reaching out to its neighbors whoever they are.

The new high school, which opened in late 2018, is a testament to the faith and generosity of many people over the decades, especially members of the CRC.

"We are reminded that this new building would not be built without the work of the Holy Spirit and the grace of God," said Ippel, sitting in his office in the administration building on the campus. "We have gotten tremendous gifts out of the blue. God is so good."

Yet the new high school opened at a time of uncertainty. Christian education isn't as important to families these days as it was in the past. Meanwhile, other options such as charter schools are opening. And challenges the school faces mirror those of the broader society. But especially crucial, said Ippel, was to be aware of and consider the painful elements of the past. Important to recall is how the native people for years had been second-class citizens in their own land. A church that should have brought a message of freedom spoke of the need to adapt to the white man's ways. Scattered across the native lands, only now are churches and the people stepping out from domination, however well-intentioned it may have been. Only recently has it become clear that God's Spirit takes everyone on a journey, a sometimes terrifying trip to self-determination, new community, and freedom. "There is a lot of baggage that comes from our past, and we have to ask 'How do we move forward with that baggage?'" said Ippel, reminding us of the Luke 10 admonition to leave our baggage behind so we can enter into the lives of people today. In this case, moving forward—without forgetting the past but not getting caught in it—is important.

Such things as the issues related to the Doctrine of Discovery have caused much grief, self-analysis, and tears. Bearing the mistakes of the past is hard, but it is necessary in order to move forward in new ways and with a new spirit. What is happening at the school needs to happen elsewhere in order to better link where we've been with where we're going, Ippel believes. Wisdom mixed with forgiveness is key. "Reconciliation is an important part of what is happening here," said Ippel. "Mistakes were made. We seek to stand with our native brothers and sisters who have a vision of how Rehoboth can be a light to the community."

## A Spirit Moving Across the Reservation

*COVID-19 rampaged through the Navajo reservation through 2020 and into 2021. At times, the reservation had one of the highest infection and death rates in the US. There were many reasons for this—family structure, widespread conditions such as diabetes making people more susceptible to the virus, and sparse medical care in many places on the reservation. Among those who succumbed to the disease was Rev. Bobby Boyd, who we had the pleasure of meeting and talking with when we visited the area for this book. We only decided to catch up with him at the last minute. He was busy that afternoon, but made time for us. And we were grateful that he did—because his story,*

*told here, adds to our book. Bobby Boyd, like many on the reservation, held
close to his faith—as best he could—during the pandemic.*

Rev. Bobby Boyd joined Stanley Jim in helping to form the leadership
network. Pastor of Church Rock CRC, he has long seen the need for native
leaders, not just pastors but deacons and elders and others as well in native
lands. Key is making Christianity their own. As a pastor, this is an important aspect of Boyd's work, both explaining Christianity and encouraging
lively worship in ways comfortable and inspiring to Navajos and others.
At his church on Sundays, members pray exuberantly, waving their arms,
speaking in English and also their native Navajo. Boyd finds this deeply
moving and heartening. The Spirit is at work at Church Rock, in other CRC
congregations, and across other parts of the reservation. Boyd stays attuned
to the Spirit, to what it is saying and how it is moving. Nearly every weekend, Boyd said, at least one Spirit-filled revival takes place somewhere on
the Navajo reservation. Some revivals are connected to Pentecostal, Methodist, or Nazarene churches while others are stand-alone, nondenominational events. Boyd has attended a few and has some concerns. Being there
he sees high emotion and praise, which can be good, but there also is often
an energy pouring out lacking the right focus. "I believe these revivals can
be the work of God, but many don't have a strong biblical background," he
said. "In some, everyone is dancing and the dust is flying, but there is no life
change. Some just want money and call for healing and prosperity."

Boyd grew up in a Navajo family in which his mother was a sooth-
sayer and his father a medicine man, both following the traditional Navajo
religion. He was formed by this approach to religion, but found something lacking. After he left home, Boyd eventually became a Christian and
learned Scripture and was mentored in ministry by Rev. Paul Redhouse,
a well-known native leader who for many years pastored Four Corners
CRC in Teec Nos Pos, Arizona. Redhouse taught Boyd how crucial it is to
hold fast to the biblical truths. Bottom line, there is no veering into misguided emotion and empty praise. Always it is the message of the cross.
"Christ came and defeated sin on the cross," said Boyd. "He was buried
and raised again to defeat death." And then came the amazing wind of the
Spirit that shook the upper room in which Christ's disciples were gathered
on that first Pentecost. The cross matters, but at the same time, a key part
in this process is the role the Holy Spirit plays in bringing about new life
for Christians. A theology of this Spirit is important—and one that Boyd
preaches. "The early missionaries didn't teach us much about the Holy

Spirit and how we are to listen to the Spirit and how we are to give back" to others and to God, said Boyd. "We need the Spirit and we need to bring the Spirit back and leaders to help that happen."

## Crafting Jewels for the Lord

Navajo artists Darryl and Rebecca Begay are members of Boyd's church. They are also silversmith jewelers whose work in recent years has been infused by the movement of the Holy Spirit. Only something as ephemeral and hard to decipher as the shifting move of God could have broken through the pain and struggles of their lives and given them the creative energy and vision to make jewelry that has now gained worldwide attention. Working out of their small home in Gallup, New Mexico, they have been able to conquer or in some cases learn to cope with serious illness and substance abuse. Quietly and with the help of friends and Bobby Boyd, they have persisted in their artwork, which includes the intricate carving and setting of precious gems into a range of jewelry that has a notably southwestern flavor. Bracelets with eagles soaring, bolo tie clasps showing desert scenes, and belt buckles featuring dragonflies are among their creations.

They are low-key people living in a home comfortably furnished with art, their own and that of others. Both appreciated how Bobby Boyd had been teaching them and others to be sensitive to the ways, through prayer and praise, God's Holy Spirit can transform lives. The Begays especially appreciated learning about the Spirit's work in the past few years as both faced significant challenges. Because of what they've been through, Rebecca has come to see that God's Spirit works in steady and yet mysterious ways. "I see that God has changed my thought process," she said. "The power of the Holy Spirit is in us, and as a Christian, I have access to it. The Spirit has helped me so much to grow as an artist."

## Drawn Together by Art

Rebecca grew up in Crownpoint, New Mexico, and attended the Christian school there before moving to Rehoboth Christian School in Rehoboth. That is where one of her teachers, Elmer Yazzie, a respected artist in his own right, noticed her talent for drawing and encouraged her to pursue a career in art.

Darryl is from Round Rock, Arizona. While Rebecca was raised in the CRC, his family embraced traditional Navajo beliefs and practices that were mixed with some Baptist teachings—so he also knew about Jesus.

Darryl grew up in a family of artists: his grandmother was a weaver and conducted Navajo blessing ceremonies, and his grandfather was a ceremonial sandpainter.

It was his uncle Bobby Begay, a medicine man and artist, who first taught him jewelry making. Darryl recalls that one day his uncle, who lived in Round Rock, Arizona, was getting ready for an art show and asked him to make some colorful bracelets out of tufa, a soft, porous desert rock similar to limestone. Moving forward in his art began there. "My uncle showed me the basics. I'd never done a tufa casting before, but it felt so easy, so natural," he said. The material felt familiar in his hands, as if it was just waiting for this chance for him to craft the soft rock into pieces of jewelry. At the same time, he admits he was a novice. "When we took the bracelets to the art show, one of the Native artists looked at them and said they weren't too bad for a beginner." Darryl was attending college at the University of Arizona in Flagstaff at the time. When he returned, he decided to forgo a career in accounting, dropped out of the university, and poured himself into working with rocks and stones and shaping them into bracelets, necklaces, earrings, and other items. At the university he had also met Rebecca, then working on her degree in art education. That was 1997. "She was taking a silver-smithing class, and I helped her get an A," he recalled in a soft voice as he glanced at his wife on the other end of the couch.

## Building Careers Together Through Hardship

In the early years of their marriage, the Begays learned how to work together as artists, each complementing the other's style and ideas. They began winning awards in Native art shows, and were busy raising their three children. But then Rebecca got sick with a rare illness and was hospitalized for lengthy periods. It was an unexpected roadblock that challenged her in many ways. "I had to lean on the doctors and medications. I was in a lot of pain and wasn't always sure what was going to happen to me," she said. She waited a few moments before adding: "But even though it was very hard at times, I was able to tap into my faith and learned more about the grace of God." Doing his best to raise their three children at home while Rebecca was in and out of the hospital, Darryl himself had a hard time steering clear of alcohol and had a long bout with abdominal pain. He wasn't sure what was happening, but needed to be strong for his wife and kids. He didn't have the time for this pain. But, finally, he was rushed to hospital and had his gallbladder removed. The surgery removed the pain and yet there were still bumpy times ahead. "We went through the storm together. . . . It was so unbearable at times that I felt like quitting, but I kept going, and God helped," said Rebecca. But during that period, Darryl wondered if a medicine man could bring comfort and healing. Christianity gave Rebecca strength; not so with him. "At times I was driven to traditional ways, but they could only take me so far," he said. Then in 2012, after a long period of searching, Darryl came to realize that Jesus was the answer for him and his marriage. Again, it was a rough process of trying to open different doors and seek different cures. But it kept coming back to Jesus, who was an unshakable presence, a person who never sent him away, who took him in and helped him deal with things no matter what they were. "I saw that Jesus was hard core. He wasn't afraid; he dealt with issues," said Darryl. "Since then, there's been no turning back. It's been all God." In 2018, he and Rebecca were taking courses from the Classis Red Mesa Leadership Development Network to learn how to be church leaders. Through it all they have also been able to keep up their art. Smiling in what can only be described as a shy, sensitive way, Rebecca credits Darryl for encouraging and motivating her as an artist, going back to when they first met and he helped her to get an A. These days she has opened up as an artist. "I've let myself go with flowers and butterflies. John 15:5 is my inspiration. By relying on [Jesus] I will bear much fruit."

# 10

# "Your Names Are Written
# in Heaven"

[or]

## Going Local in Kamloops
## and Grand Haven

"However, do not rejoice that the spirits submit to you, but rejoice that your names are written in heaven." —Luke 10:20

*In this final and concluding chapter, I (Moses Chung) discuss the evolution and power of Go Local. I describe how it began and where it is moving. We also profile two churches that have taken part in this initiative and hear from those whose lives have been changed by it.*

## The Start

When I (Moses) arrived as director of Christian Reformed Home Missions in 2011, the agency had been planting churches across North America for more than 120 years. From New Mexico to far flung places in Canada, Home Missions had been busy and successful. Vision statements and strategies about doing missions that guided the agency had changed over the decades. And as successful as Home Missions had been over its history, I knew as an agency we needed to change to meet the new challenges facing the church in the early twenty-first century. In my role as executive director, I was convinced we needed to continue to innovate and evolve. I knew there had to be something more than what we had been doing. So where to go, what to do?

Almost by accident, or rather providentially, in my early years at Home Missions, I stumbled across that "something more." Traveling to and meeting with churches supported by Home Missions, I began to come across what I call "under-the-radar" congregations and people. I slowly began to see that the real story of the church going into the future has to be about the people, the on-the-ground church members who have sought to pay attention to where the Holy Spirit is, to follow it, and then to dwell in whatever place God is at work. I saw how congregations and ordinary people, many on the edges of the mainstream church, tell the story of the small things that can reflect much larger truths. I realized that our focus as an agency must be on the vitality of a community seeking God in their midst and not on being the fastest-growing church in town. In a substantial way, this book has highlighted those people and ministries and invited others to pay attention to these under-the-radar people and places to get a clue of what God is doing in the world today. What I experienced are people worshipping and praying and living in ways that can inspire hope, encouragement, and birth a new imagination for other congregations seeking renewed life today.

To help Home Missions chart a new direction, I knew it was important to address a future filled with challenges and highly complex issues with a fresh, locally rooted, Spirit-inspired imagination and approach. Several contemporary missiologists in North America, such as Alan Roxburgh, Craig Van Gelder, and David Fitch have written recently about how over the past few decades many Christian churches have turned to secular business models and programs to address issues such as church growth and renewal. Understandably, churches want to know what the future holds and how to prepare for it, as well as how to address issues facing it today. But God needs to be first, these missiologists said. The point they are making is about taking a corrective approach; moving from having human agency at the center of the church's ministry to God's agency. This means we first ask questions such as, "What is God up to here and now and in the world?" and "What does God want?" and "How might we discern God's presence and join God's activities, not focusing on our agenda and ask God to bless it?" These missiologists write of the need to move from developing church-growth strategies to learning to become people defined by hospitality and hearts touched and informed by the shaping of the Spirit.

This book focuses on many of those people and ministries I came across—those people in church communities that had a vision focused on their own local place and ministry. In this book, you see that "rock star" pastors and church leaders aren't the main characters and don't always take center stage. Rather, we have sought to put much of the emphasis on those people—those low-profile "saints"—whose persistence and patience, often over many years, make for a church community that has taken up a lasting, faithful presence in a particular place. We have worked to tell a larger story of what it means to be dwelling in a local setting as God's people.

In 2016, in response to the need to expand our vision and emphasize personal presence over size, Home Missions launched an initiative we called Go Local as a cohort in a handful of sites. Here is a look at two churches that have taken up this ongoing, Go Local project. They, as have many other congregations, become part of the new, evolving approach and movement of joining God on mission where they live every day. This is a process that, as I say, is evolving; it is an experiment we are following, well aware that what we are doing is on the cutting edge of mission work and that ours is not the only way in which to join God's kingdom in our world today.

## Kamloops

Angelica Nunes planned to stand outside her home in Kamloops, British Columbia, to hand out candy and greet her neighbors bringing their kids by for Halloween trick-or-treating. This was a small thing, but without the inspiration she received from being part of the Go Local guiding team at her church, she probably wouldn't have thought of this as a way to connect with her neighbors. Go Local helped open her to see how the Holy Spirit was at work on the October evening that youngsters showed up at her doorstep as pirates, princesses, sports heroes, and Star Wars characters. "The idea was to meet people. We don't know what the outcome will be, but we'll reflect on it afterward," said Nunes, whose church, Sahali Fellowship CRC, was one of six congregations that took part in the initial British Columbia cohort of the Go Local initiative.

## Going Local

A journey of eighteen to twenty-four months, the intent of Go Local is to engage congregations in practices that help them discover and join God in their neighborhoods. The process involves congregational guiding teams and pastors who commit to listen, discern, experiment, and reflect together. The goal is to develop habits and practices that the entire congregation can participate in as a way to engage their communities. Ultimately, the agenda is set by God, as discerned by the guiding teams, made up of four to seven church members who guide the process. As a member of the guiding team at Sahali CRC, Nunes said, "We come together to listen to God and to one another, and we try to discern what God is doing."

## Preparing to Join the Harvest

During the first phase of Go Local, the Sahali guiding team met regularly to "dwell in the Word." In this, the team reflected on Luke 10:1–12, reading about Jesus sending out seventy disciples, two by two, "ahead of him to every town and place where he was about to go." Each time the four-person Sahali guiding team met, they reflected on how the passage hit them and discussed what new things—because there are always new things—the Spirit has been telling them. As part of this effort, they also met periodically with church members to read the same Scripture passage. The second listening practice of Go Local is to "dwell in the world," to walk prayerfully and attentively in local neighborhoods. This exercise helps in familiarizing themselves with the people living nearby—and planning for the next phase, in which they develop experiments that are shaped by what they have been discerning and that will further their understanding of what God is doing in their neighborhoods. The church leadership also participates in dwelling in the Word at its meetings. "I have had many stories of interaction with our neighbors," said Rev. Jana Vander Laan, who is a co-pastor of Sahali Fellowship with her husband, Michael. She and Michael are not members of the guiding team. Instead they meet with a cohort of other pastors. "We have not begun any grandiose programs out of this, but we definitely know God is on the move," said Jana.

## Living on the High Ground

Located in the neighborhood for which it is named, Sahali (which means "high ground" in the Chinook language) Fellowship CRC is close to a fairly large retirement home, a hospice facility, a series of hiking trails, low-income as well as market-rate apartments, and residential neighborhoods. These are all places to which their Go Local experiments could take them. Their experiments might also simply take them next door to meet their neighbors, "share peace," and "eat what is set before them" as the foundational text for the process (Luke 10:1–12) instructs.

As it turns out, it didn't take long for Go Local to help revitalize this congregation.

## Stunned but Still Strong

In 2012, Sahali was stunned by the sudden loss of Rev. Henry De Vries, their pastor for twenty-three years. "That was a very difficult period, and we put many of our ministries on hold," said Nunes.

The Vander Laans arrived in 2014. Coming into Sahali, they saw that the people's grief over their pastor's death hung heavy. Probably because of that sudden event, church members seemed to be uncertain of their future. "There seemed to be a lack of confidence in who they were as God's people," said Jana Vander Laan.

At the same time, Jana could see resilience and hope beginning to stir in the congregation. The members were close and stuck together. Initially, they tried a couple of traditional outreach programs, trying to bring new life to Sahali. "There was no traction until we got involved with Go Local," said Jana. "Now, there is a new spirit percolating."

## A New Way

People are beginning to pay attention to God's creative Spirit moving everywhere—at home, at work, in friendships, and even in "chance" meetings. They see God's hand in all things. During this journey, said Nunes, the process has been hard at times. Go Local isn't about starting a program and waiting to see the results. "Many of us are very goal-oriented, and this can be difficult for us," she said. Jana Vander Laan agrees. But the discipline of dwelling in the Word helped teach them how to listen to God and to each other. "Listening takes so much practice, even when we think we are good at it," she said.

Also challenging in Go Local is the matter of reorienting one's connection with God. Go Local isn't about praying for things we want or for things in a church or its ministries to go a certain way. It is about being available and open to whatever surprises and seemingly wild ideas God has for the congregation. It's about learning to trust by letting go of our agendas and stepping out of our comfort zones. "The whole Go Local process can be confusing because you don't know how it will end," said Nunes. "You have to trust that God will speak and move even though you don't know when or where that will be."

Ultimately, the folks in Sahali are finding that Go Local is hard; it requires a significantly different approach and mindset. It is about a change in the church arising from a close, conscious connection, among those involved, with God. It is about being able to carefully listen to the Lord speaking to them in many ways about how to be who they are in the multifaceted neighborhood in which they find themselves. Tough as it has been to shift their emphasis, several in the congregation are finding a new link to God. They are finding the ability to hear the voice of the Spirit, which—blessedly—is helping them rid themselves of the grief of losing their beloved pastor and being able to see a new light toward which they are moving.

## Covenant Life Goes Local

Wrapping up an eighteen-month journey of discernment they engaged in with other churches, leaders at Covenant Life Church in Grand Haven, Michigan, gathered to talk about the process—which held many surprises— and to discuss what might happen next. The leaders are part of the guiding team for their church and have participated in the Go Local process. At the meeting, Covenant Life members spoke of how they initially came up with a plan to make the church parking lot more available to people working and living in or visiting this Lake Michigan resort town. That was their first experiment—and it didn't bear as much fruit as they had initially hoped, but it did open people's eyes to new opportunities around them.

## The Parking Lot

Larry Schutt, a Go Local guiding team member who has attended Covenant Life for many years, said that the team read, reread, and read again Luke 10, their seminal text, and searched the passage for meaning and kept asking, If we are being sent out, what are we to do? They took many walks around the neighborhood—an area of refurbished, upscale warehouses turned into residences and businesses, located near the Lake Michigan shore—and carefully noted what they saw and tried to listen to and sense what God might have them do. Again and again, they kept coming back to the need for additional parking in the area. "We realized parking was a major issue for neighbors and visitors and our church had a huge lot that sits empty during much of the week," said Schutt, a retired certified public accountant.

Seeing the need, and initially thinking the Holy Spirit was leading them in this direction, they kept wondering how to move the idea forward. They talked with others in the church, to people living or working in the area, and considered forming a plan to present to the broader community. But they kept coming up short; it was hard to get momentum.

## Joining God in the Neighborhood

A large church that meets in a remodeled piano factory in Grand Haven, Covenant Life has multiple worship services and programs and is very active in mission outreach. When members learned of a Go Local cohort beginning in their area, they decided to join, believing the church was ripe for an effort to supplement what was already going on. Claudia Williams, a pastoral leader at the time, was among those who signed on to join Go Local. "I started to look for a group of people who would want to go on this type of journey," she said. "I prayed that God would put the right people together to do this."

Made up of six willing church members, the guiding team gathered and read Luke 10, and then discussed it, trying to discern—every time they read it—what it was saying to them about what it means to go on mission into unfamiliar places "like lambs among wolves"—as sent ones for Jesus into places where they might not be welcome—and yet also to find places where people are open and welcoming. Not too long into the process, they began to walk through their neighborhood. As they went, they tried simply to be open to what they saw, to whom they met, to what they learned. And this is where the parking lot idea took hold—in a sense, a "big idea" missional effort. But when that idea, facing obstacles from the start, hit a dead end, team members needed to pause and seriously ask what this journey meant, if it wasn't about coming up with big changes for the church. Then, they started to consider smaller things, movements of the Spirit they determined happening right in front of them. And this is when they began to see that Go Local is a project of the imagination that doesn't push changes with much fanfare. It is about God's Spirit, often at work under the surface.

## Finding God in the Cobbler's Shop

Chris Williams, owner of a cobbler shop in Muskegon, just down the road from Grand Haven, and a member of the guiding team, had already been seeking for several years to find God at work in his life, even if he wasn't quite aware of it. When Williams (no relation to Claudia) started his cobbler shop about ten years ago, they had a customers-only restroom policy. "To say that the homeless/poor community was frowned upon by most of the staff would be an understatement," he said. But it wasn't long before he rolled out a policy stating they would treat every person who came into the shop as if they were there to spend a million dollars. Williams said their shop needed to be like "a warm seat on cold days, a dry seat on wet days, and a cool place to sit when it's blazing hot. . . . A lot of people now know they can come here and be treated like people."

But lacking for Williams was a way to connect what he was doing to God. He had been struggling in that area of his life and with church: How did it all fit together?

Then he joined the Go Local effort—and it all hit home when James came into the shop one day in the summer. James is a local guy who suffers from mental illness. The shop collected cans and bottles for him. When James showed up one day to pick up empty cans and bottles to cash in at a local store, he spotted a container of cookies sitting on Williams's shoe-repair bench, and shouted, "Are those cookies?!" Williams brought him the container and offered James as many cookies as he wanted. Sticking in his hand, he took some.

About thirty minutes after James left, an apprentice cobbler came up to Williams and asked: "So, what's up with that? I've noticed you go out of your way to treat those people well. You're, like, actually one of those Christians, aren't you?'"

"Yes," he said—and from there Williams slowly had a chance to share more about his faith with his employee, a faith he has had all along but that Go Local has helped him to see more clearly—particularly in the day-to-day, often minor occurrences of his life and business.

## Running into God at the Grocery Store

Angela Vanmeurs, a substitute teacher, came to see that opening the church parking lot for more people would be nice—and to an extent that began happening without a formal program in place. Signs that are more welcoming to the public have been set up.

But, like Chris Williams, she started to see that "little things" connected with the nudging and delicate movement of the Spirit are what matters. As this began, it surprised and pleased her to realize how easy it could be. Normal experiences can be simply turned into holy encounters. When she goes grocery shopping, for example, she often sets aside time to talk with friends and others she comes across at the store. She now does this with more intentionality—God is at work and moving among people in that grocery store and in the conversations she has. With her cart of food, she'll stop in an aisle and greet a friend. Standing there, as others move past, their conversations are not necessarily in-depth; they are about familiar things. But sometimes they talk about important things. "It's really fascinating what happens when I really listen," said Vanmeurs, who works with youth at the church. "I'm always there at the grocery store for a very long time."

## Taking It to Another Level

As the eighteen-month period of the Go Local process approached its ending, members of the team at Covenant Life decided to take on an experiment that reflected a way in which the initiative could grow in a church. They recruited a few church members to go through a short, six-week Go Local cohort. And as Covenant Life's eighteen-month cohort finished, the six-week experiment also came to a close—and the two groups met to assess how it had gone. "Do we go beyond the six weeks?" Claudia Williams had asked. "How do we move Go Local beyond this group?"

Sharon Knibbe, a hospital chaplain and member of the guiding team, said she appreciated the participation of new people during the six-week cohort; it struck her that planting seeds like this can bring new growth in lives and in the church itself. "Seeing the movement of the Spirit through each of these people stepping out of their comfort zone was an example of what grassroots involvement can do in a community," she said.

Doug Einfeld, a retired hospice chaplain, and his wife, Nancy, took part in the six-week experiment to see if participants would be willing to go on a longer Go Local journey. Enfield and his wife have been interested for years in small-group ministry, believing that the mainstream church is missing the boat. "It seems that the church culture sits on an island; church people spend a lot of time with church people, but the broader culture believes the church has turned its back on them," said Doug Enfield.

As a hospice chaplain, he had the privilege of entering into the lives of people from all walks of life. He's had opportunities to learn from them and offer ministry. And after he retired, he said, he yearned for a way to connect with others who want to change the church—and to change it in low-key, enduring ways that he saw promoted by Go Local. "My wife and I have sincerely appreciated the chance to meet and pray and strategize with people seeking to find how God is active" in their lives and in the world around them. "I hope we can continue to go on in this journey," he said.

Go Local helped him to see that his leadership on the board of his condominium association provides a small way to stay connected to his neighbors. His prayer is that Go Local helps to reveal a new spirit—the Holy Spirit—more fully in the life of the church. He hopes people can learn to see that the Spirit is already present in so many ways and that, with intention and in community, and with the emphasis laid out in Luke 10, people simply need to follow the Spirit's lead.

## Going Home

As Chris and I rode from Grand Haven back to Grand Rapids, it was getting dark. Turning on my headlights, I reflected on the work the folks at Covenant Life have been doing. With every Go Local cohort, we assign coaches to churches to accompany them along. I had been Covenant's coach, meaning I sat with them and observed the process as it unfolded. I watched and listened as they sorted through whether to follow through on their "big mission" idea to make their parking lot more accessible. It sounded like a decent idea to address the parking problem in the resort town that gets very busy with tourists during the summer. I was curious to see where it would take them; I was also excited to watch as they walked their neighborhood, talked to their neighbors, and considered bringing the parking lot idea to city officials. They were working Go Local and seemed inspired by it. By the same token, and I didn't mention this, theirs was an idea that I didn't believe would lead to the transformation of lives, create a deeper connection to God, or, over time, help reshape the overall ministry of the church. "I waited and watched, and eventually, as it became clear that the parking lot idea was not going anywhere, they began to see that God wasn't showing them that was where they were supposed to go," I told Chris. "They began to realize, as they continued to meet and to read Luke 10, that Go Local is about listening and paying attention to small, ordinary, everyday things and not necessarily creating a big program." What happened with James, the man seeking cans and bottles in the cobbler shop, was a great example of Go Local revelations. Meeting and talking with friends and strangers in the grocery store, building those relationships, and seeing that God was at work up and down those aisles, was also a good example. "I know these sound like small things, but it is the small things that matter and can build into bigger things," I said. We never know where one conversation, one gentle touch on the shoulder, one smile, one unexpected act will lead.

At its foundation, I reminded Chris, Go Local is not, first of all, about getting more people to join your church—although that may, and will likely, happen. It is more about learning to ask different questions about church, building trust and friendships between Go Local team members, and slowly, patiently, and, often in little ways, connecting gently with the Spirit of God who is at work in the world around you. "Go Local is not about having a program in which you do things to please God," I said. "So often people think they are doing something wrong and maybe they should pray more, serve more, do more, go on more mission trips. But that can be a rat race. You never feel like you are good enough." The big project, growing the church to fill the seats on Sunday, is not what it's about. Instead, it is about finding ways, personal and communal, that are unique to your congregation—ways of being faithfully present with and among your neighbors and joining the work of the Lord together there.

Soon, we could see the lights of the Grand Rapids skyline flickering in the distance. We were on the road on a Sunday at the end of 2019. But, as we neared Grand Rapids that night, it felt a little like we were driving into an uncertain future. And it turns out, it wouldn't be long before the coronavirus would arrive and overturn so many things, including the work of the church. Certainly, the future was uncertain. For us, we have been able to keep Go Local alive by connecting with and training churches online. And that is good. In the midst of the pandemic, churches are increasingly seeing the significance of congregations renewing themselves through use of their imaginations; they are seeing what fits in one setting is way out of place in another. They are starting to listen to that still, small voice of God to speak to them and to lead them into a new promised land shaped by their own aspirations, intentions, and individual capabilities. They are learning to be poets, to speak a wonderful message, rich with symbols, of praise and meaning for the new world that is already upon us.

## A Return

In December of 2020, we checked back in with Doug and Nancy Einfeld who had gone on to take part in an extended Go Local process. By that time, the COVID-19 pandemic had been going on for months, but Doug and Nancy persevered online with a small group of others to learn more about the process and to further engage with it in their lives. They have tried, even under the restrictions of the virus, to meet people in their neighborhood, which is full of mostly young families, as well as to pay attention to how the Spirit is at work in their lives.

I loved talking to them; they are wonderful people who are serious about Go Local and spoke with joy about their work, as did the seventy when they returned and spoke to Jesus, about what they have seen and accomplished. Both have found a deeper connection with God and with those they meet in their daily lives and are grateful for it. "I have learned to be more conscious and intentional of being present with people that I run into in my life," said Nancy. "I take walks in the neighborhood and organized a cookie exchange and both Doug and I participated in a Facebook group for our neighborhood."

Nancy said her ability to love is growing and she has been able to more deeply appreciate and help tend to the needs of Doug's ailing father, who is now living with them. As for Doug, he is hoping and praying that the broader church can catch on to the value of going slow, of learning to listen for the tender voice of the Spirit and follow it wherever it leads. "Things are new and scary and unfamiliar. It is amazing to think we need this kind of effort to get me to think about my neighbors and be more conscious of other people," he said.

Both of them see, however, that this process, however arduous, is valuable and can eventually be a guide that the church at large can use to rid itself of traditions that have grown stale and help lead it into deeper connection with God, with one's self, and with others. They also see that this process is not one that is earning them brownie points to build up their lives or egos on earth. They are doing what they believe God has called them to do and that their reward when it comes will mean that, as it says in Luke 10:20, "their names are written in heaven."

# Epilogue

## Context-Specific
## Faithfulness

As we look back and reflect on our travels to visit ministries across North America, we think of what theologian Miroslav Volf calls "context-specific faithfulness"—the theological virtue of focusing your faith-filled efforts and ministry on one place, in one context. Many of those we met fit this category. And one image especially sticks with us: Andy Kim and Mario Pagan walking down the street in North Philadelphia, their clothes covered with plaster dust. They had just been helping a neighbor tear out a leaky ceiling and, talking and gesturing to one another, they were headed to 8th Street Community Church to talk to us. They were two men who looked happy and energetic, even though they had to get up early to do some construction work. Once we sat down in the former bar now serving as their church and ministry center, they told us the story of their efforts in this part of the city. The very building in which we spoke sat on a corner where Mario once sold crack. Now, after a stint in prison where he began to seriously read the Bible, he was Andy's partner. Andy had started this church a few years before. After we met with them, it struck us that going two by two, as stated in Luke 10, these men had entered into an incarnational ministry, in which the Holy Spirit was moving through them in what they do. They had embedded themselves quietly, subtly, and yet powerfully in this community—this context. Neither is a high-profile guy; they are low-key and down to earth. They are grassroots ministers—Andy the pastor and Mario an elder/evangelist—weaving their ways through the hearts and minds and lives of families, especially young people, on the hard streets of this neighborhood that has fought against drugs and violence and, with the support of people such as Andy and Mario, is seeking to mitigate the encroachment of these all-too-common urban problems. God is clearly with them, and they have joined with God, in their ministry in this busy corner of the city. The church, as we see it through them, comes as they hand out sandwiches to hungry people on the streets; as they hold a block party for the kids in the summer; as they sit at tables in the church to mentor students after school; as they have laid plans to open a vocational prep school for youth; and as they link in various ways with what you could call their mother ship—Spirit and Truth Fellowship. Andy was appointed to come here and Mario is from here. Together, they are an example of Christ's church at work far beyond the walls of a building.

## Ministry Amidst

Certainly, there are many others in this book who illustrate this ground-level approach to ministry; they each bring their own gifts, often in un-heralded ways, to the places in which they find themselves—often tough places, forgotten places, or places full of possibility that have reached a dead end. In many ways, Andy and Mario and others are, as we see it, on the cutting edge of God's church here in the early part of the twenty-first century. To be sure, the COVID-19 pandemic has affected them and those with whom they work. But even in the midst of the disease, they have stayed close to the God who lives as much within them as the Lord does in others and in the world itself. Without shouting or making a commotion, they are models of a new but at the same time 2,000-year-old vanguard of Christ-followers who are walking the Way. Even if they don't know it or are necessarily able to express it, they are part of this new army of disciples who have gone out into the world, often without a clear idea of where they are headed or even what they will do when they get there, to connect with those who live in the places where they land. Like Taehoo Lee, who has been a kind of neighborhood chaplain on Uber Street, also in Philadelphia, they keep all of their senses attuned to how they can join with the hurting, the broken and fallen in the places to which they are sent. And when they finally settle into the community to which they are called they will seek, day in and day out, to announce the peace of Christ.

# Ministry Close to Home and Far and Wide

The ministries on which we focus—whether in the poor, hard places or the more affluent, just-as-tough places—are about people getting their hands dirty and forsaking comfort and predictability for creating new forms of community, such as we saw with Karen Wilk's work with Neighbourhood Life in Edmonton, Alberta. The Spirit continues to show Neighbourhood Life supporters how they can join in what God is already doing in their neighborhoods and communities. In this ministry, Wilk knows the people next door; they know her; they share their lives. The Spirit is as real as a sifting wind; it is as solid as any new thought; it is the story behind the story, uncovering mystery and pointing the Lord's people in new directions. One of the early readers of this book encapsulated what we were seeking to portray when he wrote that "a faith community should be defined by the place that helps give it life." Yet another statement is in our chapter on Evergreen Ministries, which describes coming "to faith not as an event, but as a process."

As we look back on those we met, we see ordinary Christians who are not trying to do heroic, grand things for God. They are responding to simple, sometimes hard, situations—whether in poor inner cities or well-to-do neighborhoods—where they have a tug from the Spirit, a hunch or inspiration or an opportunity presented to them. Then, almost in every case, one thing leads to another thing that eventually amounts to something bigger than what they started. Often, beyond anything they would have imagined in their wildest dreams. And they say, it must be God doing the work because they know they would not be smart enough or wise enough to come up with anything like what they experience.

# Luke 10

In our book, we feature small, slow, patient, Spirit-led ministries that follow the Luke 10 framework that we have laid out. We meet and profile God's people in Christian Reformed Church congregations in "every town and place" across North America. We had the privilege to see what God was up to in these places. Called and sent, these people of God formed—and are forming—communities; life takes place often under the surface but grows and eventually begins to show itself. God's kingdom is breaking forth, showing itself in transformed lives among those we met. As solid relationships formed between them, the people started to open themselves up to the point of drawing close and near, meeting in their places of pain and finding ways to offer one another the Spirit's anointed balm of healing. Located in a shared community, in those places we visited, we found that both those who were sent and those who lived in a place linked in their sufferings as well as in their joy and hope that showed itself in revitalized worship, fresh ministry, and especially lasting friendships born out of gathering around tables of hospitality. They share the Lord's Supper as a way to nourish them and support them as members of the body of Christ in the context in which they live. As this happens—in Tucson, Arizona, Seattle, Washington, or St. Thomas, Ontario—God does something beautiful between and among them: there is healing, change brought by the Spirit that unites them and brings about something new that they never dreamed about. The circle of God's people and community is enlarged and made richer and more diverse for an even greater and newer mission because of added participants. These newer members create new possibilities that didn't exist before they joined the work of God's mission.

More broadly, we believe that the stories we have told help to reflect these questions: What is Spirit's invitation to the church today? What's the implication for the future of the church? Our answer to both questions is the option to go local, to look at what is set before you. In going local, we first need to admit that many of us are disconnected from our neighbors, meaning that person who lives right next door, that person right in front of us, those in our own families. And we need to step forward and find ways to connect with our neighbors and stay put by remaining faithfully present. We do this first by listening and not telling; by being patient; by expecting God to do the heavy lifting. The ministries we feature illustrate that the job of the church is to trust God and be faithful, not to try to bring results or make things happen by ourselves. The rest will come. Stop being anxious about your future or lack of resources. Don't be afraid of the changes around you. Embrace the place and love the people in the ordinariness of life.

Following the Spirit and going local means embracing the place where people live every day, speaking peace and wholeness to their brokenness and pain. We don't try to fix people with a specific program or through our own programs or power. We share what we have and who we are. This is about going with nothing or traveling lightly and trusting God's Spirit to be at work within us and in those we meet. Essentially, the people we met in our travels teach us of the need to follow Jesus into the neighborhoods and communities around us. And then we stay put with patience and wait on the slowness of God's work. We remain faithful with small things that God shows and leads us to do. We believe God will bring healing and the kingdom in God's time and God's way. That's much better and more beautiful than anything we can bring. This is an upside-down process; it challenges structures already in place. It is like a slow, underground earthquake, rattling the familiar; it is quietly seismic; it is about allowing the Spirit to arise within us and help us to see what is right in front of us. It is about a fresh way of recognizing the incarnation—the flesh and blood of Christ in us all. It is about going local. It is about love in motion. Disassembling the norms, it is about transformation. It is about, as Volf says, "context-specific faithfulness."

## Incarnational Tables

We think of mission leader David Fitch and how he talks and writes about the importance of people gathering around tables—inside and outside church—to eat and talk and share in meals, in which we all bring what we have to the table and in return receive a bounty of God's grace. These are incarnational tables; at these tables we share the Lord's Supper in different ways. We partake of a eucharistic meal that fills us with joy, solace, and strength for the journey ahead. Looking back on the places we visited, we think of the many tables around which we sat and ate. We think of the final meeting we had over authentic Philadelphia cheesesteak sandwiches with workers at Spirit and Truth Fellowship. There was a meal of hot dogs, salad, and warm conversation with members of The Village in Tucson. And there was the coffee we shared at Rick Abma's coffee shop in that small prairie town in Alberta; the pre-Christmas brunch at Karen Wilk's home in Edmonton; the lunch with those creating a new church in a movie theater in Vancouver. Also, there was eating lunch in the cafe in downtown Window Rock, New Mexico, with Stanley Jim, who told us stories of Navajo saints and the faith he received from, of all people, Dutch folks who came to the Navajo reservation more than 100 years ago to evangelize his people. We ate Korean food with a businessman who told us of how going on mission trips with Ttokamsa Mission Church in Los Angeles has reshaped his life. We ate a potluck dinner after a service for recovering addicts in Hudsonville, Michigan; shared bagels and cream cheese with students involved in the Wine Before Breakfast campus ministry at the University of Toronto.

We sat around a long table during lunch at Loyola University's busy cafeteria with a mix of students involved in the campus ministry at Loyola. Breakfast, lunch, and dinner; long meals and meals on the fly, we had them all on our travels; and the food was good, but what mattered most was the chance to spend time together. To listen to stories of God at work in so many lives; to realize this is how God's mission gets done. When you go, you go slow because then you can more easily see God working with others. For us, we had the chance to realize—from those dozens and dozens of people we met and with whom we ate—that by staying put we become part of a family that depends on one another. We share what we have and we receive freely in return. We wait for the actions we'll need to follow. We wait for our lives to fill and expand with God in us and God outside of us. And we take chances—we break out of our comfortable routines—in order to see more fully the contours of the Lord's architecture in the world. The key, as our book professes, is to share and to receive, to worship God in the rich praises that pour into and then flow from our hearts. To break bread and, as we sit at tables, see a mysterious God revealed in our midst. Whenever we can and with the help of others, we take chances to see into our neighborhoods anew and communities more clearly. If we remain open to it, our world will be enlarged; grace will continue to flow.

## Go Local and Stay Put

In closing, consider this metaphor. It might be stretching things, but use your imagination: Ministry can be like riding in a car on a Ferris wheel, going slowly up. Gears grind; wind blows across and into us. Your car wobbles. Time ticks down as, climbing into the sky, we see vistas and features of the same place—our community and its context—we've missed until now. Below, our neighborhood is spread out in great detail, reminding us of the blessed place that it is. We recognize where we live and work—and why. As the ride reaches its peak, we clasp our hands on the car's bar. We don't want, anxious about what is to come, to let go. But in the plunge we let go, allowing the motion to take us down—even more deeply into the place where we already are. We laugh and our eyes fill with tears. Taking this ride is exciting, at the same time it is scary. Pounded by the g-force, we give ourselves over to the ride.

Setting the metaphor aside, we know that, through the ups and downs of ministry, things will continue to change. Whenever we can and with the help of others, we take chances to see into our neighborhood anew and our mission more clearly: through the call of God we are where we are. Side by side with those we have gotten to know, we stand on solid ground and—despite the thrills and spills, the joys and tragedies, and the grueling challenges—we don't leave. Like a strong tree, our roots will go deep and we will stay rooted.

Together, we break bread and drink wine in which the reality of God's vast sanctuary—the world itself—is revealed. In going fast, we slow down; in venturing out we find new vistas; in staying put we expand; we feel the rush of the Spirit through us; we share meals—because together we can support one another and by following Christ we can get all we need by allowing our lives to flourish right where we are. Whether it's a banquet or a pizza party, a chance to have hamburgers cooked on the grill or to sip soup in a church basement, we can have the chance as we sit around tables to listen, really listen to what our neighbors are telling us and be blessed and powerfully sustained in the process. Despite the joys and tragedies and the grueling routines of ministry, we hold on. Come hell or the high water of heaven, this is our home. We are on holy ground. We are in an ordinary space that is at the same time sacred.

And now that we are there, by going local, we stay put!

# Afterword

Reading the manuscript for *Joining Jesus* fifteen months into COVID was painful *and* inspiring. Until recently there have been no gatherings at my local church. I miss the little things of being together in community. The tactile experiences of handshakes, hugs, passing the peace, and especially of feeling the reverberation of voices boom around me. I miss seeing others hold my young son and watching children play together carefree. The stories in this book of people sharing space, air, touch, and in-person conversations are a reminder of what we've been missing for so long.

Yet these stories are precisely what the church needs to be reading at this moment when the desire to "get back to normal" threatens to hold our imaginations captive. Amidst our societal and ecclesial pain I hope the church recenters its vision around the priesthood of all believers. Our structures of worship, discipleship, and mission need to teach Christians to follow the Spirit of God's leading in their neighborhood, workplace, and public life. Otherwise, the momentum will continue along the lines of an inward, private spirituality disconnected from the outside world.

Now hear me out, I am not saying that we should approach models of church as if working from a blank slate. Pursuing creativity for the sake of novelty is not a path of wisdom. Creativity requires limitations, and I am convinced that our imaginations need to be seeded with the long histories of suffering and reflection in the church. But the creeds and confessions that the Reformed tradition holds dear must always be read *missionally*, as texts that guided the life and witness of the church in particular sociohistorical contexts. Their enduring authority resides in prayerful discernment of the Spirit's leading through them and Scripture to form the faithful witness of the church in each age. A brief example of how to read theology *missionally* will illustrate this point.

John Calvin once wrote that the church doors in Geneva should remain locked outside of Sundays.[1] This odd instruction becomes more comprehensible when we see that Calvin was counteracting superstitious practices among the medieval masses. The theological pay dirt underlying his thought was that the world is a theater of God's glory—the sanctuary and mass were not the sole domains of the Holy Spirit's work and presence in creation. The daily workshop, field, marketplace, home, and town square are domains in which the *priesthood of all believers* are called to encounter God and love their neighbor. These daily places and activities are all part of God's mission to embody shalom and hope in the world.

It is this type of theological imagination for the formation of the priesthood of believers that the church desperately needs to cultivate today. And it is exactly this type of vision that *Joining Jesus* inspires. Through careful attention to the Spirit's presence in several Christian communities, Chung and Meehan offer helpful windows into how God is forming the priesthood of believers in North America today.

## "Every Square Inch" and A Comprehensive Vision of the World

I grew up in the Bible church movement in the Sierra Nevada mountains of California. In my mind, as a kid, the Trinity consisted of Scripture, Jesus, and evangelism—in that order. The Bible is the exclusive source of truth, Jesus is the only Savior, and my neighbors need to hear the gospel. On these, my imagination was fixed. It was not until I was well into college that some of the anti-intellectual streams of fundamentalism became apparent and presented intellectual problems for me. The dualisms that were shot through my worldview created points of doubt, and eventually, crisis.

It was around the time I became the director of college ministries at a nondenominational church that I encountered Reformed theology—or, I should say, a winsome expression of Reformed theology through the likes of Tim Keller and Richard Mouw. It was in the Dutch Reformed accents of their teaching that I found a deeper theology that remained centered on Jesus and Scripture but articulated a gospel that was far more cosmic and world-encompassing. I remember getting a lot of mileage from Abraham

1. Calvin, "The Ordinances," 79.

Kuyper's famous line, "There is not a square inch in the whole domain of our human existence over which Christ, who is Sovereign over all, does not cry: 'Mine!'"[2]

My imagination began to expand with this newfound theological depth. I came to learn that Jesus cares about the eternal destiny of people's souls, but he also cares about how we run our businesses, pursue racial and economic justice, and cultivate culture through art and politics. He even cares about how we care for the earth by studying the "book of nature" and learning from God's providential workings in creation! This theology had immense implications for pastoring young adults who were choosing majors, wrestling with possible vocational futures, asking deep theological questions about life and death, and searching for identity and purpose.

Over time cracks began to show in my Reformed worldview even as my appreciation for it continued. This showed up especially in the absence of a lived theology of place in my practice of discipleship. Looking around, I realized I wasn't alone in this. There was something wrong, sick even, with my imagination. I was enamored with Kuyper's vision of the cosmic scope of God's purposes and mission, but I was disconnected from the pain and suffering in those "square inches" one block over and in other parts of the city. To complicate matters further, my congregation never wrestled with this question: "what responsibility do we have for life in *this* place?" We were unbothered by our participation in societal practices that reduced creation to a commodity and disconnected us from our neighbors suffering under oppressive racial and socioeconomic systems. I came to see that adherence to an orthodox Reformed worldview was significant but insufficient. Deep healing and transformation of our imaginations needed to take place.

## The Work of the Spirit In A Sanctified Imagination

*Joining Jesus* is a gift to those churches desiring a sanctified imagination of discipleship and mission. It is written with Luke 10 as a framework for curating numerous stories about ministry in the way of Jesus. This passage features Jesus' instructions to his disciples on how they are to extend God's shalom to the ordinary lives of hurting people they encounter. Luke 10 is a very fitting passage for this book.

2. Kuyper, "Sphere Sovereignty," 488.

This book could also have been written with Acts 10 as a framework. In this passage, the Holy Spirit is the lead actor while the Apostle Peter gradually learns to follow God's leading in the world. Together, the narrative we read in Luke-Acts shows the intimate relationship between the ministry of Jesus and the work of the Spirit. Luke teaches us that the Holy Spirit bears witness to Jesus throughout his life and ministry. And Acts shows us that the mission of God continued in the Spirit's work through the apostles. Together Luke-Acts offers us a vision for understanding how the church is to faithfully participate in God's mission.

Throughout their book, Chung and Meehan regularly reference the Holy Spirit as they describe their encounters with many Christian communities. This is a unique genre of writing drawing together practices from ethnography, journalism, and missiology. I would argue that this book is not so much journalistic reporting as it is a form of careful *testimony* tracing the work of the Spirit at the grassroots level, in the lives and communities of ordinary Christ followers.

I am convinced that it is precisely this holding together of the ministries of Jesus and the Holy Spirit—*in the ordinary spaces God has placed his people*—that should be central to a vision of the church in North America today. So it is alongside Chung and Meehan's account of the Spirit's activity in these churches that I offer my reflections as a theologian and missiologist. I hope that the three points of reflection below will help elucidate the significance of what we read and encourage readers to allow the Spirit to sanctify their imagination and live out their faith *where God has uniquely placed them.*

## Reflections for Healing Our Imagination

### 1. From Place to Parish

Richard Mouw once wrote a chapter titled "Abraham Kuyper, Meet Mother Teresa" as a corrective to Christian triumphalism.[3] In it, he offered a corrective to us Kuyper-quoting Reformed folk who emphasize the Lordship of Jesus over every square inch but neglect an embodied presence with those who suffer in those places. While we boldly proclaim Christ's rule over all creation, we must never fall into thinking we can inhabit those places as victors and rulers. Mother Teresa's practice of seeing the face of Jesus in the

3. In Mouw, *Uncommon Decency*, 159–69.

suffering outcasts of Calcutta is a model for us as we inhabit Christ's square inches. In *Joining Jesus* we encounter several people who have taken up this Kuyper-Teresa approach to discipleship and mission.

I see another dimension of lived wisdom in this book as well—one that displays a radical commitment to place. Through stories of people like Beth Fellinger in downtown St. Thomas, Clarence Presley on the football field on Sunday morning, and Karen Wilk's neighborhood presence in Edmonton, we learn how Kuyper's "square inches" have become *deeply loved parishes* for these Jesus followers. They sense that the Spirit has led them to take responsibility for life in *this* place. They don't act like owners or possessors of their parish, but responsible actors in touch with the joys and sorrows, the beauty and the pain of the people and place. Each one has developed practices for inhabiting their parish with knowledge, wisdom, and love.[4]

## No Global Without Local

Throughout the modern missionary movement, many churches drew upon a particular interpretation of the Great Commission. The emphasis was placed on *going* into "all the world" (read "overseas") and making "disciples of the nations" (Matt 28:18–20). Unreached people groups in distant lands were where "mission" took place, while the various people groups in the "Christian West" fell outside the mission scope. This global vision of mission had its merits but may have contributed to the anemic theology of place we see in the Western church today.

When the resurrected Jesus repeated his commission to his followers, the importance of place showed up clearly. "But you will receive power when the Holy Spirit has come upon you; and you will be my witnesses *in Jerusalem*, *in* all *Judea* and *Samaria*, and to the ends of the earth" (Acts 1:8). This emphasis on *place* as instrumental to faithful discipleship shows up again in John's vision of the new creation. In Revelation 5:9–10 we read that Jesus has made a kingdom of priests "from every *tribe* and *language* and *people* and *nation*"—this is the climactic fulfillment of the Pentecostal outpouring of the Spirit on peoples from particular geographic places both near and far (Acts 2:5–12). Pentecost corresponds to Jesus' commission as we see the initial stages of this *glocal* movement.[5] We must

4. Chung and Meehan, *Joining Jesus*, 85–90; 37–40; 48–56.

5. *Ta ethne*, the Greek words commonly translated "the nations" in Matthew 28:19, should be understood against the backdrop of the Hebrew *goiim*—the multitude of

hold fast to the global trajectory of the gospel message while insisting that the task of witness is deeply and permanently *local*, bound to *all the places* to which people groups belong. It is precisely these eschatological texts that should infuse our imagination about how to inhabit daily places and spaces as our parish.

In the 1970s Lesslie Newbigin called for a recovery of a "parish" mind-set amidst the fallout of industrialization in the United Kingdom. He argued that if the cchurch is to be the "first-fruit" and "sign" of God's new creation it "must be the Church in and for *this village, this factory, this suburb*. In other words, the structures of the Church must be organically related to the structures of the secular world. *That is the enduring theological justification for the idea of the parish.*"[6]

Newbigin's words still ring true. A recovery of parish in the church's imagination must center on the ways the Holy Spirit is at work empowering witnesses to Jesus in the particular communities where the Father has placed them.

## 2. From Royals to Priests

The transformation that takes place when we inhabit the particular places God has called us to as "parishes" entails a profound change in our identity. Unlike external disciplines we take on such as New Year's resolutions, the testimonies of individuals and communities in this book reflect an inner transformation of identity and mission. Refracted through distinct personalities and cultures, these stories reveal a *priestly identity and calling* that each person has embraced over time.[7] There are important theological lessons for us here in terms of what it means to be the church active within God's mission.

families, clans, and people groups outside the boundaries of the Jewish people. Lesslie Newbigin used this more precise interpretation of *ta ethne* as the basis for his calling for the church in the West to see various industries and business sectors as strategic sites for mission. It is in those communities and people groupings that the gospel needed an embodied witness. See Newbigin, "Mission to Industry," 100–101. See also Kaemingk, "Lesslie Newbigin's Missional Approach to the Modern Workplace."

6. Newbigin, *The Good Shepherd*, 88.

7. Chung and Meehan quote Alan Roxburgh's discussion of a poetic role and calling for God's people. Roxburgh's discussion is incisive and helpful. What I am discussing here regarding a priestly calling and identity corresponds to his discussion of the poet as a "secular priest" (Chung and Meehan, *Joining Jesus*, xix).

The Reformed tradition has done a lot to draw out the "royal" dimension of Scripture's teaching on the people of God being a *"royal* priesthood" and a *"kingdom* of priests" (1 Pet 2:9; Rev 5:10; Exod 19:5–6; Isa 61:6). This royal theme has been effective in cultivating Christians who seek to reflect God's character and purposes in the world through their daily work. But reflecting God's image and character should not be viewed solely through this royal lens.[8] The *priestly dimension* of our calling and identity is essential if we are to be faithful to God's mission. This has profound implications for how we inhabit our daily habitats as a *parish*. Here we are helped by another insight from Abraham Kuyper.

While the kingship of Christ was an abiding preoccupation in Kuyper's writings, he also spoke provocatively of the priestly ministry of Christ and its implications for redeemed humanity. Commenting on Genesis 1 and 2, Kuyper wrote that God created humans *as priests* who were to engage in *"consecrating . . . the entire creation to God"* through their daily work.[9]

True, our mission is rooted in a vision of God's royal rule—"the earth is the Lord's, and the fullness thereof" (Ps 24:1a). But it is *as priests of God* that we are called to be attuned to all the diversity of those square inches around us and offer them up as an offering of worship to God. The ministry of Jesus and the Spirit is to restore us to this priestly calling as redeemed humanity. This priesthood involves at least three dimensions.

## How The Priesthood of Believers Participates in God's Mission

First, as priests, we are called to be *deeply connected and attuned to all that is around us.*[10] This stands out clearly in the multiple expressions of shared life in Aurora Commons in Seattle. From social gatherings around meals, coffee, and football, to services for wound care, support groups, and risk

8. For an extended discussion of the royal and the priestly dimensions of human existence and the Christian life, see Kaemingk and Willson, *Work and Worship*.

9. "According to the original arrangement [in Eden] the unity of [creation's] coherence comes to expression in humanity as the creature that gathers everything else—all other creatures—under its dominion [to] *consecrate, in a priestly fashion, the entire creation to God*, and dedicated it to him, in a kingly fashion, forever" (emphasis added). Kuyper, *Pro Rege Vol. 1*, 474. See also Kuyper, *Honey From the Rock*, 664–72.

10. Eden was the first parish and Adam and Eve's creative work of tending and cultivating creation was itself priestly work. See Beale, *The Temple and the Church's Mission*, 68; and Middleton, *The Liberating Image*, 89–90.

reduction for drug use, this intentional community has become part of the fabric of Aurora Avenue. Second, this *attunement goes beyond the limits of what we see physically with our eyes.* Part of our priestly calling is to break the shackles of the "immanent frame" in our Western social imaginary, which is choking out our awareness of the transcendent God and his grace.[11] Priests must maintain a prophetic vision that insists that there is more to behold than physical eyes can see.[12] When Taehoo Lee frames his annual youth summer camp under the Exodus theme "Our Children Matter," he provides a prophetic vision that challenges the pharaonic bondage of racism that holds his community captive.[13] Third, the power of our priesthood resides in *practices that harmonize creation and humanity by facilitating connection to God and his shalom.* One example of this is the story of how church members at Spirit and Truth came around Joe Sanderlin to walk with him on the path of sobriety and recovery. Having come into contact with the God of shalom through the Esperanza Health Clinic, Bible studies, and church services, Joe himself became an artisan of God's shalom to others.[14]

## Priestly Attunement and the Change of Subject

There are many stories in this book of Christians who have chosen the Mother Teresa path of following Jesus the king. Several contain testimonies of how *Christians* have undergone profound changes as they love their parish. These stories of priestly attunement are an important part of cultivating a sanctified imagination of discipleship and mission.

My colleague, theologian, and psychotherapist Danjuma Gibson has written powerfully about the need for Christians to cultivate a "hermeneutic

11. Charles Taylor uses the term "immanent frame" to diagnose the secular Western mindset that has blocked out all possibilities of supernatural order. See Taylor, *A Secular Age,* and Smith, *How (Not) to Be Secular.*

12. The rise of the prophets in Israel was in part a response to the failure of priests (and kings) to guide the people into proper worship of God through their daily work of farming and commerce. See the discussion of Amos, Hosea, and Isaiah in our chapter on the prophets in *Work and Worship* for more on this.

13. Chung and Meehan, *Joining Jesus,* 22.

14. Chung and Meehan, *Joining Jesus,* 12–14. Another example: when Emily and Kurt Rietema secure mortgages for immigrants who are denied access to loans due to language barriers, they are embodying God's shalom in the lives of their Latinx neighbors (Chung and Meehan, *Joining Jesus,* 75–78).

of affective attunement" as they engage with others. "Affective attunement" is the ability to be aware of and responsive (attuned) to the affective state of another person. People who are developed in this manner of relational connection generate a sense of intimacy with others. The other person intuitively feels that their emotional state and experience is deeply understood. Like a doting parent with their infant child, affective attunement involves giving others space and encouragement to express themselves, actively listening, and then responding accordingly.

Gibson goes further and argues that a hermeneutic of affective attunement also means receiving the other person as your teacher and being open to allowing their inner world to challenge and inform you. This is especially true as we encounter those whose backs have been against the wall in society and "who have existed on the underside of history." Gibson explains, "Empathy, understood as an epistemological category, is a critical skill and function in any discipline . . . [T]he use of self [our affect, including empathy, but also responses of fear, shame, guilt] is critical when seeking to understand and interpret the context and worldview of another individual."[15] In other words, the kind of attunement that God calls us to requires giving up the habit of approaching relationships, church outreach, and missions as if we are the *subject* and people and parish are the *objects*. In seeking to love and serve we must first open ourselves to being transformed by others.

I believe that it is this type of transformation through attunement that is taking place when Hayden Wartes says that listening deeply to the suffering of others has changed *her* and "is an important part of my spiritual journey." We also encounter this in the story of the Grimmius family who experienced the Spirit's transformative power in their lives as they opened their heart and home to Erica Martinez and the Cisneros family.[16] Here again, the book of Acts is illuminating.

In Acts 10 we learn how the Holy Spirit worked through the Apostle Peter in the conversion of Cornelius's household. In a rush to celebrate the missionary success of Peter it is tempting to overlook the real hero of the story. We need to read this passage from the vantage point of a hermeneutic of affective attunement. Far from being the sole *subject* of the story, Peter,

15. Gibson, *Frederick Douglass*, 14. A hermeneutic of affective attunement offers "a much-needed corrective to the ideological tendency in the academy, scholarship, the church, and society at large to exclude, erase, or claim as irrelevant the histories and traditions of those who have existed on the underside of history . . ."

16. Chung and Meehan, *Joining Jesus*, 27; 66–71.

along with Cornelius, are *recipients* of the Holy Spirit's powerful work. There is an intersubjectivity—a dynamic mutuality—between the Holy Spirit, Cornelius, and Peter. The story begins with Peter attuning to the Spirit through prayer. The Spirit then invites him to witness the profound conversion of Cornelius's entire household. This becomes the pathway to dismantling Peter's ethnocentric vision and distorted mission practice. In this story, we see an amazing revival in a Gentile's household, but perhaps more importantly, a deep transformation of *Peter*.

Walking attuned to the Spirit, Peter was led to crack open his narrow, ethnocentric vision of the church and God's mission. This cautious ambassador entrusted with proclaiming the good news of Jesus was given a front-row seat to the wild and seemingly reckless working of the Holy Spirit among the "impure" Gentiles. Despite his prior convictions Peter succumbed to the Spirit's leading and welcomed Gentiles into baptism and the church (Acts 10:47–48). At first, this brought about controversy among the leaders back in Jerusalem (see Acts 15:1–19), but over time it sparked an ongoing succession of crises and transformations within the church as more people groups embraced the gospel of Jesus.[17]

The stories in *Joining Jesus* belong to this long mission history of attunement and transformation of the church. The life and imagination of the community is sanctified by the Spirit as we practice attuning to the joys and sorrows, beauty and brokenness of those with whom we share life in our parish. Such is God's design for his priestly people to participate in his mission in this world.

# 3. From Teachers and Professors to Learners and Confessors

What I want to focus on in this final point flows directly out of what I discussed above about parish, priesthood, and a hermeneutic of affective attunement. If we are to be faithful priests in God's mission we need to expect the Holy Spirit to confront and transform us. Practicing ongoing receptivity to the Spirit's sanctifying work in the church is foundational for faithful mission. The importance of this should be kept front and center as we read chapter 9, "Navajos 'Shake the Dust off Their Feet' in New Mexico

---

17. Andrew Walls has written detailed accounts of church history tracing this theme. See Walls, *The Missionary Movement in Christian History* and *The Cross-Cultural Process in Church History*.

and Arizona." Before we discuss the stories in this chapter, I want to return briefly to the book of Acts and discuss a prescient insight into the Reformed Confessions from Kuyper.

## Transformation—Through Mission—in the Early Church

Following the leading of the Holy Spirit is not for the faint of heart. Growing up I heard a lot of stories about the risks that missionaries were taking overseas amidst harsh landscapes, poisonous snakes, and cannibalistic tribes. But the mission we read about in Acts 10 of the Holy Spirit's work in Peter points to a mission filled with greater risks and fears. These fears are not of hostile environments and dangerous wildlife, but of losing our fragile religious identity and the comforts of our inherited communal boundaries. In Acts we learn that the Holy Spirit's transforming work within the church continues *amid its participation in the mission of God* throughout history. *The church should expect to be convicted of sin* as we live out our priestly calling in our parishes.

Acts 15 and the book of Galatians provide windows into the deep resistance to the Spirit's transforming work in the early church. Those of us who are not of Jewish descent find it difficult to understand how much it cost the first Jewish disciples to embrace us as full sons and daughters of God. Peter's revulsion to eating unclean animals reveals the visceral response Jews had towards fellowship with Gentiles (Acts 10:14–16). We were seen as "impure," "untouchables," and "contaminants." Even after Peter had witnessed the powerful outpouring of the Holy Spirit on an entire Gentile household—and had himself baptized them and argued for their full membership in the church—he fell back into his ethnocentric, exclusionary behavior (Gal 2:11–21). This cultural superiority threatened to tear the church apart and prompted Paul's scathing public chastisement of Peter in front of the entire community. Paul knew there could be no healing and reconciliation in the church if there wasn't truth telling about Peter's public sin.

Sadly, the focus of a lot of interpretations of Galatians has been placed on the doctrine of justification by faith, while little has been said about the deep prejudice and ethnocentrism *that occasioned Paul's theological treatise.* The rebuke of Paul *and the sin of Peter* must continually bear down on the life and imagination of the church until Christ's return.

## Living Into the Theology of Our Confessions

I find Abraham Kuyper's reflections on the Three Forms of Unity of the Reformed churches especially relevant to the Christian practices of rebuke and repentance. Kuyper helps crack open our propensity towards using theology to buffer us from acknowledging our *communal* sins. On the one hand, wrote Kuyper, "the church is the salvation of the world." And yet, "*the church remains so far below its own standard.*"[18] So the honest person will find themselves confessing that very often "the world turns out to be *better than expected* and the church *worse than expected.*"[19]

Article 29 of the Belgic Confession describes the True Church along the following lines. On this side of the final resurrection, the True Church is marked by ongoing weakness and sin, continual reliance on the sanctifying grace of the Spirit, and a constant appeal to the atoning blood of Christ.[20] The line between sin and grace *does not reside* in the boundary between the church and the world. Instead, sin and grace *are mixed* in the world *and the church*. Total depravity applies not just to individuals, but the church as well. We are the community of the redeemed, but sin still resides in us. We should expect to see the church's sin and failure to love God and neighbor show up again and again. There is no exemption clause for the church community when it comes to sin.[21]

We should expect that the church will have moments when we act like Peter and embrace "untouchable" outsiders (Acts 10:34-35), or even speak out against prejudice and exclusion (Acts 15:7-11). But we must always be mindful of our propensity towards oppressing marginalized groups as Peter did in Galatians 2. This is why we must remain vigilant in our openness to those who rebuke the church. Practicing "receptive humility" and confession of communal sin are essential parts of embodying the theology we profess.[22] We must confess not simply that "I am a sinner" but that "we as a church are sinful and participate in corporate and systemic sins."

It is also revealing that in the Belgic Confession the tell-tale sign of the *False Church* is active violence towards those who seek its health by calling it

---

18. Kuyper, *Common Grace,* 2d (italics mine).

19. Kuyper, *Common Grace,* 2f. (italics original).

20. Belgic Confession, "The True Church."

21. Kuyper, *Common Grace,* 2gh–2gi.

22. See Shady and Larsen, *From Bubble to Bridge,* 99–101.

to repentance.[23] This sober reality should lead us to embrace fervent practices of listening to others when they rebuke the church, grieving over our sin by honoring the pain and trauma others bear because of us, and repenting by engaging in sincere efforts towards reconciliation. The church should see itself not simply as *professors and proclaimers* of the gospel, but also as *confessors and lamenters* of our sins. It is against this important theological backdrop that we can better appreciate what the Spirit of God has to teach us from the experience of our Native American sisters and brothers.

## Sin and Grace in Our Mission History

Chung and Meehan set their interviews with Navajo and Zuni Christians in the context of the Doctrine of Discovery and its violent legacy. What emerges from the stories they tell is that the CRC's Mission to the Heathen reflects a mixture of sin and grace.

Chung and Meehan explain how "white superiority was the driving force" behind the Doctrine of Discovery and its horrific impact on Native Americans. This racist doctrine provided the religious sanction for the genocide of native peoples and the "blueprint for conquest and the various forms of oppression that followed." They go on to explain that "this doctrine helped shape the CRC and especially how it conducted its ministry among the Navajos and Zunis . . . in the southwest starting from the late 1880s."[24]

True, some former native students like Donovan Carlile are appreciative of their experience at Rehoboth—the boarding school operated by the CRC for much of the twentieth century. Carlile says it was "the building block of my faith."[25] At the same time, Caleb Dickson reminds us that in numerous ways, both explicit and implicit, "[Native Americans] were devalued as people. Stripped of our humanity. That was [considered] part of our heathenness. *We were punished for being Indian. Let's not whitewash over the pain.*"[26] This meant, for example, that in boarding schools native children

23. Belgic Confession, "The Marks of the False Church."

24. Chung and Meehan, *Joining Jesus*, 143–144.

25. Chung and Meehan, *Joining Jesus*, 151.

26. Quoted in Libolt, "Synod Encourages Churches to Use Blanket Exercise" (emphasis added). Bob Ippel shares this perspective as well: "Native people for years had been second-class citizens in their own land. A church that should have brought a message of freedom spoke of the need to adapt to the white man's ways" (Chung and Meehan, *Joining Jesus*, 152).

were not permitted to speak their language or maintain the cultural ways of dress and lifestyle.[27] The lasting impacts of the Doctrine of Discovery and its dehumanizing mission practices have meant that native cultures have been suppressed or wiped out and Native American Christians have been kept "on the sidelines of their own faith."[28]

As we reflect on our mission history we must not give in to the temptation of thinking that "the ends justify the means" or that gospel proclamation somehow absolves the church of its sins. Yes, the working of God's grace through missionary work should be acknowledged. But sins and injustices—whether consciously deliberate or not—must never be glossed over.

## "Shaking Off the Dust" to "Start A Dialogue of Love"

The primary focus of Chung and Meehan's work in this chapter is on providing windows into ways in which native people are shaking the dust off their feet and embracing their native heritage and Christian faith.[29] In a book published in 1996, Reverend Stanley Jim provided a clear and prophetic vision for a healed and whole Navajo church. He said, "The music has to change to become true to who we Navajo are as people. Churches down here have been seen as being 'missioned' . . . Instead of being on the receiving end, we need to be on the giving end."[30]

What Jim is teaching us is that a "dialogue of love" must be undertaken between the gospel of Jesus and Navajo history and heritage.[31] And that indigenous leadership is essential if this movement is to have lasting roots. He explains what this looks like in his ministry. By speaking the language of my people "I'm able to connect Jesus' work and God's whole mission with the culture that I'm in. I'm able to speak with the medicine men from a point of view that *I'm not condemning them, but bridging that gap in love.*"[32] This dialogue of love can only be taken up by shaking off the dust of past mission approaches and external dominance.

27. Chung and Meehan, *Joining Jesus*, 150.

28. Chung and Meehan, *Joining Jesus*, 144.

29. Chung and Meehan, *Joining Jesus*, 141–156.

30. Hoezee and Meehan, *Flourishing in the Land*, quoted above, 149.

31. José Míguez Bonino, quoted in Sinclair, "Prologue," 15.

32. This quote from Stanley Jim was printed in the Calvin Theological Seminary 2021 Commencement materials. (Emphasis mine.)

The process of reclaiming their beautiful and God-intended Navajo culture through the power of the Spirit is well underway through the Leadership Development Network in Classis Red Mesa. "The best thing that ever happened to us here is leadership development," said Jim. "It is helping people rely on themselves instead of someone else coming here to help us."[33] This sentiment was echoed by Alice Dickson, "We realized we needed to step out of our comfort zones and be servants of the Lord and build up the churches in this area."[34] This work of proclaiming the gospel in ways that speak to the Navajo context, and especially to the younger generation, is a vital part of how people like Janelia Smiley see the Holy Spirit at work today.[35]

What does this history mean for us Christians who are not Native American? How might we be faithful participants in God's mission in light of this past reality and its present consequences? The Belgic Confession and Kuyper are very clear guides for us on such matters. As priestly people, we are called to be *professors and proclaimers* of the gospel, but first, we must be *confessors and lamenters* of our sins. It is easier to see ourselves as Paul in the Galatians 2 story. But the Spirit's sanctifying work in the church requires us to see ourselves as Peter.

The process of unlearning and relearning how to follow the sanctifying leading of the Spirit lasts from the cradle to the grave. The legacies of colonialism, white supremacy, and the Doctrine of Discovery cast long shadows over the church in North America. The truths and the sufferings of our native sisters and brothers must be listened to by Christians in denominations like the CRC. Communal sins must be confessed and lamented, and genuine reconciliation must be pursued.[36] I want to add one final admonition, in the spirit of Richard Mouw, that addresses our propensity towards silencing rebukes and suppressing the truth about our sins as the church.

## When Good Motives Still Fail Us

It takes no great act of imagination to see how Kuyper's "every square inch" quote might be co-opted within the greedy and rapacious imagination of the

33. Chung and Meehan, *Joining Jesus*, 149.

34. Chung and Meehan, *Joining Jesus*, 146–147.

35. Chung and Meehan, *Joining Jesus*, 147.

36. The Blanket Exercise is just one practice that can help churches engage in truth-telling, confession, repentance, and reconciliation. See Kairos Blanket Exercise.

Doctrine of Discovery. If Scripture says, "the earth is the Lord's and the full-ness thereof," and we are following this Lord as our King, then it is a short step to think we are justified in saying that *"your* square inch is *'mine!'"*[37]

The temptation towards this "settler" mentality is subtly present in churches in North America today—even in those churches who see themselves as "missional" and "seek the welfare" of their city. It shows up in churches who desire to help their neighbors but who decide on their own what their neighbors need and how those needs should be met. No harm is intended and yet real harm and disrespect are dealt out. It also shows up in churches that, having once been a church in the community, now find themselves as a "commuter church" with few members living in the neighborhood around the sanctuary. Still, the church's outreach is often taken up from the position of being the "host" in a place they do not call home, while the actual residents are made to feel like guests in their neighborhood.[38] As we attempt to go local and stay put, we need to first be mindful—not about our well-intended motives—but how our actions do real harm and betray our distorted imagination of superiority.

## Abraham Kuyper, Meet Chief Joseph.

At the CRC's synod gathering in 2015, I met Stanley Jim and Caleb Dickson for the first time. As the newly confirmed missiologist at Calvin Seminary, I took to heart Jim and Dickson's recommendation to read more about Native American history and experience. Dee Brown's *Bury My Heart at Wounded Knee* was at the top of their list of required readings. Brown's book is a meticulous recording of history from the Native American perspective of "how the West was lost." In it, I encountered this profound theological statement from Heinmot Tooyalaket (Chief Joseph) of the Nez Perce. In the following quote, Chief Joseph protests the violent displacement of his people from their land by white Christian "settlers."

> Say to us if you can say it, that you were sent by the Creative Power
> to talk to us. Perhaps you think the Creator sent you here to dis-
> pose of us as you see fit. If I thought you were sent by the Creator
> I might be induced to think you had a right to dispose of me. Do

37. James Bratt offers helpful commentary on how Kuyper's phrase might need to be retired for a few years in some Christian circles. See Bratt, "Why I'm Sick of 'Every Square Inch.'"

38. Pohl, *Making Room*, 119. See also Gittins, "Beyond Hospitality?," 399–400.

not misunderstand me, but *understand me fully with reference to my affection for the land. I never said the land was mine to do with it as I chose. The one who has the right to dispose of it is the one who has created it.* I claim a right to live on my land, and accord you the privilege to live on yours.[39]

Chief Joseph's words reflect a profound theology of place that resonates with Scripture itself. The Creator is the owner of the land, *not us* (Lev 25:23; Ps 24:1). Deep affection for the land and place where the Creator has placed us is natural and God-intended (Ps 137). Respecting others as God's creatures means honoring their relationship to the land—for they belong to that place.

Those of us who have embraced Kuyper's cosmic vision of the Lordship of Christ must also listen to the wisdom of Chief Joseph. Our relationship to God is bound up with how we treat our neighbors and uphold their dignity and relationship to the land. If we are to faithfully inhabit Christ's square inches in our parish, we must learn the history of *those who belong to that place.* We must open ourselves to the power of the Spirit operative in their affection for their land and culture. Living into the theology of our confessions should entail listening to what the Spirit is doing among our contemporary Navajo and Zuni sisters and brothers. It should also involve learning from the culture they hold dear and are working to redeem through the gospel. It is time for our reading of Kuyper to incorporate the wisdom of Native American communities. Abraham Kuyper, meet Chief Joseph.

## Conclusion: An Invitation to a New Hermeneutic of Word, Spirit, and Parish

What is subtly happening in *Joining Jesus* is that a new way of reading the Bible is being offered to you. Starting with the stories of the Spirit's work in diverse communities, Chung and Meehan bring us again and again to Luke 10 to see new dimensions of this text. In the book, we read about many people who have embraced their priestly identity and parish and have encountered God afresh in Scripture. This is vividly portrayed in the story of Carol Scovil. Chung and Meehan tell her story in this way:

> Scovil divides her time between the weekly fellowship, rehabilitation research, and working in a clinic that helps people paralyzed

39. Quoted in Brown, *Bury My Heart at Wounded Knee*, 316.

from spinal cord injuries to access and find assistance from computer and smartphone technologies. Living and working in the two worlds gives her a unique perspective and has helped her to reflect on God's role in helping people. "You can't skip over the painful things," said Scovil. "But we know that [no one] understands pain and suffering and injustice better than a loving God who will be with us so that we can sit and lament together—which is a holy and beautiful thing."[40]

The groaning of the Spirit of God that Scovil encounters in her work parishes is the same Spirit that meets her in the liturgy of Word, sacrament, and prayer with fellow believers. What happens in the clinic and research lab enriches her experience in gathered worship. And the God she encounters in the liturgy accompanies her in her parish throughout the week. In worship she not only experiences the open arms of a loving God but also grows in "self-awareness and recognition of the forces at work that shape and misshape the world."[41] In the words of Brian Walsh, as she turns her eyes upon Jesus and looks full in his wonderful face, "the things of this world grow strangely *clear* [not dim], in the light of his glory and grace."[42] Scovil's testimony and Walsh's reflections summarize succinctly the impact that this hermeneutic of Word, Spirit, and parish can have on the life of the church as God's priestly people.

In reading this book an invitation is offered to you and me. Will we attune to the Spirit's presence around us in our parish—whether in the home, neighborhood, workplace, or some other third space? Will we bring the joys and sorrows, the beauty and brokenness in and around us to our engagement in prayer and Scripture? Having done so we will be transformed by the compassionate yet untamed Spirit of God as we are sent out to our daily parishes where God has placed us. May God's priestly people be enriched, empowered, and humbled by the Spirit's presence as we participate in God's mission.

40. Chung and Meehan, *Joining Jesus*, 116.

41. Chung and Meehan, *Joining Jesus*, 116.

42. This line was taken from Walsh's review of *Work and Worship*, "Work and Worship Must Be One."

*Cory Willson is the Jake and Betsy Tuls Associate Professor of Missiology & Missional Ministry at Calvin Theological Seminary. He is also Director of the Institute for Global Church Planting and Renewal.*

# Bibliography

Beale, G. K. *The Temple and the Church's Mission: A Biblical Theology of the Dwelling Place of God.* Downers Grove, IL: InterVarsity, 2004.

Belgic Confession. "The Marks of the False Church in the Belgic Confession Article 29." https://www.crcna.org/welcome/beliefs/confessions/belgic-confession.

———. "The True Church Described in the Belgic Confession, Article 29." https://www.crcna.org/welcome/beliefs/confessions/belgic-confession.

Bratt, James. "Why I'm Sick of 'Every Square Inch.'" *Reformed Journal,* October 12, 2013. https://blog.reformedjournal.com/2013/10/12/why-im-sick-of-every-square-inch/.

Brown, Dee. *Bury My Heart at Wounded Knee: An Indian History of the American West.* New York: Holt, 2007.

Calvin, John. "The Ordinances for the Supervision of Churches in the Country (1547)." In *Theological Treatises,* translated by J. K. S. Reid, 76–82. Philadelphia: Westminster, 1954.

Chung, Moses, and Christopher Meehan. *Joining Jesus: Ordinary People at the Edges of the Church.* Eugene, OR: Cascade, 2021.

Gibson, Danjuma G. *Frederick Douglass, a Psychobiography: Rethinking Subjectivity in the Western Experiment of Democracy.* Cham, Switzerland: Palgrave Macmillan, 2018.

Gittins, Anthony J. "Beyond Hospitality? The Missionary Status and Role Revisited." *International Review of Mission,* vol. LXXXIII, no. 330 (July 1994) 397–416.

Hoezee, Scott, and Christopher Meehan. *Flourishing in the Land: A Hundred-Year History of Christian Reformed Missions in North America.* Grand Rapids: Eerdmans, 1996.

Kairos Blanket Exercise. https://www.kairosblanketexercise.org.

Kaemingk, Matthew. "Lesslie Newbigin's Missional Approach to the Modern Workplace." *Missiology: An International Review,* vol. XXXIX, no. 3 (July 2011) 323–33.

Kaemingk, Matthew, and Cory Willson. *Work and Worship: Reconnecting Our Labor and Liturgy.* Grand Rapids: Baker Academic, 2020.

Kuyper, Abraham. *Common Grace: God's Gifts for a Fallen World. Volume 2: The Doctrinal Section.* Edited by Jordan J. Ballor and J. Daryl Charles, translated by Nelson D. Kloosterman and Ed M. van der Maas. Bellingham, WA: Lexham, 2019.

———. *Honey from the Rock: Daily Devotions from Young Kuyper.* Translated by James A. De Jong. Bellingham, WA: Lexham, 2018.

———. *Pro Rege Vol. 1: Living Under Christ's Kingship.* Translated by Albert Gootjes. Bellingham, WA: Lexham, 2016.

———. "Sphere Sovereignty." In *Abraham Kuyper: A Centennial Reader,* edited by James D. Bratt, 165–202. Grand Rapids: Eerdmans, 1998.

Libolt, Clayton. "Synod Encourages Churches to Use Blanket Exercise." *The Banner,* June 16, 2015. https://www.thebanner.org/news/2015/06/synod-encourages-churches-to-use-blanket-exercise.

Middleton, J. Richard. *The Liberating Image: The Imago Dei in Genesis 1.* Grand Rapids: Brazos, 2005.

Mouw, Richard. *Uncommon Decency: Christian Civility in an Uncivil World.* Downers Grove, IL: InterVarsity, 2010.

Newbigin, Lesslie. *The Good Shepherd: Meditations on Christian Ministry in Today's World.* Grand Rapids: Eerdmans, 1977.

———. "Mission to Industry." In *The Good Shepherd: Meditations on Christian Ministry in Today's World,* 100–104. Grand Rapids: Eerdmans, 1977.

Pohl, Christine. *Making Room: Recovering Hospitality as a Christian Tradition.* Grand Rapids: Eerdmans, 1999.

Shady, Sara, and Marion Larsen. *From Bubble to Bridge: Educating Christians for a Multifaith World.* Downers Grove, IL: InterVarsity, 2017.

Sinclair, John. "Prologue." In *Juan A. Mackay: Un esocés con alma Latina.* Mexico City: Cambridge University Press, 1990.

Smith, James K. A. *How (Not) to Be Secular: Reading Charles Taylor.* Grand Rapids: Eerdmans, 2014.

Taylor, Charles. *A Secular Age.* Cambridge, MA: Belknap Press of Harvard University Press, 2007.

Walls, Andrew. *The Cross-Cultural Process in Church History: Studies in the Transmission and Appropriation of Faith.* Maryknoll, NY: Orbis, 2002.

———. *The Missionary Movement in Christian History: Studies in the Transmission of Faith.* Maryknoll, NY: Orbis, 1996.

Walsh, Brian. "Work and Worship Must Be One." *Christian Courier,* March 22, 2021. https://www.christiancourier.ca/worship-and-work-must-be-one/.

# Acknowledgments

M any people, including friends and family, deserve our warm-hearted thanks for playing a role in helping this book become a reality. To begin, we have to express our gratitude to the dozens of people in churches across North America who were willing—over the last four years—to show us hospitality and to sit down with us to share their stories. Unfortunately, the stories of some of these people didn't get into the book, but they still helped to shape the writing.

We couldn't have even started this book, which required extensive traveling, without the support of Rich and Helen DeVos and Ginny Vander Hart from the DeVos Foundation. Along the way, so many people helped us with wise advice at crucial times. These folks include John Witvliet, Susan Felch, Alan Roxburgh, Sarah Jane Walker, Cory Willson, Dean Heetderks, George Hunsburger, and Eun Hong Kim.

People who read the manuscript and gave us feedback: Amy Schenkel, Mark Wallace, Kevin De Raaf, Claudia and Keith Williams, and Karen Wilk. Paul Faber was an early editor of many of the stories that were published on the Christian Reformed Church in North America website. Zach Meehan spent many hours compiling research on the history of church planting in the early stages of this project.

Assistance from our generous editor Rodney Clapp and others at Cascade has been invaluable as this book has moved through the stages leading to publication.

Support from the Christian Reformed Home Missions Board and Zach King, director of Resonate Global Mission, and many others in that agency has been constant and unwavering.

Family members deserve special recognition for putting up with our regular absences and the love they have shown throughout the process: Eunae, Alvin and Jewel Chung, and Mary Meehan, who often wondered what exactly her husband was writing for hours on end in the basement.

Finally, I (Moses) want to express my heartfelt gratitude to the following Christian Reformed Home Missions coworkers (and those who continued in Resonate Global Mission) between 1996 and 2021. They constantly worked hard and without recognition behind the scenes of the stories that appear in this book and many more beautiful stories of heartrending but faith-filled struggle not told in this book: (Alphabetically) Luann Abma, Dan Ackerman, Drew Angus, Diane Averill, Marco Avila, Ben Becksvoort, Ernest Benally, Sarah Boonstra-Boer, Gerry Borst, Rich Braaksma, Janice Buist, Tom Bratt, Martin Contant, Sue Contant, Viviana Cornejo, Peter DeBoer, Elaine DeJager, Kevin DeRaaf, Jack DeVos, Afton DeVos, Larry Doornbos, Michael Dykema, Terry Etter, Jean Faber, Cindi Fairchild, Diana Klungel Garrett, Lois Githinji, Betty Grasman, Margaret Griffioen-Drenth, Nelson Grit, Lois Haagsma, Dirk Hart, Jack Heinen, Ruth Hiemstra, Jerry Holleman, Norma Holleman, Marideen Holtrop, Peter Holwerda, Jan Hondred, Sam Huizinga, Erica Eizenga Jensen, Stanley Jim, Catheryn Kim Jo, Cindi Johnston, Marjo Jordan, Douglas Kamstra, Ben Katt, Peter Kelder, Ruth Kelder, Charles Kim, Audrey Kinder, Marian Lensink, Allen Likkel, Julie Louwerse, Don McCrory, Jul Medenblik, Scott Meekhof, Delaine Meyer, Howard Meyer, Larry Meyer, Keith Meyering, Al Mulder, Amy Navarro, Jim Osterhouse, Grace Paek, Jane Park, Tong Park, Steve Pearson, Ron Peterson, Robert Price, Laura Posthumus, Gert Rotman, John Rozeboom, Amy Schenkel, Kristie Schrotenboer, Kevin Schutte, Peter Schuurman, Judi Sjoerdsma, James Steenbergen, Faith Steensma, Shirley Stel, Denise Stevenson, Joyce Suh, Jack Stulp, Jack Tacoma, Gary Teja, Javier Torres, Duane Vander Brug, Alvin VanderGriend, Delaine VanderLaan, James VanderLaan, Nancy VanderMeer, Margaret VanderSchuur, Nate Vander Stelt, Ben Vandezande, Arlan Vanden Bos, Fran Vander Molen, Adrian Van Giessen, Bill Van Groningen, Ben Van Houten, John Van Til, Rick Van Til, Betty Veldman, Ryan VerWys, Joe Vriend, Mark Wallace, Henry Wildeboer, Scott Witteveen, Stan Workman, and Lori Worst.